Big Life

Also by George Huitker and published by Ginninderra Press

Poetry

An Unfamiliar Sea

The Actor Is Happy

An Unfamiliar Actor

Prose

Not Just Footy

How To Succeed Without Really Winning: Not Just Footy II

Little Life

George Huitker

Big Life

Big Life
ISBN 978 1 76041 131 2
Copyright © George Huitker 2016
Cover photo: George Huitker

First published 2016 by
GINNINDERRA PRESS
PO Box 3461 Port Adelaide 5015
www.ginninderrapress.com.au

Contents

Foreword	7
Introduction	11
Track #1 The Time Has Come	15
Track #2 I Am Ready, Let's Begin	33
Track #3 Arm Wrestle On the Altar	51
Track #4 Grow Anything In My Heart	75
Track #5 Drive That Mystery Road	101
Track #6 Shifting Sands and Broken Plans	132
Track #7 You Don't Give In	149
Track #8 The Dreaming Never Ends	169
Track #9 No Place To Retire	200
Track #10 Court Fines On the Shopfront Walls	211
Track #11 Build Materials At the Side	214
Postscript	223
About the Author	224

To Dad's Army.

To Jeane's Team.

To Matt Pye and all who cross divides.

To all Junk Sculptors, past and present.

To the Oils.

(And of course to Ronnie Hilton.)

No amount of make believe can help this heart of mine.

Foreword

I first met George when he showed up at the tiny school in north-western NSW where I taught in what must have been late 2011. Someone in the playground called me over to meet this energetic man with a glint in his eye and a manic grin spread across his face. He was running around with a group of primary students and high-fiving them with not a shred of self-consciousness – it was as if he had been on staff for years. I later learnt that he has an uncanny ability to quickly break down social barriers, particularly with the younger generation. We shook hands and he proceeded to express his passion for remote rural communities and in particular the Indigenous people of the area, stating that he had was in the process of developing/expanding a program for his school, a Radford College in Canberra.

I am embarrassed to say that I was somewhat gruff and dismissive on that first meeting, moving off as soon as possible. You see, I had become jaded by a myriad of promises and pledges of support from people, institutions and organisations from all levels of society for my program Crossing the Divide, which is designed to give young disadvantaged, predominantly Indigenous people a second chance at education and subsequent employment. People have too regularly come, extolled the virtues of what we are trying to do, made promises to the program – or worse, to the individuals in the program – and then left, never to be heard from again. This still goes on today and I expected this oddball of crazy energy to do likewise, hence my uninterest and mistrust. But I am happy to admit that, boy, was I wrong...

George, who has since become a very close personal friend and a massive tower of strength and support for me personally, first introduced me to the term 'service learning'. His passion and dedication to the notion of action not words and his emphasis on returning, to me at least, embodies the very essence of what this service work should be about. It is George's shoulder-to-shoulder approach and his commitment to the long haul that is required by private and government sectors if we are to truly make a difference that is both lasting and generational.

His G-trip program stands a very real chance of achieving great things from both ends of the social spectrum. On the one hand, there are the young Radfordians who have had their eyes opened to the social injustices occurring in their very own backyard, having experienced first-hand what no textbook or video clip can hope to adequately convey. They will, no doubt, take this new-found knowledge with them on their life journey. At the other end are the young Indigenous boys and girls from the north-west of NSW, who may not fully grasp the bigger picture. Yet they indisputably know that there are a whole bunch of young and gentle souls from a place called Radford, somewhere 'out there', who seem to genuinely care and who, better still, keep coming back to spend time with them and share love and joy and happiness. This is a much-welcomed certainty in their lives and an important constant. The longer-term benefits of the 'G trippers' are yet to come to fruition but the seeds have been well and truly sown and carefully tended. It is only a matter of time.

There is a place for think tanks, symposiums and extended dialogue; these undoubtedly play their part in the betterment of service approach. For mine, though, I will take the action-oriented, shoulder-to-shoulder approach of Huitker any day. As far as I am concerned, if you are not in it for the long haul, don't be in it at all.

In this memoir, George embarks on his own personal pilgrimage of self-discovery (in accordance with his innate understanding of the concept of returning) in parallel to that of his idols, Peter Garrett and the members of Midnight Oil. Towards the end of the journey, he included the incredibly talented members of his band, Junk Sculpture. Their journey saw them playing free concerts for fans, followers and the blissfully uninitiated from Canberra to the Warrumbungles, from Tingha to Bundarra, and then back home again, touching lives and hearts along the way. Connections are made that will last a lifetime and these have transcended class, status and life experiences. As one astute, young Crossing the Divider asked me after the band played for them in our workshop amidst cars in various states or repair/disrepair, 'Why would they do this for us?' Hidden was the implication that no one, in his experience, does nothin' for nothin'. This was, in itself, a challenging, if not sobering assessment.

The Junk Sculpture tour, like the G-trips, acts as a powerful and unconditional response to this sort of world view and provided a symbol of hope, joy and solidarity between communities from the 'big smoke' and the downtrodden from 'the bush'. They are both a testimony to the foresight and big heart of one man, and prove that anyone can effect change if they try hard enough.

I hope this book resonates at least half as strongly with you as it does me. The journey described in it has really only just begun. And I, for one, cannot wait to see where it leads next…

Matt Pye
January 2015

I don't wish to listen and not understand.
>> Midnight Oil, *Arctic World*, 1987

And he told his people let the stars keep on turning
We have friends in the south in the cities and towns
>> Kev Carmody & Paul Kelly, *From Little
Things Big Things Grow*, 1991

Music is a source of reconciliation…
>> Anthony Storr, *Music and the Mind*, 1992

I only know that every act which has no heart
will be found out in the end.
>> Cormac McCarthy, *Cities of the Plain*, 1998

… There was and could be no direct connection between my physical whereabouts and the place referred to by the song that I was hearing on the radio. It was coincidence. I knew that. But that fortuity invested the moment with a shock and a magic that reverberated down the next forty years.
>> Michael Chabon, *Manhood for Amateurs*, 2008

If he had something to offer,
something to contribute,
okay, do it.
Go north.
>> Robert Hillman, *Gurrumul: His Life and Music*, 2013

Introduction

I had a dream of sorts.

I was looking at a map after a long journey.

I have often found it easier to get a sense of where I have been, and perhaps how well I had travelled, by finding a flat piece of red earth and there, amidst an absence of spinifex, unwrapping each well-worn fold and opening it all out. After laying the paper on the ground, I place tiny desert rocks on the corners in case a wind should stir, and then finally, and with some excitement, begin to survey things from above.

Without lifting my magical marker, I retraced my trip, following miles and miles of rarely straight and often squiggly routes, unfazed by those sudden shifts and jerks of direction that I had spontaneously made. When completed, I gazed down at the untidy, somewhat unpredictable and often strangely-twisting serpent I had created, connecting all the spots where I laid my head, filled the tank or taken a look around (hoping not to step on a smaller, browner little brother). For a moment, and just a slight one, the messy line seemed to rise up from the page, possibly to strike, before something settled it back into its natural habitat on the page.

My tribe came to watch me at my work and after initial hesitancy and caution, took my marker from my hand and began to superimpose their own squiggly existences right there upon mine. At every intersection the marker briefly stopped and the ink began to glow like embers in a fire. The younger ones loved the dazzle from the orb of light, while the elders nodded in recognition. A few from each age group stood away from the map and refused to participate; some even hid behind the more substantial clumps of spindly grass. Another group had begun to play football.

As the map got messier and warmer, I suggested the need for a celebratory song and dance for the journey undertaken thus far.

One of the elder men laughed. A very old woman next to him, probably his wife, had a gift for weaving ideas into conversation. She started by telling us that people are like songs. Some you cannot get out of your head. Some you pull out at special occasions. Some are ceremonial. Traditional. Some don't go for all that stuff. Some, like little brother brown snake, suddenly surprise you. Some stay dusty and forgotten. Some are special, stay with you a lifetime. Some you tire of. (She cackled briefly.) Others remind you of good times. Others old times. A few...bad times. Collecting them? Well, some folk do that but it is fool's work. Still, it is mostly good work. What better way to add meaning to your world.

She cackled once more and asked me what did I think?

I replied by riffing in return and said, that to me, music is like a cloud. It drops, scatters and sometimes even pelts its songs down onto all those squirmy, wormy lines below. Some of the time, the offering is collected and if the cloud appears at the right place and at the right time, its rainwater can last forever. (Sadly, these days, most people put up umbrellas.) I told her about one particular cloud I knew, that spent far too long hovering around a big city miles and miles away, until its whiteness lost its bright – mixed in with all that toxic dirt, dust and diesel rising from the pits below – and it thus needed to follow a long, straight and endless highway out of that hell. And none too soon.

As legend would have it, a tribal prophet, early in his career, had announced that a shitstorm was coming. He warned us all that its first shower might be heavy and tainted. But he also promised that in the end, in time, clean rain would fall and refresh and cleanse and heal and please. And eventually the dirty water dropping from the heavens would transform once again into droplets of songs that would sprinkle their melody upon any maps that had been laid out to dry amidst the random clumps of spinifex.

The elder then pointed to the children of the tribe who were playing football under the stars. It gives them meaning, he told me, shaking his head, as he could not see what that meaning was because the ball bounced so *unpredictably. And sometimes went flat. It was a young person's game, unlike storytelling, singing...* He redirected his pointing finger towards my open map and asked me to sing for the other children, particularly them quiet ones, some of the melodies sent down from that world-weary, city-visiting cloud.

I looked at him hopelessly. I confessed to him that I am often asked to sing for people, usually children or the childlike, and often to those who prefer to not do so themselves: those who have chosen to remain silent, those whom life has encouraged to clam up... Yet these days I often caught myself making old-man excuses not to open my mouth. Perhaps singing was also a game for the young and that was all in my past and I am now too tired and heavy and damaged to do the singing of songs any real justice. I could no longer pry open those little pods they wear with these shaking, arthritic hands. I could no longer light fires under muddied imaginations or set free shackled feet that only wish to dance. I am now a grown-up. A forgotten song. On those rare occasions when I do sing, I desperately struggle to weave my tune over unfinished buildings, through the abandoned lots of broken promise, and in and around posturing suits filled only with the hot air of hollow apology.

The old man threw up his arms and appeared to have given up on me.

But the old woman simply nodded and I could not tell if she was angry, disappointed or accepting of my weakness. She explained to me that even that old bald-man prophet, he sang songs of peace, of love and deeper understanding. (He could have sung more on the middle topic by the way.) She pulled my map close and in the space of a few seconds traced with her crooked, wrinkly finger across the forty or so years of my existence. She playfully repeated its shape with her finger in the air in front of her nose. She then gruffly asked me what the point of all that walking around was if I did not sing some of the songs collected along the road. These kids, she said (capturing them all once again in an invisible circle drawn by her finger), needed the musical equivalent of a deep, glistening and glorious waterhole.

She allowed the silence to speak as she looked at me with her gentle but penetrating eyes. And the silence said,

So.

When you gonna stop feeling sorry for yourself?

And when are you going to start singing up a storm, big enough to fill a wide, gaping hole?

I awoke suddenly, as you do when confronted in dream. I realised that I was an hour away from having to deliver on the promise of a song to some kids I had volunteered to care for, entertain and enliven. I also calculated that I was twelve hours away from my own home and the relative safety of musical manuscripts and large, clunky instruments most of which needed a power cord.

But I knew what I had to do. I would sit them all under a big tree at the back of the school, planted by a friend in his own childhood, and then point to a little cloud. I'd say to them,

There! See it! That small, fluffy feller's been hanging around my sky for ages. Decades even.

It hovered above me when I was just a short, wobbly line on the roadmap of life, barely connecting two spots on it…

And then one day, when I was your age in fact, it rained out – or squeezed out if the truth be told – a strange little 'songlet' which I happened to catch.

It's about this cheeky, little mouse who lived in an oddly shaped building with spinning bits added to the front; there in an old, old city in an ancient country where my parents once came from.

And, if the truth be told, where they lived quite peacefully, a long, long time ago.

It goes like this…

Yup. That's as good a place as any to begin to sing.

Track #1 The Time Has Come

For as long as I can remember, I have wanted to be a rock star. It even trumped my other boyhood wish to one day save the world. I was never particularly precise about what I might be saving the world from. Possibly Bono.

When rock 'n' roll's Irish High Priest sang that he didn't believe it could really change the world,[1] he was quite possibly dumping on two of my childhood dreams at once. As a result, and for not the first time in my love-hate relationship with U2, I found myself hoping that on their next Australia Zoo tour I'd somehow find the $500 necessary for the ringside privilege of sitting close enough to throw a pie at him. Bono should not have a monopoly on indignation, even the childish kind, despite his lofty status in the rock hierarchy.

As a child, I remember seeing footage of those with even loftier status, the Beatles, being bustled about by fans who seemed intent on expressing their dedication by hurling themselves at the Liverpudlians. From my recent experience at preschool, I had come to be quite accepting of the lack of restraint in those who see fit to hurl their frames at any objects worthy of their affection, even if they should bruise, break or bust up the said object. At South Curtin Pre, that was exactly how we welcomed anyone friendly at the gates. 'Ah, they look kid-friendly! ATTACK!'

I watched the Huitkers' black and white telly with envy and admiration as the Fab Four struggled to walk freely out of houses, dressing rooms, elevators, public buildings and all modes of transport including cars, trains, helicopters, planes and yellow submarines. I concluded at the tender age of five that the manic and at times precarious adulation they received would far outweigh any inconvenience had from tripping over a roadblock of mostly hysterical female teenagers. In under a decade, the thought of drowning in a sea of girls would become my third largely unfulfilled wish.

But hey, life isn't all about idolisation, fame and sex. The Beatles also produced a lot of good music in and around the sideshow of hysteria. So let us start there.

When Mum passed away in 2013, like many trying to cope with grief, I found myself revisiting dusty boxes under the house in the hope of discovering lost things to remind me of happier times past. I had hoped to find the first record my mother had given me – a 45 rpm single of a cute *kinderliedje* called 'A Windmill in Old Amsterdam'. I do not remember the artist's name, sadly enough, because being a self-obsessed child with a hyperactive imagination, I assumed as I sang along that it was me who was the recording artist. What is even more tragic, is that now as I near middle-age, I still sometimes feel this way. Lost in my hyperactive imagination, I will often sing along loudly, in the kitchen or when driving the car, fully believing that I actually recorded and wrote 'Hey Jude', *par exemple*, and made so many people's sad-and-sorrowful days just that little bit better. What a nifty and talented bloke I certainly am in that selfsame imagination.

So there I was, suitably immersed in my performance of that little ditty about a lucky rodent in Holland, ably backed up by my natty and reliable little red record player. I'm not sure what my parents thought as I clog-tapped in and around and sometimes through the family furniture in positively reckless, joyous, verminous abandon. While I loved that catchy tune – which to most adults would be the musical equivalent of Chinese water torture – it was its lyrics that truly excited me. I mean, let's face it, if you're a mouse, then you'd want to be in a country that makes pretty good cheese. I was in particular awe of the word play in the lyrics and, in deference to Bono, I would admit to sometimes getting a little carried away by what I was singing. I remember being smitten by the crafty ingenuity of the line 'A windmill with a mouse in, and he wasn't grousin'! What is clearly, to any adult, an irredeemably ludicrous attempt at rhyme, was to young George pure poetry. Pretending I had written it myself, I would sing this couplet in my own smarmy, pre-Bono self-righteousness and as if it were as worthy as any poetry sprinkled forth by Dostoyevsky or Shakespeare.

I would perform the song to the whole of Allan Street and even when shopping with Mum. Family and friends were forced to enjoy the song or would be ostracised for decades. As I sang along word-perfectly with the record, audiences were never ever – at least in my presence – to acknowledge the existence of the original artist, nameless and unknown as he was. There was to be no one else but me in the room credited with creating and warbling such wonderful music. Yes, even then, I was exhibiting the alarmingly high levels of self-absorption necessary to become a successful lead singer.

Being a somewhat precocious and far from modest mouse, I had, by a five-year-old's standards, a somewhat developed ear for emulating a singer's pitch, phrasing and intonation. This helped me in my deception. It meant that it was quite conceivable to never hear any original singer's rendition behind my own. (These skills were to become handy for me in future life when I performed in tribute shows.) So you can imagine my delight when I realised, some years later, that you could wipe away the Beatles' lead vocals on some tracks of *Rubber Soul* simply by turning down the left speaker. I re-recorded and appropriated many of that LP's classic songs and peddled tapes to my now long-suffering family and friends, claiming they were my new hits. (It made no difference to me that I was not old enough to possess a car to permit my baby to drive in, or for that matter did not know anyone called Michelle with whom to practise French or kissing or a combination of both.) That said, I was bewildered and a little miffed that, weeks after their release, absolutely nobody threw themselves at me when strolling through the Curtin shops.

Not that I am any expert in the field, but I think the best tribute artists need to be a little nutty themselves and, like an obsessive method actor, should start to believe that they actually are the performer, reincarnated if the latter is deceased. This helps one to overcome bitter realities like when you are struggling at a rural or coastal RSL and a scattering if not spattering of drunken pundits implore you to break out of character to play 'Khe Sanh'. (This is also based on the assumption that you are not performing in a Cold Chisel tribute show. Hypocrisy surrounding the performance of this song will occur throughout the course of this narrative.) I'm not sure who or what was being channelled back then when I was five and performing in my first (albeit one-song) tribute show to an anonymous artist. But remain assured that it was a minimalistic set list of devotion to whomever that geezer actually was that sang 'A Windmill in Old Amsterdam'. One thing was certain, I performed with a passion and intensity that many of the rock geriatrics sporting Zimmerman (sic) frames on their fourth or fifth reunion tours these days could ever hope to match. Never, absolutely never, underestimate a five-year-old's devotion to a cause.

I remember sitting down over a pipe with a cantankerous and strongly caffeinated Dutch relative (who incidentally thought 'A Windmill on Old Amsterdam' to be a real low point in the lyrical content of *kinderliedje* specifically about the Netherlands and/or mice). I informed him that I was frustrated with the Beatles' producer George Martin and was considering writing him a letter as I couldn't sufficiently turn down John, Paul, George and Ringo's vocals on any of their albums post *Rubber Soul*. (My mother's answer to all of life's problems was to write a letter, usually on floral stationery; this has rubbed off on me.) My relative, with typical and somewhat harsh if not age-inappropriate Dutch honesty, pointed towards my toy piano and said, 'Why don't just write your own songs?'

Despite my desire to one day write a catalogue of classics to rival the Fab Four's magnificent *oeuvre*, I argued that across the universe there were already so many good songs in existence that there would hardly ever be a real need for me to add to its back catalogue. Uncle Edam-Face then bluntly informed me that I had nothing to complain about and should go to St Vincent de Paul's and buy a lame, unwanted LP of instrumentals to sing along with. I didn't have the heart to inform him that I actually had raided Mum's record collection and started to do just that. (The crusty old fart was pre-dating karaoke here and could have made a million if he hadn't been destroying little kids' dreams.)

Nebraskan musician Matthew Sweet once sang, 'Why don't you write your own song, if mine doesn't do it for you?'² While I suspect he was venting a little frustration at his critics, I remember wanting to write him a letter as well, stating that there was absolutely no need for me to compose even a measly note when people like him were producing classics like 'Sick of Myself', 'Someone to Pull the Trigger' or 'Girlfriend'. I would much rather sing those than my own lame compositions. If you'll pardon the word play, songs as sweet as these quite accurately mirrored my own unrequited love and adolescent angst. Thus, I never felt the need to progress beyond performing cover versions at tribute shows. Other real artists were saying and singing about exactly what I was experiencing in life so much better than I ever could or would. In the concluding paragraph of my letter, I would share with Mr Sweet that Mr Picasso once said, 'To imitate others is necessary. To imitate oneself is pathetic.' So I humbly continued, for perhaps a little too long, happily humming along in a spiritually vacuous, karaoke version of life. That was until I finally stumbled across a band and a body of songs that would stir me beyond mere mimicking and vicarious emulation and out into the real world of action.

Even then it took close to two decades of packing instruments, sound gear, lighting equipment, home-made costumes, used set lists and empty bottles before I recognised that solely performing safe and standard covers was akin to throwing a blanket over my own creative fire. In time, there would be nothing left to do but face the fact that I was comfortably hiding and smothering myself in the persona of the artists that I was paying tribute to – and their largely successful and well-known music, the creation of which I had had absolutely nothing to do with. (Except that I had actually purchased it, as opposed to illegally downloaded it, so that the artist could survive to create some more art.)

As it turned out, that band which finally forced me to take a turn onto the road less travelled were very much about exposing wrongs. Often through incendiary lyrics, they would demand of their listener to light fires in the darkness of modern Australia in order to see clearly the truth not only about their own country and its people, but in their very selves. This band challenged many to realise that the time had come to say fair's fair and to get up off the proverbial seat and discover not only our own national voice, but a way to help the disempowered and dislocated to find theirs.

It took me a little while to get around to this.

When folk used to say to me that an album changed their life, I would find it it hard not to scoff.

I would perhaps too harshly question why historical shifts, socio-economic forces, blessed good luck, tragic circumstance, the alignment of the planets and even – God forbid – actual living people might not have a larger sway in how someone's life pans out. Could a dozen or so songs really ever do that?

I could have been persuaded to concede that an uplifting or stirring collection of tunes might change one's mood for a day, possibly a month, if the CD gets stuck in that unreliable car stereo that you should have replaced with an iPhone socket years ago. It would also be fair to add that my fellow rock music tragics are often prone to hyperbole when espousing their musical enthusiasms. (I am about to provide some examples of this.)

Due to spending far too much money on musical purchases through Amazon or at JB Hi Fi, they are prone to being poor eaters, unfashionable dressers and social misfits. With nothing really going for them, they take comfort in presenting loud opinions about rock and roll bands and revel in an unusual delight in the verbal and often public assassination of boy bands. Might I add to this that they are also always the last to upgrade to modern, music-playing technology, forever claiming their antique, rusting and scratchy mode of sonic-reproductive machinery maintains an authenticity in playback missing in sterile, digital advancement. This may be so, but for most with untrained ears, all that is really maintained is a big, annoying scratch in the middle of a good track. At this point I await an angry pie thrown at me by Neil Young.

So surely it is fair to suggest that these ELP (Evangelists of the Long Play) aficionados might be similarly slow in facing the ugly truth that as time relentlessly moves on, an album they adore may not have necessarily moved on with it. That their futile efforts to resuscitate an idyllic moment of the past may have found them metaphorically stuck in a groove, rather than having any real transformative bearing on the future. Like all of us, I can vividly remember a selective roadmap of albums that possibly shaped my temperament and even my way of thinking for the finite period that they were on heavy rotation. None are likely to appear on many people's lists of the Best Albums of All Time. Their quality greatly varies, depending on whom you talk to. And did they change my life? I really do not think so.

Morrissey warns us of a time 'when all were judged squarely and fairly on their musical tastes, and a personal music collection read as private medical records'.[3] Well, I am about to throw caution to the winds here and peg the Huitker musical X-rays up for all to see like the dirty laundry they are/were.

I was hypnotised by my mother's very scratchy and now lost LP of songs from the Roaring 40s, convincing myself and others at South Curtin Pre that the Andrew Sisters in fact lived over the back fence and baked a mean blueberry pie, despite periodically succumbing to the sweet temptation of that irresistible rum and Coca-Cola. Even the most gullible of my preschool posse knew that I was perhaps stretching the truth here. But I still recommended to my gang that if the Andrew Sisters should ever visit the preschool, we should ambush them then hurl ourselves at them at the gates and cling to their kid-friendly stockings for dear life.

Next came *Explosive Hits '75* – the first LP I ever owned. Its crazily eclectic range of pop classics opened my nine-year-old ears, eyes, mind and rock 'n' roll heart to some (far from memorable) Top 10 artists. My favourite was the band Pilot who, in turn, opened the album if not the calendar year with the desperate yearning and world-weary sick and tiredness of their No 1 hit 'January' (paradoxically set to the most infectiously saccharine of ear-candied melodies).

As already hinted, from there I arrived at the Beatles, well and truly after the horse had bolted from Junior's Farm. I came at the Fab Four through unusual means and what I suspect was, to any discerning rock historian, an utterly unlistenable collection of covers from the late 70s movie version of *Sgt Pepper's Lonely Hearts Club Band*. This 1978 film redefined the non-existent Album-to-VHS genre and inexplicably starred the cigar-chewing George Burns along with a host of Hollywood C Teamers, their family, neighbours and any friends with time to spare. Oh yes, and the Bee Gees. Yet hearing my very first rendition of 'Strawberry Fields Forever' sung by Sandi Farina ('Who the…!?' I hear you exclaim) it was there and then I became joined at the hip with John Lennon's beguiling songwriting. This was to eventually culminate in my emulating Australian performer John Waters in creating yet another tribute show to the curmudgeonly peace-loving Beatle, when I myself had reached the age (forty) Lennon had been when he was shot. I will also endeavour to do a Sandi Farina tribute show one of these days, as I love performing for the picky rock connoisseur. That and having an early night.

And speaking of 'One of These Days', the needle next drops (at least four times) onto Pink Floyd's double album *The Wall* in 1979. This time, I was introduced to the original version of an album – as opposed to some bizarre movie adaptation's soundtrack featuring men singing in extremely tight undies. *The Wall*, a cranky, bombastic, nihilistic, yet occasionally symphonic, lush and melodic concept album, whispered many antisocial words of wisdom to an evolving but only theoretical teenage anarchist.

Society (and mothers) sure as hell were building walls around the real me and, from the safety of my bedroom workshop, I wanted to break if not batter it all down into a malleable piece of putty from which I could mould a braver and better new world. Yeah! Take that, fascists! This album was also to stage a comeback of sorts in my life when I eventually settled down and joined a theatrical society twenty-nine years later. In 2008, Roger Waters inexplicably awarded the performance rights to the fortunate SUPA Productions, a Canberra-based theatre company, at the dogged and dedicated badgering of fellow Floyd-enthusiast and sagacious director Ron Dowd. I was cast in the dream role of Pink and then got to break and batter the set and supporting cast to smithereens, all to some gloriously operatic rock music. Every night. For a three-week season. Now that was very cathartic.

Drama by prog-rock classicists Yes followed just under a year later, an album I thought broke all the rules of rock music, even *sans* Jon Anderson's glass-breaking soprano, Rick Wakeman's RSI-inducing seventeen-notes-a-second synthesizer runs, or the band's mystifying lyrical revelations about fairies from outer space. It was all a dose of massive musical nerdiness augmented by sonic steroids. It would lead me through a wormhole in space and time, towards the interstellar Yes back catalogue, replete with LPs with only three songs or four on them and a host of the band members' solo albums and collaborations, including Anderson's own unlikely duo with Greek synthesizer wizard Vangelis. In 1973, Yes released a double album with one song on each of the four sides. If that wasn't silly enough, they chose as a conceptual base a (lengthy) footnote on page 83 of Paramahansa Yoganandra's *Autobiography of a Yogi*. It was probably the first time in rock history that songs and/or album sides were imbued with the four classes of Hindu scriptures (known collectively as shastras). I was never put off by the mega-mysticism and polished pretences of this band, absorbed as I was by the hyperspace ear candy, dexterity and impossibility of Jon Anderson's vocal range and some incredulity that anyone from the planet Earth could entitle and release a song called 'The Revealing Science of God (Dance of the Dawn)'.

My tastes, like the religion Mum strongly encouraged me – but strangely never my father (!) – to take up, were very catholic. I have always fluctuated somewhere between the glow of the progressive space-cadet canon and the raw power of three-chord (four at the most) wonders. When in the USA on a family visit in 1983, smack-bang in the middle of my festering prog-rock infection, I remember locking myself away with a new spew-green Walkman – purchased at a California flea market by my saintly Aunty Joyce – and listening to the first tape I could get my mits on at Walmart that day: Bruce Springsteen's *Nebraska*. The Boss was, at the time, in no mood for too many pesky chord changes. This inspired but somewhat harrowing fluke-grab at the mall gave me a veritable musical haunting; its downbeat, dusty, stark, slightly outta tune and outta step lo-fi music, and those irredeemable first-person lyrics, hardly sent the first-time listener grasping for a travel brochure to Lincoln.

Bring on 1987 and U2's *The Joshua Tree* which appealed to the self-serious, slightly-older but none-the-wiser wanderer of the no-named streets and barren deserts of existence, who unabashedly heard deeper truths and found great personal significance in nearly every couplet sung by the ridiculously named Bono, over the ghostly pedal effects of the equally name-impaired lead guitarist, The Edge. This was only to be stamped as redundant by Bob Mould's incredible, indelible and ultimately self-combusting trio Sugar, whose assaultive *Copper Blue* (1992) and its delectably abrasive companion-piece *Beaster* (1993) took grunge to a whole new level. Both releases were crammed with provocative lyrical content and huge, concrete Hoover Dams of sound which seemed to crack the foundations of the very social mores, ranks and files I was about to join.

The new millennium belonged to the mellowing discontent of Nick Cave & the Bad Seeds. Their lush, tuneful and snowflake-inflected release of 2001, *No More Shall We Part*, I somewhat pompously believed displayed an increased maturity in both the artist and this listener. It did not matter to me one iota that this album, and those recorded before and after it, severely irritated fans of the Birthday Party and Boys Next Door. I had come to welcome blunt and baffling stylistic shifts in musical style, including those from mayhem to meekness. There was also dogged Pete Townshend's formidable *Lifehouse Chronicles* box set in there, revealing to me over many hours of listening a disquieting reality that even with major, successful rock practitioners, art works can sometimes take years if not a lifetime to finish, if they get finished at all.

I felt I had become more open-minded and adventurous in my musical tastes as I got older, while remaining oddly unwilling to take the risk of producing any of my own musical creations. As already indicated, I remained strangely satisfied in 'interpreting the music of others', a kinder way of saying that I just played covers. While revisiting the likes of John Lennon, Pink Floyd and Bruce Springsteen through tribute shows (the latter artist coming to Australia twice in 2013, and then again in 2014 to do a tribute to my tribute show – and I played more of *Nebraska* than he did), I was still allowing myself to be drawn to hidden musical wells away from the madding crowd.

The unfortunately surnamed Canadian songwriter Ron Sexsmith is a case in point – and God love him for continually returning to small venues in Canberra to perform whenever in Australia. His sublime sleeper, *Retriever* (2004), was to me pop perfection without the sell-out sensibility or McCartneyesque cuteness. In fact, it is so wholesome that it almost inspires a sense of guilt at the ease with which it is experienced and aurally consumed; it is the sonic equivalent of eating a salad or perhaps even a perfectly rounded stack of golden pancakes appropriately doused in maple syrup.

And finally, five years later, there came an inexplicable admiration for an album my erudite, yet equally unpredictable Iron Maiden-adoring guitarist Rob Marshall casually threw at me one day at rehearsal: Glen Campbell's quintessential and stirring swansong, 2009's *Ghost on the Canvas*. (Whenever a music enthusiast casually recommends something to you, follow it through. They may still be wishing to convert you to their cause, but should always be given street cred when being subtle in promotion.) My championing of this at-times-sentimental album is due to a compassionate response on my part to Campbell's suffering from Alzheimer's during its recording – and some of it sounded as if Glen is trying to convert the listener to Jesus, so be wary if you are an atheist with a short fuse. When listening to it, I like to imagine that gritty old gunslinger fighting time and memory while being unapologetic and unwavering in his faith – a little like my own dear mother had been near the end – to sing just one more soaring, simple and sweet melody for us all, for old time's sake. Yup. That'll do me. The title track, a Paul Westerberg tune, is near glorious. If you find it too schmaltzy or churchy, Rob and I are fine with you going back to *Number of the Beast*.

I knew the words and most chords to nearly every song of every album mentioned here, the Yes epics excepted, but would be tested to do so now. I knew it could be true that these albums, like so many that are rolled out of the sleeve at high school reunions, might not be the life-changing artworks we once proclaimed them to be – even though they sure as heck seemed to be at the time. It certainly does sadden me to think that they are now relegated to being dated soundtracks of the past, musical artefacts of only subjective significance which the iPod generation will either unceremoniously mock before deleting, or unequivocally worship after download as precious if not wacky curios from the age of dinosaurs. (Being young means you get to be world's taste-police without needing to do any research into the past.)

Yet if all this is the case, it does not tidily explain away Midnight Oil's *Diesel and Dust* for me. This is an album which, like the Gunbarrel Highway, stretches out across many miles of my life's desert, out into the horizon and possibly beyond it. Whether through intelligent design or not, it has plainly effected change in both me, and those in my orb, in profound and largely unfathomable ways.

Even now, as I commence writing about it, I feel myself shifting my tired writer's butt and wanting to read the signs and come alive along its long and dusty highway.

Let's get this clear. It is not my favourite album of all time. It is not even my favourite Midnight Oil album. (*10 9 8 7 6 5 4 3 2 1* and maybe even *Breathe* hold higher rankings.) But of all the albums that have survived being gathered, boxed and sent to church fetes, this is the one closest to altering or, at the very least, gently messing with the steering rod of my life's direction.

1987. My third and last year of uni. I was about to enrol for another year's study – a teaching diploma, no less – and was armed with a certainty that if I could not be a rock star, I would still somehow be fully destined, equipped and able to follow Option B and change the world for the better.

After all, I had read George Eliot's *Middlemarch* from cover to cover in my final year. (In the yet-to-be-released *Sounds From a Distant Past* recording from this time, a collaboration with Wollongong-based actor/musician Lajos Hamers, I read/infused chunky passages from *Middlemarch* over some – let's just say 'experimental' ambient music and collected sounds. Lajos and I, and the two of us alone, considered it a masterpiece.) With the intellectual muscle that my ANU (Australian National University) Arts degree afforded, I was now a qualified and articulate rager against a social machine whose workings were as foreign to me as the inside of a car bonnet. I still do not know the essential difference between a fanbelt and a fantail.

I recall earlier in my final year, heading with fellow *Middlemarch* readers to my future educational institute's refectory, that being the CCAE (Canberra College of Advanced Education, now University of Canberra), to hear the increasingly popular Midnight Oil trial-run some songs from their upcoming and yet-to-be-titled album. The Oils evidently liked trialling stuff in Canberra. In 2009, when they temporarily reformed for *Sound Relief* to raise funds for victims of the Victorian February bushfire disaster, they performed two gigs at the National Conventional Centre, to the delight of the territory's many designer-flannie wearing, but nonetheless generously spirited pub rock enthusiasts.

The CCAE venue was a nightmare for sight lines, with a plethora of fat and unsubtle concrete pillars holding the high cafeteria roof in place and proving a nightmare to get stuck behind mid-concert. I'm always prone to being the one who gets lucklessly caught behind these edifices, or behind a member of a visiting local sumo wrestling troupe. The Oils were similarly rock-solid, upright and uptight on an elevated stage overlooking a swarm of enthusiastic students and late-80s' revolutionaries, now tired of sporting Howard Jones haircuts. Uncompromising in their self-belief, Garrett and the gang played perhaps a few too many of their new songs. Wishing to impress the George Eliot fan club which I had dragged to this rival educational establishment, I offered up enlightened and glibly dismissive critiques of the concert such as 'This is not as good as their old stuff' or 'I prefer it when they played pubs' or 'Geez, I wish they stuck to their surfie ideals.' Yes, I know. What a wanker. (I was third year Arts remember.)

I made further intellectually stimulating friendships with some drunken economics students who agreed with me when I added, with studied irritation, that 'the band is getting way too political for my liking. Why,' I decried, 'can they not simply bash out "Surfing with a Spoon" and be done with it?' Yes, what I said was as nonsensical as stating that Slim Dusty is a little too country, or that Nick Cave should stop brooding and lighten up a little. Nonetheless, my English-majored posse all nodded and I mistakably thought, like most pontificators of taste, that all the bobbing head movements were in support of my vast rock acumen. There was a group consensus occurring, that's for sure, but I was blissfully unaware that it was hardly an endorsement of my superior concert reviewing. No, there was a mutual and unspoken agreement happening here between those third-year English majors that never again would they go out and see a band with such an opinionated tosser.

Upon leaving, Dorothea Brooke came up to me and said, 'I think you were a bit unfair on Peter Garrett and the band.'

'How so?' I chortled.

'If they don't act as spokesmen for Indigenous Australians, who else will?'

'Err, perhaps the politicians who are paid to do so.' (I can see myself swaying smugly, awkwardly.)

'But who actually listens to them? You indicated tonight that you switch off the second any of them open their mouths.'

(Swaying ceases.) 'You're taking my words out of context and –'

'So surely a rock group that is revered by both young and old across the nation has a greater chance of raising awareness of the plight of Aboriginal Australia than most?'

'You make a good point but –'

'And that new song – it sounded pretty good to me. It might even raise international awareness if it became a big hit overseas…'

'You didn't really like it, did you?'

'I thought it was quite catchy.'

'Catchy, you say!'

I told her Howard Jones was 'catchy' and that people would be laughing wildly about his music and hairstyle in a decade's time – if they remembered him at all. (As it turned out, Jones had a slick, slightly static and successful comeback tour of Australia in 2009 with solid ticket sales and happily nostalgic audiences. Shows how much I know.)

I then reassured her that I knew my rock music a lot better than late nineteenth century English novels by women with men's names and that there was no way that the songs I heard tonight, including that one about flammable mattresses, would have any influence into the nineties, let alone the new millennium. On that note, and not for the first time in my twenty years on the planet, an intelligent, cute, young and articulate female of the species left me with an agree-to-disagree shrugging off. And a sinking feeling that perhaps I had missed something special. That I should have had the sense to keep my opinions to myself, lighten up and actually *listen* to the girl.

In late 2010, in *100 Best Australian Albums*,[4] Midnight Oil's 1987 masterpiece *Diesel and Dust* was voted the most influential Australian rock and pop album of the past fifty years.

Yup. There it is. Came it at Number 1. No less.

By the end of 1987, I had softened in my criticisms of the new music. As the legend surrounding its writing and recording became more widely known, and 'Beds Are Burning' became the international hit Dorothea predicted it would become, I had to begrudgingly admit my initial assessment had been way off the mark. Not even close in fact.

I have never loved it in its entirety. But I concede that I had an unfortunate tendency back then to need to find flaws in any masterwork, instead of admiring the beauty of even the crudest of brushstrokes. 'Warakurna', a slow-burning, multi-layered track which guitarist/keyboardist Jim Moginie feels is the centrepiece of the album, took me two and a half decades to truly understand and eventually appreciate and enjoy. I felt 'Whoah' should have been what was exclaimed when the band decided to include it on the album. I even found the catchy and successful third single, 'Dreamworld', a little too lyrically smug, preachy and musically uninteresting to warrant any repeated listens, despite a constant appearance on live set lists right up until the band broke up. But here I am sounding just like I did at twenty, once again.

To the positives. I fell in love with the first single, 'The Dead Heart'. A song with anthemic qualities often bugs me, but if I ever was coerced to sing a chorus of this type without blushing or hesitating, this would surely be the one:

> We carry in our hearts the true country
> And that cannot be stolen
> We follow in the steps of our ancestry
> And that cannot be broken.[5]

These were words that would be filed in a drawer in my brain and stored in a compartment of my heart long after the album's needle lifted from it. The song's heavy acoustic strumming to a droning didge, the haunting tribal doo-doo chants, and the occasional percussive flourishes by Rob Hirst, had me thinking that this was a near-perfect Midnight Oil single that would never be topped.[6] Wrong again.

The second single, 'Beds are Burning', went to number one in many other countries, including New Zealand, Canada and South Africa, and became the song that sold *Diesel and Dust* to the world. It was not long until folk living in places as remote as the Arctic Circle were turning up their Walkmans under their earmuffs and wondering how on earth they could ever slumber with their bedding on fire or dance on a planet which, like the song, was shifting in heavy rotation. Never before had anyone considered that the town of Yuendumu, Holden wrecks, frightened cockatoos and most importantly the dispossessed Pintubi tribe – some of the 'last contact' Aboriginals[7] – might be sympathetically mentioned in a top-selling song.

While 'Beds are Burning' was a sensational opener to the album, it flowed seamlessly into another one of my favourite Oils songs, 'Put Down That Weapon'. I often sang this tune in front of the mirror, pretending

I was pointing a finger at the wayward Ronald Reagans or Mikhail Gorbachevs of the world (my timing is generally a decade late), as well as my sixth grade cane-wielding teacher, seedy drug or arms dealers, militant despots, pampered patriarchs, unfeeling past employers, unreasonable bouncers, Joan Collins, and even the bus interchange bullies from my childhood at the Woden Plaza who targeted anyone wearing a private school uniform. The song's brooding fury, gently nullified by a warm symphonic synthesiser sound, literally exploded two-thirds of the way through with incendiary Pixies-like bombast, as Garrett, bewildered and frustrated and fed-up and possibly affected just a smidgen with a hint of Bono-esque self-righteousness, repeatedly denounces

> We keep talking about it
> We keep talking about it
> We keep talking,
> We keep talking, talking, talking…[8]

In truth, I could talk ad infinitum about the album and perhaps produce unintentional bewilderment and possibly yawns from even a pro-disarmament audience.

I will return to this album's songs sporadically throughout this narrative. However, a parting word needs to be provided about the near-final track, which also happens to be my favourite Midnight Oil track of all time, 'Sometimes'.[9] The Oils sometimes closed their shows with this song and from memory they did so at the CCAE Middlemarch concert. The jerky verses, so helpful for inducing Garrett's own robot-gone-haywire dancing style, were followed with a resounding chorus about discovering self-belief during times of adversity. It would leave even the most insecure of psyches marching toward the car park feeling ready to take on the world. Or even that nasty crook who stole their hubcaps.

> Sometimes you're taken to the wall, sometimes
> Sometimes your face is gonna fall –
> DON'T YOU LET IT![10]

It got me thinking that if the Oils could plug up the leaks in the engine of my own fluctuating self-esteem, maybe they could do so on a political and spiritual level as well. Was Dorothea Brooke correct in what she had said? What if they really *could* do the same for other disappointed, disempowered and disaffected folk, black or white, and effect positive change on the national stage? Maybe even go further and rock the entire world *while* saving the planet? These were two of my childhood dreams now fused into one.

It was probably during that sobering walk to the mustard, hubcap-liberated Chrysler Gallant that a slow-sprouting seed was sown in me by the Oils and *Diesel and Dust*. Despite my public protests, many of the songs from this album remained vividly glued in my consciousness, along with those wonderful accompanying videos and the striking cover image by Ken Duncan of the run-down shack near Burra in South Australia – and *not* as I had hoped the similarly named tiny NSW town forty-five minutes from the ACT. (I spent four hours trying to find the shack in the late 80s.) I remember vowing, as I reached for my car keys, to one day close my own concerts – be they tribute shows or otherwise – with that uplifting song 'Sometimes'. It was a vow which took me twenty-six years to honour. But that too is a story for a little later.

As I drove home, I reflected on my own poor performance that evening and its stark contrast with Midnight Oil's sublime one. I was about to start a teaching diploma and I suddenly realised, on the Tuggeranong Parkway, that in a little over a year I would be presenting more of my ill-informed, poorly considered opinions to impressionable and hungry young minds. Finally thinking like an adult, I started to question the damage that could be done if those future Australians sitting there in front of me were to blindly take as gospel the rotting fruits of my own limited understanding of the world.

I had a lot of growing up to do. That's for sure. And for not the last time in my life, I could hear Garrett singing with utter conviction, insisting inside my head that

> The time has come...

Despite his insistence, it took me well over two decades to respond to his call to arms.

Track #2 I Am Ready, Let's Begin

I have always been fascinated by coincidences. I have wasted many hours on mountaintops pondering over their possible design. I generally end up bracing against a cold, slapping wind of logic, which states that improbable events have simply happened, despite their unlikelihood. Coincidentally, while recovering from scaling such heights, I came across this curious passage in John Banville's *Ancient Light*:

> The statisticians tell us there is no such thing as coincidence... And yet I ask myself, why not? Why should I not allow of a secret and sly arranger of seemingly chance events?[1]

So once again, I found myself closing the statistician's book and entertaining those more mystical, perhaps less grounded thoughts, depending on the reader's perspective. At the very least, I approach coincidence like an unmarked track in an obscure national park: I give in to an almost childlike urge to explore it further, often times to my detriment. As Neil Gaiman recently wrote,

> Adults follow paths. Children explore. Adults are content to walk the same way, hundreds of times, or thousands; perhaps it never occurs to adults to step off the paths, to creep beneath the rhododendrons, to find the spaces between fences...[2]

I am equally inspired by a phrase that DBC Pierre once coined about how

> ...we write our lives while accidents write us, linking, honing, dramatizing every minute, using all the tools of the novelist.[3]

The exciting promise that coincidence and associated accidents often lead to high drama, miles away from the grind of routine, is perhaps what has made chasing them both so damned appealing to me.

So for instance, if I knew you in my childhood and bump into you in a thermal spring at Mataranka, or whilst strolling through Leicester Square, there is a certainty that I will insist that we go and have a coffee. Or, say, I am lost on a mountaintop in the Grampians and am guided off them by an expert rock-climber researching for his book on bouldering, who just happens to be a friend of my literary mentor's son (whom I once met over a family lunch) – *if* that should ever occur, I would unflinchingly buy and promote that book amongst all the granite clingers I know.[4]

My Aboriginal elder friends would say there is no such thing as coincidence, that there is *nothing* improbable about it. Coincidence is simply when one songline, or possibly one thousand, criss-cross at significant junctions in life, in a timely and cosmic manner, the way that they do.

Those more religiously sympathetic, would empathise as a character in Donna Tartt's *The Goldfinch* attempts to identify who said that coincidence was just 'God's way of remaining anonymous'.[5] Whether plausible or not, I am partial to this notion that places of convergence, those cosmic points on the map where paths strangely intersect, are imbued with a power of sorts. Such hotspots along my own journey, such as the Warrumbungles,[6] seem to have a strange magnetic pull on my own internal compass, so much so that I feel regularly compelled to return. Others, like the one I am about to write about, may be somewhat less accessible for a return visit, but nonetheless were busy intersections.

When my band, Junk Sculpture, performed at the Lodge in November 2009, one might suggest there was more than just a traffic jam of songlines. This wasn't simply because of the limited parking and lengthy queues for ultra-pedantic security checks. Here, at the grandfatherly-white residence where (most) Prime Ministers choose to live, matters personal and less egocentric were about to take one of those sharp and unexpected turns.[7] As we are all probably more than aware, just under two years earlier, and months after being elected to office, Kevin Rudd became the first

Australian prime minister to officially apologise to the Stolen Generations and attempt to publicly 'remove a great stain from the nation's soul'. In doing so, he pushed and pleaded for a reconciliation 'across the entire history of the often bloody encounter between those who emerged from the Dreamtime a thousand generations ago and people like himself' – and probably ourselves, dear reader – 'who came across the seas only yesterday'.[8]

I seem to make a habit of being distant from both civilisation and the media – two things not mutually related – whenever significant historical shifts occur. In February 2008, I had been accompanying a Year 7 camp in Jindabyne, enjoying hanging from ropes, steadying canoes and strolling through ancient scrub with privileged Radford College kids doused in UV protection. Upon return, while reading a transcript after a long shower, I could feel a tear or two welling in my eye. With my own mother slowly losing her sense of her identity through vascular dementia, I had grown sensitive to those who, for any reason, were experiencing an acute loss of self. I was struck by the responses of those immediately affected, like Lyn Austin, the chairwoman of Stolen Generations Victoria, who remembers the little girl she once was:

> crying myself to sleep at night, crying and wishing I could go home to my family. Everything's gone, the loss of your culture, the loss of your family, all these things have a big impact.[9]

Her challenge that 'a few hundred words can't fix all this but it's an important start and it's a beginning' were to resonate with me long after my own tears dried up.

While relieved that Rudd had articulated what John Howard and previous leaders would not, I found my head starting to spin with the messages and moods, lyrical snippets and striking video images from the *Diesel and Dust* album. I remember feeling ashamed that after its songs were no longer on heavy rotation, the emotions it had stirred up in me had never been acted upon. Upon meeting Archie Roach, Michael Hohnen[10] was made curious about Indigenous Australia; made him embarrassed to know so little of the vital life of people who could call Australia home in a way that went far beyond the glib sentimentality of a pop song.[11]

I could definitely relate to this embarrassment. Was it my responsibility to know more as an Australian citizen? If I didn't act, who would? And surely as a teacher, if not a trainee rock star and world-saver, I had a brief to at least inspire those near me into deeper thought and meaningful action – to engender in my charges/audiences some form of what Rudd termed the notion of 'intergenerational responsibility'? There was also an underlying fear that, as potent as this apology was, it might remain, like the groundbreaking album before it, yet – or possibly never – to be acted upon.

Rudd's words about working towards a practical response and solution challenged me. Elaborating on Australian pragmatism, he stated,

> For us, symbolism is important but, unless the great symbolism of reconciliation is accompanied by an even greater substance, it is little more than a clanging gong.[12]

I hear you, Kev. Merely *talking* about reconciliation was clearly not doing it for me either. I'd often hear Garrett repeatedly chanting in my head how 'We keep talking about it!'[13] and I always felt caught short. One of my mother Jeane's oft-repeated maxims to her highly verbose son was 'I want deeds, not words.' Beyond declaring solidarity for the plight of my Indigenous brothers and sisters through zealously, if not at times ferociously, singing 'The Dead Heart' with my band, I could not hide from an uneasy feeling that I was actually just flaccidly gong-clanging. There must be more that I could do.

I learnt a lot from observing Bono. Between songs at a gig, it is quite easy to lecture and lobby for any humanitarian cause, shout it out loud from the rooftops and rally those recreating around you against injustice – particularly when, in my own case, you are the lead singer of a covers band in middle-class society. Unless you are woeful or overly-radical, most rock audiences these days are agreeable and accepting (including that irritating guy at every gig who has to have a personal exchange with the lead singer), lulling the performer into reassuring thoughts: I am accepted. I am terribly cool. I am hip, aware, edgy and savvy. But when, to paraphrase Elvis Costello, lip service is all you ever get or give,[14] those quieter, reflective audience members, with a finely tuned social and moral radar, would be forgiven for feeling a little dissatisfied about the emptiness of your rants when the gig is over and the flashing, coloured lights have been packed away.

I suspect that is partly why Midnight Oil travelled into the heart of the continent and its history. As Garrett once said,

> we need to go out there and see them first-hand and be a part of it, if you like. We're less inclined to believe what we read and what we see on the box than we are to go out and experience first-hand, and I think that Midnight Oil's always had a direct relationship with the people that it's played to anyway.[15]

With the benefit of first-hand experience and a willingness to journey many thousands of miles to get it, let alone the rigmarole associated with 'performing', the band could hardly be accused of merely talking, singing and occasionally shouting about the issues they wore on their sleeves. And perhaps more importantly than the issues, the band wanted to make a real and direct connection with the people concerned.

As the Lodge Gig got closer, my thoughts would often wander towards the newly appointed Minister for the Environment, Heritage and the Arts. Peter Garrett would probably be working in an office very close by my family home these days. He might even be sneaking quiet coffees at the Curtin shops. I often wondered how the Oils boys had felt on 13 February 2008; where they actually were when hearing the speech; and what it all must have meant to them at that precise moment. Did they feel that *Diesel and Dust* had been more than just an entertaining time capsule? Had it made a difference in steering the national psyche towards an apology twenty-one years down the track? Had it made any effective changes to the Pintubi 9 and those who follow in their ancestral footsteps? Or did they still feel, to use Jim Moginie's blunt phraseology, that they had essentially been 'screaming into a fog of indifference'?[16]

Well, at least they could say that they had tried to do something.

As the twenty-sixth prime minister gave his apology and followed it with a twenty-minute speech, the man who was to eventually become my school's fifth principal was, I imagine, most probably shedding tears like Lyn Austin and myself. As the speech was broadcast, Phillip Heath was in St Andrew's Cathedral, gathered with the entire St Andrew's Cathedral School cohort, in downtown Sydney, New South Wales. Around him would have been the twenty-five students of the Gawura School, Indigenous children, aged between five and twelve, who mostly hailed from Redfern and surrounding inner city suburbs.

During the apology, Heath described to me how the Gawura kids and their families were in the front row of the cathedral, seated in places of honour. When Rudd finished his address, the congregation, most with tears in their eyes, rose from their seats. Heath ended the auspicious gathering with a few short remarks and invited the Gawura kids and their families to leave the cathedral first, in pride of place, as the remaining, upstanding members of the St Andrew's community applauded as they filed out through the western door into Sydney Square. 'What a day,' recounts Heath. 'Nothing was the same after that moment.'

Heath had been instrumental in the set-up, development and growth of Gawura School, a literal school within a school, for Indigenous children. As he explains,

> On the eve of ANZAC Day in 2007, a personal essay in reconciliation commenced with the establishment of the Gawura School in the centre of Sydney CBD. Inspired by a visit to the Vuleka Schools in Johannesburg, I witnessed the immense power of a vision for justice. The children of Soweto were receiving a first-rate educational experience in the under-utilised church halls of well-to-do suburbs of a city whose international reputation stood on mining and on the atrocities of the apartheid movement. Nelson Mandela called upon his country to rise by saying, 'Education is the most powerful weapon which you can use to change the world.' The Vuleka School was changing the world, one life at a time. It was impossible to remain unaffected by the sight of optimistic faces of children who had trundled across

Johannesburg from Soweto in makeshift transportation so they could access schooling of a high standard. The venture pursued justice for the years of disrespect. Does this sound familiar? It did to me.

The establishment of the Gawura School was laborious and involved complex and even painful excursions into the political frustrations and anger felt within the inner-city Indigenous communities. It was the first time I witnessed the pain of dispossession and the anger of disrespect that had been the daily experience of the people of Redfern. My visits to the area were complicated further by the appalling tragedy of the death of seventeen year old Aboriginal local, T.J. Hickey, and the subsequent Redfern Riots of 2004, which was still very fresh in the memory of people living on Hugo Street and the Block.

With the help of my saintly colleague, Cathy Miscovich, who lost her battle with cancer in 2009, we spent many months in 2005 and 2006 speaking to hundreds of Aboriginal and Torres Strait Islander people in Redfern, gauging their level of interest in the formation of a new Primary School for Indigenous children. After scores of unsuccessful attempts to secure a suitable site for the school, we resolved to commence within the premises of the school of which I was then principal, St Andrew's Cathedral School located in Sydney Square. The new school was named Gawura by an Aboriginal advisor, Sharon Minniecon, who chose a word from the Eora people who for 40,000 years had lived in the area known as Sydney Harbour. Gawura means 'whale' – for, as Sharon said, 'It was from the belly of a whale that God saved a nation.'

To hear or read of Gawura should give most Australians relief that something was being done in the big smoke to balance the damage caused by less enlightened educators of the past. Australia's contemporary fictional landscape is replete with stark narratives and indelible characterisations that reflected a reality that was far from fictional: the insufferably pompous, harmonica-hating Reverend Theodore Hollower from Xavier Herbert's *Capricornia* springs to mind. In films such as *Rabbit Proof Fence* and *Bran Nue Day*, the spectre of Kenneth Branagh's uncompromising Chief Protector of Aboriginals, Auber Octavius Neville, or Geoffrey Rush's harsh and hypocritical, do-gooder German priest, Father Benedictus, ominously march across the screen in my head as portraits of what we should never place at the front of the modern Australian classroom.

(Spoiler warning: Rush's character, Father Benedictus, for sundry reasons, including breaking his vow of chastity and having a child out of wedlock with an Aboriginal parishioner, does come to eventually realise the error of his ways. He then joins the cast for a resounding song and dance routine at the close of a quite bizarre film.) I find myself at such times wishing to ask the likes of Lyn Austin, Molly Craig,[17] Rachel Perkins,[18] Gawura families and the Pintubi et al., how it is we can effectively do good for, or preferably *with*, modern Indigenous people in an educational setting. And, without inflicting upon them our subjective interpretation of what is 'best'. To do otherwise would surely make us no better than the Reverend Hollowers and Father Benedictuses of this world.

The indicators are strong that the Gawura School is getting it right, with largely Aboriginal educators, counsellors and advisors teaching children of Aboriginal heritage close to their homes and amidst the shared facilities of those considerably more fortunate. One can only hope that this schooling model does something to address the cultural loss Lyn Austin identified and rekindles a deeper sensitivity, understanding and passion for Indigenous culture in all of St Andrews' students.

I suspect it must have given Phillip Heath modest pride to be sharing the Rudd apology and accompanying speech with those particular kids, sitting in an actual school where they were voluntarily attending and in an environment concerned with the thoughtful shaping and sharing of lives. I hope it truly was a lasting moment in the life of that college, its principal and students, the ripples of which would eventually hit the (artificial) shorelines of Lake Burley Griffin when Phillip Heath agreed to take the reins of Radford College Canberra as its fifth principal only two years later.

The temper of the times might have suggested to shrewd marketers that a Midnight Oil tribute show would be a winner for what we had originally and somewhat unimaginatively labelled the Lodge Gig.

Firstly, the band members were Australian; secondly, it could be considered somewhat controversial, depending on which songs were chosen – and controversy draws crowds; and thirdly, Peter Garrett's portfolio meant that he would still be keeping an active interest in and eye on the arts. Heaven knows, he might have busted some moves with me if I asked him nicely. (I should have written him a letter of invitation on Mum's floral stationery.) I might have even caught him off-guard during a caffeine high at the Curtin shops[19] and convinced him to join me in a rousing medley of head-turners like 'Short Memory', 'US Forces', 'If Ned Kelly Was King', 'Hercules' and even the topical 'Truganini'. Perhaps we could even let bygones be bygones and do an encore less lyrically or politically sensitive and bang out 'Surfing with a Spoon' as a duet? I could even dedicate it to beautiful Dorothea Brooke.

Then reality set in. It would surely have been a little surreal, maybe even inappropriate, for me to suggest to the Rudds that I was going to play a collection of greatest hits by one of Kevin's own staff from just over the hill and down the corridor at Parliament House. The lyrical content of any of the songs shortlisted above would probably not have sat too comfortably with many of Kevin's fellow ministers on speed dial. Let alone the former-rock-star-cum-politician himself.

So it was that the omni-influential, universally adored Beatles won out as the tribute act of the day. In the lead-up to the the Lodge Gig, I knew that I would be on long service leave, driving freely and drifting aimlessly along the Great Ocean Road with my compass pointing towards Kangaroo Island and from there on to Mauritius. Hence, with their wayward lead singer on walkabout, and because the band had recently played a John Lennon tribute show, it meant – with respect to George, Paul and even Ringo – that close to half (if not more) of Junk Sculpture's set list was primed and ready to go. Also, the charitable nature of the event dictated that all you really needed, besides excruciatingly thorough organisation and security, was a lot of…love. That, and three fat set lists full of classic and iconic tunes that everybody knew.

The Lodge Gig was to benefit the Black Mountain School (BMS) community. BMS is an exemplary educational institution that caters for approximately 110 high school-aged students with a range of disabilities. As principal, Frank Fogliati shared with me about its history and vision,

> Koomarri School was opened in 1955 after considerable lobbying by parents for a facility to provide education and therapy services for their sons and daughters with disabilities. The school was established in O'Connor with an enrolment of 12 students and two staff. The original building consisted of two classrooms, principal's office, three storerooms and a first aid room…
>
> In 2003 Ms Katy Gallagher, the ACT Minister for Education, officially renamed the school Black Mountain School. The name change was initiated by the Parent and Citizen Association and involved consultation with the whole school community.
>
> The school has had many achievements over the past 60 years and continues to provide an outstanding educational program that encourages students to develop their maximum potential. Every student participates in both an individual learning plan and a personal futures action plan that promotes development of skills, independence and inclusion in the community.

For years now, Radford College had been sending its students to BMS to share class and playground time with their kids on a weekly basis. My teamSUPPORT boys also independently organised three or four themed activity days each year as part of their leadership program. (The teamSUPPORT history is recounted in my previous book, *Little Life*.[20] In a nutshell, it is a leadership program designed to encourage more males into service endeavour.) Kevin Rudd's son, Marcus, who had joined the program, was instrumental in suggesting that his 'rents' house be opened for a fund-raising concert to assist his mates at BMS. Coincidentally, Marcus had seen me perform in SUPA's production of *The Wall* the year before (see, it is all linked) and I suspect had read in the program that I had a fully functioning band called Junk Sculpture. Enlisting them as the house band was thus a given. I often imagine what it would have been like if we had done a Pink Floyd show instead? To be fair, the Lodge's unsmiling security detail had enough to contend with as all the former hippies and their offspring swaggered in for the Beatles show. So I suspected a bunch of anarchists with mother issues questioning the need for education and thought control and punctuating it all by marching in jackboots and chanting in unison 'TEAR DOWN THE WALL!' may well have been pushing things.

The teamSUPPORT boys had an almost supernatural gift for pulling off big, intricate and complex events even though organisation and planning – and even agreement on what was actually happening – rarely commenced until quite late in the piece. In fact, often the night before. But it was clear right from the outset that everyone from the Lodge staff to the HBSGSF (Humourless But Slick Government Security Folk) that *nothing* could be left to chance. Thankfully my long-suffering and hyper-efficient buddy 'Rufus' Wainwright (who last appeared saving the day in a previous book *How to Succeed Without Really Winning*[21]) would come to save the day, but I knew I was really pushing the boundaries of our friendship. Similarly, I was testing the patience of Junk Sculpture, the members of which I had asked to rehearse and prepare songs while its lead singer was inspecting rows of grapes in McLaren Vale (and about to get geographically embarrassed in the Grampians.) By the way, I left express orders to include 'Strawberry Fields Forever' and to retain the eloquence of Sandy Farina's interpretation if at all possible. My similarly long-suffering and hyper-efficient bass guitarist, Chris Brown – who shares his name with a notorious American hip-hop recording artist from Tappahannock, Virginia – agreed to undertake the near impossible job of arranging the personnel, charts and schedules for Junk Sculpture (and humouring me about Farina) while I attempted to secure rigs and equipment through sketchy emails from various internet cafés with variable reception, situated along a bendy line along the Fleurieu Peninsula up into the Adelaide Hills.

If we pulled this gig off, both Rufus and Brownie would deserve an OA.

The concert went extremely well. The band, purely and simply, rose to the occasion.

Marcus opened proceedings with a heartfelt introduction, diplaying an inherited comfort when public speaking. Around him, his teamSUPPORT minions were directing people away from ponds, checking on portaloos, running activities for the kids such as face painting, assisting with African drum workshops and their infamous chestnut – the good ol' sponge-throw. Kevin Rudd was wisely nowhere to be seen when the sponges were being dunked.

I shared the vocals with the operatic Patrick 'Phantom' Oxley[22] and the sizzling Toni Maxfield; youngsters Mikey Bell (a teenaged John Petrucci) and Dan Miller (a slightly older Jimmy Page) played show-stealing fireworks on their guitars; and Michael 'Obama' Kulesza tickled the electronic ivories with his customary elegance and idiosyncratic salute to his believers. And last, but not least, there was Cooma's favourite son, Matt Swain – whom I met while performing *The Wall* – firing on the drums.

I remember casting my eye out over the lawns covered in streamers, garments and auras of bright, fluorescent rainbow colours. People of all abilities and ages were dancing in the world's first user-and-kid-friendly moshpit or enjoying the tunes from the grassy embankments. I pulled a BMS boy called Bradley onto the stage, threw him a tambourine and let him take the spotlight at the heart of the magnificent mayhem. I will never forget the joy I saw in his face as he stood there, playing lead tambourine, and looking every bit the centre of the known universe.

The PM, who I wanted to believe was making video conference calls to the other, non-pianistic Obama in the USA, made sporadic appearances on the deck, behind the euphoria, surveying his kingdom and surely declaring that it was good. Did I see him busting some funky dad moves up there on the driveway or was it just my imagination again? It was certainly in the realm of fantasy that when he finally got back on that conference call, he looked the camera in the eye and said, 'Barack, baby. You should hear these dudes rippin' through "Back in the USSR". The groove is sweeeeet. A veritable antidote to global tension. All you need is love, Barack. Grab Michelle and sing along with me. All together now…'

As the band warmed, I had that rare feeling as a performer that it could never get much better than this. I was getting by, if not (naturally) high, with a little help from my friends. There were many highlights: 'Phantom' Oxley's vocal majesty in 'Lady Madonna', with Obama Kulesza trickling up and down the keys like an over-caffeinated alley cat; Swainy's dependable and undaunted dexterity when confronted by the multiple time signatures on 'Here Comes the Sun' and 'A Day in the Life'; the fun and frivolity as Toni took the kids and those with a kid in their heart on a swim through an 'Octopus's Garden'; Mikey's sweetly sad and soaring solo in 'While My Guitar Gently Weeps' or Dan's brash and bluesy brilliance in 'Dear Prudence'; or when I looked up at the rainbow-coloured Lodge slopes during that selfsame song as the band slowed to double time and I sang with as much joy as I ever had in my life:

> The sun is up
> The sky is blue
> It's beautiful
> And so are you[23]

Yet it wasn't the so-called headlining act which made the event so sunny and beautiful. It was the BMS kids and their families. I think it was a day that will stay with Connor McClure forever. Connor and I have spent many hours together at BMS over the years. His love of music, particularly with a sprightly beat and catchy tune, is often shared when I visit the school. Both Swainy and I wheeled Connor to the back of the raised stage so that he could road test Matt's drum kit. I will long remember the utter joy on his face[24] as he was given free rein to bash and thump out an irregular but emphatic series of whacks of delight. It was hard to eventually prise him away from the drums. But Connor had had a big day: hanging with Kevin Rudd and Therese Rein, showing Junk Sculpture how to keep the beat, and even having his photograph in the newspaper the next day to prove it.[25]

Frank Fogliati, that wise, caring and softly spoken principal of BMS,[26] caught me during the bump-out. He began to tell me about how a family had approached him after the gig, thanked him and indicated how they had never thought they would ever be important enough to be admitted to the grounds of the prime minister's residence. He recollects being amazed at the sheer wonderment of looking around and thinking holy crap, we're here, we're really here, we are actually at the Lodge. Several times I would just walk off somewhere quiet and look. I'd scan across the grounds and see our students and parents having a ball. And always there was the backdrop of the Lodge which made it both surreal and inspirational. I know the parents were overwhelmed.

I do recall one parent tearfully telling me she was so moved that the PM of Australia, the leader of a nation, would do such an amazing thing for a group that are often the most marginalised and isolated. The particular parent told me she would never forget the moment when Kevin came up to her and personally introduced himself. From memory I think she squealed and said, 'Can I hug you?' But she never waited for his reply, she just threw herself upon him. It was a pretty special moment.

The event was a truly generous act. It was a lot of trouble and effort for everyone – staff at Radford College, Marcus, the Rudds, AFP – but it seems the planets aligned favourably that day for the Black Mountain School community.

Looking back on the gig now, it did have a tremendously surreal quality, appropriate to most latter-period Beatles compositions. Richard Browning, the Radford chaplain, perhaps best summed it up in saying,

Geez, H. It was like the prime minister of the country had flicked you the keys to the Lodge and said chuck a party. Lots and lots of boys had jobs; there was a big buzz from among the BMS/disability community but it wasn't so much about being at the Lodge, the event itself was just so much fun.

But with that fun now completed, the task of cleaning up after it all brought us back to reality relatively quickly.

With exhausted band members retiring to their families and friends, I returned from handshaking to assist with the bump-out. Phillip Heath was still about, helping with the removal of the staging at the end of the day. I thanked him for hanging around and asked him what he felt about the whole extravaganza. He said something along the lines of having 'a bigger plan ahead and the need to harness this sort of energy and make it possible to create more nation-changers'.

I was exhausted by then and did not know how or where to take these grand comments my new boss had made. But when I had seen the smiling faces of the BMS kids and their families that day, I deduced that an extremely potent and positive energy had been harnessed indeed. And figuring that my new employer's agenda would always include the Indigenous of this country, especially after his amazing work with Gawura, I began there and then to seriously consider whether my own school and its community, the teamSUPPORTers, my generous-hearted rock band and anyone interested enough to follow my madcap swings of personal, professional and artistic focus, might clang a tuneful gong and move onto something of even greater substance *alongside* the Aboriginal people.

When lost in the Grampians, I remember singing Pink Floyd's 'Is There Anybody Out There' to cheer me up. This may well have been the first time in history that a Roger Waters song had been used to create an uplifting mood. In any case, I am glad I was found by the rock-climbing/book-writing David Pearson and made it back alive and in time to perform at the Lodge Gig. And on the topic of Pink Floyd, I also have a lot more to be grateful about concerning Ron Dowd's production of *The Wall*. Not only could I relive an inspirational piece of music from my childhood; not only would I discover a drummer in touch with the rhythms at the heart of a song and then share them in a precious moment with an incredible boy from BMS; not only had that production drawn in and inspired a teamSUPPORT member who just happened to be the son of a prime minister; not only all of these things…but, with perhaps the greatest irony of all, *The Wall* tipped over a sequence of dominoes which resulted in a very real societal wall being similarly tipped over: one that separated those in power from the many who had none. Ah, the interconnectedness of it all. (I never got to perform 'Strawberry Fields Forever' à la Sandy Farina. But I guess there is only so much serendipitous nostalgia one is permitted in a single day.)

At the Lodge Gig, I received an awakening of something I suspected Midnight Oil already knew: that a community, particularly a disempowered or disabled one, could find some joy, significance, identity and even relief or solution through the sharing of music. There exists here a blissful hotspot indeed: when a performance of relevant, timely and sensitively chosen songs can steer a gathering of artists and its audience towards something bigger than the sum of all its parts.

I wanted to organise more of them.

I was proud of all that had been achieved in 2008. Even the harshest of critics would have to agree that it was a useful, if not commendable, exercise in empathy. After all, this was the year Obama diagnosed his country as having an empathy deficit on top of a financial one. In *The Audacity of Hope* he had written how empathy pulsed at the centre of his moral circuitry and that it was 'not simply as a call to sympathy or charity, but as something more demanding, a call to stand in somebody else's shoes and see through their eyes'.[27]

Yet, silky as this all sounded, I was now becoming unsettled and unsure that empathy without action; without a genuine response to a calling; without sincere gestures as opposed to empty arm-waving; without pure and simple doing – was nothing better than a dormant idea. It was like a novel left in a desk drawer never to be read by anyone. Rudd went further in an interview with John Pilger for his 2013 film *Utopia*,[28] when responding to attacks over his apology being merely 'gesture politics':

> if you have deeply wronged a people, or deeply wronged a person in your own life, you cannot begin to conduct a normal relationship until you've set wrongs to rights at that level.

Pilger then characteristically and somewhat pompously pushes him about a perceived lack of action in the post-apology period. Rudd replied that he was 'not going to stand up here and sort of wave some flag and say, guess what, it's all fine and dandy and we've fixed it'. He then, bluntly, grasped at what he attributed to be one of the great Australia proverbs for describing such grand assertions, and stated, 'That's bullshit.'

The Lodge Gig was where a richer engagement with the real world was to start for me. I was in my early forties and knew in my heart of hearts that this may have been way too late. I had sat in my comfortable place on the couch, wallowing in my own ignorance about self and country for just a little too long. Although well-intentioned, I was as guilty as the next person of gesture politics and flag (and arm) waving.

Yet I went to bed with some hope that I'd wake to the new day hearing Lyn Austin's words echo on through it…

'It's a beginning.'

My mother's voice is there too. 'I want deeds not words.'

And then the prime minister's. 'It is not sentiment that makes history; it is our actions…'[29]

George Huitker

Service Learning Palmcard

I offer the following service palmcard as an equation for our approach towards service learning for discussion and reflection.

Best to question...
Do-Gooder Service = Relationship/s x Returning x 1
D-G Relationship = Provide Quick Fix
D-G Service + D-G Relationship = Quick feel-good sensation
with largely short-term outcome/s
with limited empowerment
leading to dependence
Motto = To and for people
Leading Question = Where do I put the gifts?
Leading Exclamation = I want to make a difference!

Best to work towards...
Authentic Service = Relationship/s x Returning
Authentic Relationship = Respect, Listen, Imagine
Authentic Service + Authentic Relationship = Active love
Longevity of concrete outcome/s
through empowerment
leading to independence
Motto = Never to, not for, but with people
Leading Question = How can we work alongside?
Leading Exclamation = This is not about me.

(Author's note: most service learners start out approaching service as per the 'Best to Question' section above. The author certainly did. He wishes his potential hypocrisy noted. DGS can result in many good things happening and act as a wonderful introduction to service. But for a genuine service relationship to be formed, which empowers both parties in a lasting manner, the second approach is highly recommended.)

Track #3 Arm Wrestle On the Altar

When I was appointed the first Director of Service Learning at Radford College by Phillip Heath, in late 2012, I figured I had better lay down some rules of engagement.

Ideas had fermented over many years, particularly through my sharing of some glorious time with folk with disabilities through RAID (Recreation Activities for people with an Intellectual Disability) basketball, teamSUPPORT, the school visitations previously mentioned and the deepening relationship with Black Mountain School, post-Lodge Gig. I had also been developing programs which incorporated teenagers visiting the elderly and/or working in and around their environs; assisting at fetes, markets or similar fund-raising events; and even ventured into working in large national parks or smaller wildlife reserves, attacking everything from weed removal to bushfire remediation. Phillip was keen to invite me to keynote speak on the school's service practice alongside himself and Richard Browning at a national AHISA (Australian Heads of Independent Schools Association) conference at Twin Waters in 2012. I felt compelled to quickly formulate – or respectfully appropriate – some innovative, concrete and defensible service learning practice.

When all was said and done, I did not have to look too far for inspiration. In fact, I only had to turn to my fellow keynote speaker.

He might deny it, but our school chaplain is lead singer of sorts. He provides as abundant an amount of inspiration as he does perspiration. I have oftentimes felt that we must be blessed, if you will pardon the pun, with one of the more liberal-minded and huge-hearted priests in the universe, if Father Benedictus and Reverend Hollower are anything to go by. I wondered if this was because Father Richard initially studied to become a physiotherapist for four years, and in doing so has always kept the body and soul in equal check.

It was during his study of physiotherapy between 1987 and 1990 that he first met his future wife, Mel. Initial impressions he gave her must have been unique. This is because their relationship apparently developed over a cadaver, with six peers during Anatomy 101. In Richard's own unforgettable words, 'We would be leaning over quarter parts of human cadavers. I think I might have caught her eye the day I put a brachial plexus in her pencil case. It was a bit of a winning move and I have not lost that deft romantic touch.' Evidently not. Despite replacing flowers and chocolates with a brachial plexus, their friendship evolved, particularly when one of Richard's schoolmates, Sam Bailey, had a car accident and became a C6/7 quadriplegic.[1] Richard, with his arm in a sling from a shoulder reconstruction, required Mel to take lecture notes and also accompany her beau to visit Sam in the spinal unit of Princess Alexandra Hospital. 'We would visit Sam a couple of times a week, he explains. This went on for months. It became a bit of a fixture. We ended up taking many of my physio buddies, and this included all six from the anatomy lab table. It became a bit of a stand-up comedy routine. Sam seemed to enjoy our company. We had lots of fun visiting.' It would seem that inspirational folk magnetise towards each other. Sam would go on to become a successful beef cattle producer, ultralight pilot, focus of ABC's *Australian Story*, bestselling author and inspirational guest speaker, and aims to become the world's first quadriplegic to fly a helicopter.

Richard began to question his own desire to become a physiotherapist through his involvement in AYR (Anglican Youth Rallies), a spiritual and artistic extravaganza held six times a year in Brisbane. I suspect these rallies, with their fusion of creative, service and spiritual energies, had attractive sway in what was shortly to become a change in career path, if not life journey. His involvement with AYR certainly rallied him to listen to a calling to become an Anglican minister. In the back of Richard's mind he found there existed 'the sense that I may not be working as a physio forever. It started as a vague idea'. It was an idea probably heavily informed by circumstance, some outlined above, but perhaps also subconsciously by his father.

Richard had a rather significant role model as he warmed his chops at the spiritual hearth at his childhood home. His Brighton-born father, George, was ordained a priest the year *Sgt Pepper's Lonely Hearts Club Band* was released and similarly decided, after emigrating to Australia, to look at and attend to 'all the lonely people' down under. He subsequently worked as an assistant priest and vicar in New South Wales, in New England townships such as Armidale, Inverell and Warialda (where his son's friendship with Sam Bailey began), a region with many dots on the fringes of a map significant to this narrative, and where our roads are about to wind. From 1993 to 2008, his father was active as nothing less than the Bishop of Canberra and Goulburn, which may have played more than a small part in the decision his second, back-massaging, soul-restoring son made to travel south with his family, after numerous church posts around the Gold Coast,[2] to take up a position at Radford College in 2003 and hang with the 'rents.

Richard has spent many years shaping together a whole-school philosophy around a holy trinity of religion, service and rugby union. He has had his most ostensible success in the first two, but persistence and possibly a lot of prayer have evidently won through with the latter. (The Radford First XI won their first games under Richard's coaching in 2013. Like Pete Townshend's *Lifehouse* project, Richard took a very long his time to sculpt his winning sporting masterpiece. By 2015, they had made their first ever grand final.)

I suspect, like me, Richard has always wanted to be a lead singer. He commands attention through a series of unrestrained, spasmodic, awkward and often spontaneous bursts of arm flailing, which could possibly decapitate any unsuspecting Hobbits in the front row of his congregations, were they not already aware of this predilection. Peter Garrett would be proud. Like the Oils front man, he similarly does not let pitch get in the way of emphatic delivery, and sings hymns with total conviction and enough volume to be heard, unamplified, above a school of over 1,600.

When retelling passages and parables from the Bible, he is happy to take on characterisations which often involve the spontaneously casting of Hobbits as anything from prodigal sons, Ishmaelites, doubting Thomases, costumed angels, weeping or bleeding women, stable animals or even as live props such as burning bushes, mountain ranges or music stands; perhaps, if lucky, one could be enlisted as impromptu sound technicians and set builders or decorators (butcher's paper and crayons often used in abundance) should the day's themes and/or homily require your services. You could not claim chapel was boring as either a staff member or student. Something, usually unpredictable, always happens. This is definitely a man who raises a sweat for his beliefs and demands it of his entire front to back row.

No other chaplain I know incorporates sumo wrestling, writes in chalk on the chapel walls, drenches students with water, uses *Life of Brian* (unedited) in a pro-religious context, and allows himself to be covered in Glad Wrap to get a story told; or, to be more precise in my segueing here, to help its message get untangled, imprinted, awoken and unwrapped. Like all good storytellers, he leaves an (often striking) impression or image or reaction with the listener, one that later reignites, replays and reviews the narrative in both the memory and imagination. It is then for them to take it where they will.

Regardless of your own take on his methods, Father Richard has quite obviously inspired many with an encompassing and all-embracing approach to religions and belief systems. His careful inclusion and weaving of Indigenous culture ('I try to propagate the culture of the Dreaming') into chapel proceedings has always been respectful and unforced. Robert Hillman once described a similar marriage of beliefs when relaying the attitude on Elcho Island where Indigenous people 'are able to accommodate the Christian narrative without surrendering their engagement to their far older cosmology'.[3] Of course, this has its critics. These often come from the same corner: folk who are distressed about the following of hip new spiritual trends, yet simultaneously complain about the repellent stuffiness and soulless repetition inherent in traditional religious service practice and philosophy. Phooey to all bet-hedgers.

During Radford's Foundation Day services, in particular, Richard encourages the whole school to recognise the grand act of foundation/creation – and not just that of the college;[4] not just that of the traditional, tribal founding fathers of the Ngunnawal and Ngambri land, upon which early white Canberrans proceeded to build an unnecessary number of roundabouts and artificial lakes; no, the service in many ways is gargantuan, attempting to encompass the very foundation of all existence. Nothing less. As with his rugby team, Father Richard asks nothing but an unprecedented appearance in the semi-finals of existence, and asks his congregations to always rise above their weight, no matter how lowly their state of origin. Inspired no doubt by his days of Anglican rallies, he has created an extravagant spectacle incorporating dance, booming percussion, prayer, song, chant, face and body paint, abseiling ropes, levitating cauldrons, artwork and spoken word.

Yet amidst all this, he has also opened up an incredibly important space in the crammed order of proceedings for the student body to open up in turn, and speak out about their own personal dreamings and songlines. It is here, in my favourite part of the service, that something powerful is often released when a bunch of courageous students – and often those who you might doubt would speak unguardedly to a congregation of near 2000 – reveal something about their understanding of the essence of life. It was in fact during one of these Foundation Day services that I was provided with one, if not two, of my most inspirational moments as a teacher of twenty-five years at the school. It was a moment when Indigenous Australia and Radford College made a momentous and highly symbolic connection, then saw it repeated the following year with a new and different voice. I will come back to this later.

Wiradjuri elder, Duncan Smith, is often invited to these Foundation Day celebrations, perhaps to add another brick to the glorious bridge between the Anglican and Aboriginal sensibilities, in a ceremony that would do Peter Jackson proud. As with a lot of what I am about to share, you may just have to come out and witness it all for yourself, in order to really fully experience the breadth of what is being attempted. You will never be the same.

Give me a call and I'll arrange seats next to some Hobbits. And sit there alongside you.

As both Richard and I continually placed our occasionally provocative ideas on service in the firing line at national educational conferences, staffrooms and informal gatherings – or whenever Phillip Heath enlisted us – it became abundantly clear that open debate on service practice was long overdue. It needed to be approached with sensitivity, as no person engaging in seemingly selfless activity likes to be told they need to lift their game. Both of us would be the first to acknowledge that the search for an authentic service formula is ongoing. It is also one for which we do not seek or claim authorship or copyright. If any service idea is to be effective, it belongs to the community in a place emphatically distant from ego and bank statements.

Imagine. Listen. Respect. A bunch of verbs. A holy trinity of a different sort.

Young lives – if not lives of all ages – can be augmented through nurturing the skills of imagining, listening and respecting. They can be invaluable tools for anyone deciding to engage in service activity. In striking a balance between them, and sensing the appropriate time to utilise each, the basis of an effective code for service outreach[5] can be formulated and evolved.

Spoiler alert: in time, those three verbs were to become the ingredients which constituted a fuel which inevitably kick-started not only a school bus filled with students heading out into the land of the Gamilaraay (G-trips as they became known), but eventually Junk Sculpture's tour van replicating a revised version of *Blackfella/Whitefella* and heading to the bush to play some special music. This power trio of words was certainly the base on which I was to encourage my own students to enter into an authentic and lasting service *relationship* – as opposed to some isolated project or one-off visit. I would find myself asking them to reconsider a 'do-gooder' approach, worried that an antiquated Aunt Daphne or Uncle Derwent style of no-nonsense service pragmatism might be philosophically and practically ill-advised for the development of teen service learners. Before you start getting riled up in defence of Daphne and Derwent, or start hitting me an umbrella, allow me to explain.

Richard stirs me greatly when talking about his Aunt Valerie Browning and her amazing work among the Afar nomads in Ethiopia. It is from this impressive woman that Richard came to fully understand the precarious and dubious nature of do-gooding. The reason why both of our service values can challenge, sometimes inflame, other folk at times – to the point of them wanting to lash at us with parasols – may well be due to an unabashed adoption of Valerie's notion that service work should not be undertaken through thoughtless and possibly self-righteous action towards those we have somewhat arrogantly appointed as worthy of our charity and compassion. We must never place ourselves in a position of power to 'fix things'. Rather, we should seek solutions with and alongside those who are impoverished and disempowered, thus nourishing and empowering them, in turn, to overcome this situation. As Richard sums up, 'Poverty is first the absence of power to do anything about your situation. Service must increase power.'

Wallaby captain David Pocock, who experienced immense poverty and powerlessness in his own home country of Zimbabwe, understands inherently the need to change the approach of solution-and-fund provision and look towards increasing the capacity of those in unfortunate conditions. As he writes in his inspiring autobiography, *Openside*, his charity, Eighty Twenty,[6] aims

> to achieve a sustainable future by collaborating with people with the aim of building their capacities so that they can empower themselves, rather than just trying to provide solutions from the outside. I think we often, mistakenly, think that we simply need to go and help people who are in poverty or are

oppressed because they are incapable of helping themselves, but this does not acknowledge a person's amazing skills and resilience.[7]

So when Benjamin Franklin once stated, 'I think the best way of doing good to the poor is not making them easy in poverty, but leading or driving them out of it,'[8] I find myself angrily reaching for an umbrella handle myself. What gives one the right to treat the poor like cattle who need herding? What arrogance underlies a self-appointed expert to casually assess another's powerlessness as something they might be easy with or comfortable in? A lifestyle choice perhaps? And what short-sightedness permits one to lasso the poverty of those we consider as cows, and 'do good' upon them without any contemplative research, open-eared discussion or apparent empathy to their context? *Thwhack!* Benjamin. *Thwhack!* (I should acknowledge here that Benjamin Franklin's ideas of paying forward acts of kindness, explored in the book and film *Pay It Forward*,[9] were the basis of the teamSUPPORT philosophy. I should also admit that he goes on to write about the poor in the document cited above stating, 'the less was done for them, the more they did for themselves, and became richer'.)

In her amazing book *Maalika*, Valerie Browning highlights many examples of how the poor and powerless have been kept in that state by mismanaged and misinformed good intentions (and sometimes sadly less so) on the part of those vested with the responsibility of distributing aid. These include overseas aid workers and organisations close to the ground, from government officials through to those in private enterprise. Two stories from it have stayed in my mind.

The first centres on UNESCO piloting teacher's packages in Afar, which included items identified by Valerie and her colleagues as useful resources for both staff and students. At a training workshop run by an educational expert from UNESCO in Andabba, Valerie became concerned about two elderly Afar desert men, with rifles hanging from their shoulders, who broke into proceedings and demanded to join in. Valerie assumed, before speaking to them, that they would be disappointed as the training course was about education and 'not treatment for malaria and health things'.

But when spending time to discuss matters under a tree, she was surprised when the elders exclaimed,

> We send our camel caravan from Afar all the way into Tigray… They tell us that the Tigrayana are meeting, they're doing, they're building, their changing their lives. They tell us fantastic stories. We wonder about ourselves. We are sleeping under trees. The Afar are going nowhere. We have no future and you are trying to stop us being involved in education? How dare you.[10]

Valerie's reaction said it all: 'I'd thought they would be resistant to education; instead, they were demanding it.' So, after negotiating the involvement of female students from the clan elder, she admitted each of the leaders' sons, who had travelled with their fathers for over 300 kilometres to be there with them, to commence the training under the UNESCO expert. 'This was the first time I really understood,' she explains, 'that the Afar were desperate for a future where they could be empowered to do things for themselves.' It certainly highlighted to her, as it should us, the danger in making assumptions about what exactly is needed in a service situation, before actually sitting under a tree and talking.

The second is her inspiring example of how working alongside one another, in community, is so much more likely to produce a unified and lasting solution to a problem. In 2002, Valerie began receiving reports that people in the Dubte region were dying of measles. Her account of the governmental response is unsettling:

> Someone in an office somewhere makes up a plan on a computer about how many vaccinations they're going to do, and allocates a certain time for the job – say, a week. The administration office dishes out the money. There will probably be a few arguments about how it's going to be divided up, which takes a couple of days, so they've got five days left to do the job. Vaccines have to be kept refrigerated. The government workers collect their ice in some regional centre like Dessie or Dubte, which might be 400 kilometres away from where they're working. Then they drive as close as they can to the vaccination area. They might still have to walk 24 hours to get there. Most government workers won't walk, they want to be driven, but they can't be because there are no roads. By the time all this has been sorted out, the ice has melted anyway and the vaccines have been ruined. Sometimes the

government workers just dig a hole and bury the vaccines, then sign the forms to say they've achieved 90 per cent coverage. I know. I've found them.[11]

This failed experiment in good intention would be laughable were it not lethal. But rather than being overwhelmed by cynicism, Valerie found a solution which involved working with the very communities she has chosen to serve alongside. What strikes me as telling in what follows, is that she engages the young of the community to play a vital part in the solution:

> Our vaccination method is to take a refrigerator, and a generator to run it, on a truck as far into the area as possible. We set up base near a water source, load the vaccines into ice chests and use camels donated by the community to carry them into the wilderness. When the vaccines have been used, the camels return to base and pick up another load. A boy stays with the generator and ice chest under a tree, filling up plastic bags with water and freezing them so they're ready to send out with each foray.[12]

Utilising seventy-five highly motivated Afar health workers, and travelling over hundreds of kilometres, Valerie and her community somehow made this solution work, sometimes 'running camels by the light of the moon'. And most striking is not only that they achieved a 93–94% vaccination coverage in this manner, but that they would unwaveringly administer to all in their reach, even if it meant chasing down every single child: 'If we found that the child had gone away with the goats, we'd wait for that child to return.' No single small or seemingly 'statistically insignificant' member of the community was left out of the aid. This is because the community themselves were empowered in a solution solely concerned with looking after their own.

When asked why the government could not do this good work, especially while claiming otherwise? 'It's not in their guidelines,' writes Valerie. 'Their programs are drawn up for the town where people take their children to a clinic. This program was a classic example of why you should involve community effort.' She applauds government and international aid agencies for their good intentions with contributing money and vaccines, 'but they should keep their hands off implementation'.[13] After reading passages like the one above, one can understand why some people might use the phrase 'Dogooder' with occasional vitriol.

It could well be the sad state of my own psyche, but I have always associated 'doing good' with infliction: such as force-feeding, tidying up a room, or necessary dental procedure. Or as Patrick White once described his mother in his autobiography, *Flaws In the Glass*,[14]

> She sincerely believed in the necessity for doing good. It never occurred to her that she often forced her charity on its object with what almost amounted to physical violence.

That said, I wish to hedge my bets. I am not, at the end of the day, a callous gent. I feel, on a daily basis, the need to be encouraging, thankful and congratulatory of anyone desiring to engage in *any* act of kindness. But then, I also share that niggling feeling of annoyance with those who have had Aunt Daphne constantly filling your freezer with fish casseroles when you are allergic to seafood (and then staying for a three-hour coffee while your stomach churns), or Uncle Derwent insisting that you put aside the inconvenient issue of your dyslexia, as he insists that your education would be dramatically enlightened by reading *The Brothers Karamazov* – in fact, stop what you are doing now, turn everything off right this instant, and get cracking on them 776 pages.[15] Or, on a more suddenly sombre note, the feeling of despair you may descend into when removed from your family, so that you can get an apparently better education, necessary socialisation, formal religious instruction, clearer perspective, a straighter back, a modern world view and a wholesome upbringing for some predetermined future life, some place else, in the hands of total strangers.

That phrase about the road to hell being paved with good intentions is not my favourite one, but heck I use it a lot. Good intention is a noble cause. Hearing people, of any age, stating that they want to make a difference to this world is actually inspiring, were it not equally as brazenly rash. *This is because wanting to make a difference through service work can be a precarious path.* It is often paved with the alluring promise of saintliness.

Its travellers, armed with a pack of nifty tools for the trade of good intent, sometimes set off intuitively, half-baked and without contemplating the map of their service terrain. Something akin to my trek in the Grampians. Remember? I got very lost.

We have all heard the apocryphal story of the group of missionaries insistent on building huts for a tribe they had come to 'do good' for in some foreign land.

As the tribal leader began to speak, the head missionary exclaimed, 'You can thank us later, dude. We've got work to do. You lot go rest with your camels under the shade of that sole tree over there and we'll have a village built for you in a week.'

The tribal leader lifted his hand in protest and began to open his mouth to speak, but was once more waved down and had his response spoken over by the missionary.

'We've got it in hand, good buddy. We're here to help you. Don't you worry about a thing.'

After a surprisingly tiring week of building with overpriced tools and shoddy materials, the missionary announced the job was complete and that their organisation might come back the following year to complete the car park, that is, if the funding came through.

So for a third time, the tribal elder attempted to speak but was once more stopped in his tracks. 'No, no, no. No need to thank us. We just want to do good to other people.'

As the missionaries left, the tribe gathered their camels and slowly, but sadly, walked through the village that had been generously and spiritedly built for them. They took a few small items of need from the buildings as they passed through, before heading off into the horizon themselves.

As the sun followed them behind the rise in an explosion of crimson, the tribal leader turned to his travelling companion, solemnly shaking his head, and said, 'I tried so hard to tell them we were nomads. If only they listened…'

'Did you even get his name?' his friend enquired.

'No. He was too busy building buildings to build a relationship…'

In a striking performance as John Quincy Adams in the film *Amistad*, Anthony Hopkins questions a fellow anti-slavery campaigner about his approach to his well-intentioned work and the people in his care: 'You and this young so-called lawyer have proven you know what they are. They're Africans. Congratulations. What you don't know, and as far as I can tell haven't bothered in the least to discover, is who they are.'[16]

There's the crux of the matter: the server needs, right from the outset, to find a way to move away from work that focuses on 'what' they are doing, towards work that stems and grows from 'who' they are working *with*. From my vantage point, the only way this can be effectively done is to commence a relationship where stories can be shared and deeper context provided.

On numerous occasions now, I have heard leadership guru Paul Porteus[17] explain how it is often best to 'lead with a question' when wishing to guide, inspire, nurture or help other people. So when a student is spontaneously ignited into action by something they may have seen on the internet, read in class, heard at assembly, or maybe even the need to impress a boy/girlfriend, they usually proclaim, 'I want to make a difference!' I might reply in a Morrissey-like fashion, 'Why does it matter what you want?' (I resist the urge to add here that most despots also wanted to make a difference. So what makes us any different to them?) This is often met with a stony silence and often an aggressive 'Don't diss my vision' look that accompanies a soul grappling and probably lost in a fog of zeal.

But before the crusader draws a lance, I then ask, 'Is there a way you could find out what the person, group or organisation you desire to work alongside might actually need?' Some may reply 'the internet'; others will advocate you pay 'the experts' to find out; and some have even proposed that you give your target person/group/nation a lot of cash and observe how they spend it. To each response there is an equal degree of validity as there is naivety. Without being too smarmy (although it is hard not to when leading with a question, as you often feel like a priest in a confessional), you then ask, 'What is stopping you from asking those you wish to work alongside what it is they might need?' The answer to this is often the exorbitant expense of a plane ticket. 'But surely you need to understand their context before you go running off doing good for them or acting on their behalf – let alone purchasing pricey airfare?' Valerie Browning is even less equivocal about the perceived need to do good overseas:

> We shouldn't try to manipulate other people's lives. I think a lot of missionary work is manipulative. In my mind, I'm not sure about mission services. I think anybody can have a mission. Say you live in Bondi or Vaucluse, you have an ordinary life, you go to the office, you come home, you have three kids, you're a member of a few clubs…if you live out a godly life amongst these people, that is your mission. You don't have to buy a plane ticket to a foreign country.[18]

Thus begins the age-old 'charity should begin closer to home' debate. I concur with Browning that perhaps doing some work with poverty 'in our own backyard' may be a judicious way to start out on a service adventure, before hitting the tarmac with untested ideas, ideals and approaches in someone else's.

And there's the rub. The only way one can commence authentic service work is to engage in a relationship and, like any relationship, commence with exploratory research and, where possible, dialogue. I recently wrote in an article for Anglican Schools Australia[19] about the necessity for our trips to Gamilaraay country to initially be *exploratory* in nature, particularly as the Radford contingent began

> looking for ways to better understand the country, townships and people of rural Australia. Participants also hoped to learn more about themselves and the realities associated with authentic service endeavour. We did not go to do much but to learn to build relationships and respond to things as they emerged.[20] Over time these ideas have been simplified into the phrase 'never to, not for, but with people' to describe what we do on our trips. These seven words convey a very powerful message and as such have come to form one of our service rules of engagement. They also offer useful advice for engaging with a part of Australia that has suffered from misplaced or misinformed good intentions and short-term or empty promises.

I stand by such rules of service engagement, which are only reinforced by Richard Browning's reminder that 'service can only occur where there is a real relationship being formed'. The best way to create a relationship is to find common ground with those you assist. This can be as specific as artistic and cultural interest, or as broad as a united quest for freedom. As Aboriginal activist and educator Lilla Watson is often credited with having said, 'If you've come here to help me, you're wasting your time. But if you've come because your liberation is bound up with mine, then let us work together.'[21]

Setting aside ample time in the building of a service relationship to imagine, listen and respect *together* – and you can do these in any order – is frankly essential. (Richard Browning confirms that the ordering of ILR does not matter so much: 'The business is in doing all three. They are not separate compartments that can be given individual attention, they are the necessary notes of the same one chord. When one is diminished, the other two will immediately suffer.') Surely, armed with a willingness to firstly respect those you are working alongside (that is, not walking into their village suggesting a car park would look nice under that shady palm tree, or perhaps over there where those stones and sticks are neatly arranged, or better still over there where that big family lives); secondly to *listen* to what they have to say about anything and everything – be it whimsical or profound – and to be alive to their feelings, opinions, needs, wants, dreams, what makes them happy or what makes them sad, as well as their personal, family's, town's and country's histories; yes, all of this – and then thirdly to *imagine together* a way of creatively and effectively making a difference that might steer all towards independence and empowerment – this is going to set you on the correct service course.

Just a little more on the idea of imagining. Nick Cave & the Bad Seeds hauntingly lamented at the turn of the century that perhaps a more burdensome evil lies in our inability to creatively conceive and configure:

> The burdens that you carry now
> Are not of your creation
> So let's not weep for their evil deeds
> But for their lack of imagination.[22]

When one revisits Paul Keating's Redfern Park speech from 1992, it is consistently critical throughout of a seeming inability within us to *imagine* not only the context of another's poverty or powerlessness, but also how we would respond if we were, if you pardon the timely and provocative choice of image, in the same boat,

> We took the traditional lands and smashed the traditional way of life. We brought the diseases. The alcohol. We committed the murders. We took the children from their mothers. We practised discrimination and exclusion. It was our ignorance and our prejudice. And our failure to imagine these things being done to us.[23]

He then proceeds to ask of us to imagine, more profoundly, a list of scenarios specific and familiar to all non-Aboriginal Australians. Although bulky and challenging, I feel they are worth repeating here.

> It might help us if we…imagined ourselves dispossessed of land we had lived on for fifty thousand years – and then imagined ourselves told that it had never been ours. Imagine if ours was the oldest culture in the world and we were told that it was worthless. Imagine if we had resisted this settlement, suffered and died in defence of our land, and then were told in history books that we had given up without a fight. Imagine if non-Aboriginal Australians had served their country in peace and war and were ignored in history books. Imagine if our feats on sporting fields had inspired admiration and patriotism and yet did nothing to diminish prejudice. Imagine if our spiritual life was denied and ridiculed. Imagine if we had suffered the injustice and then were blamed for it.[24]

Imagine indeed.

For in doing so you come to slowly realise that in serving others, you might actually be serving yourself; that your own liberation is bound up with that of others; and that in an alternative universe, that sickly child given birth to in a different place and time and in a less fortunate context – might well have been you.

I realise that in writing all of this I am putting myself up for possible if not severe scrutiny. But so be it. (Just be polite.) To coin a phrase attributed to Socrates, 'the unexamined life is not worth living'. I similarly assert that 'the unexamined service act is not worth doing'. Especially as the unexpected and occasionally negative outcomes from misguided and misinformed service rarely affect the 'do-gooder', but more markedly those inflicted with its best intention.

At the risk of being overly harsh, it is the 'good intent' practised by the Mrs Whites, Aunt Daphnes, Uncle Derwents, Father Benedictuses, Reverend Hollowers, missionary leaders, those who stole generations of children, and all who consider that they have had their 'hearts in the right place', that needs to be refined, rejigged and revisited in order to evaluate and maybe compensate for any shortfall.

The necessary attributes to commence such review includes the *ears* and *eyes*; a heightened sensitivity to correct time and place; and the capacity to be alert and aware of what is happening around you and the person/people you serve. At a recent first aid course, I was told to remember 'DRABC' in order to pass the test at the end of the day. The 'D' stands for 'danger' (that is, an awareness of the surroundings), and it tellingly comes before the 'R', which stands for 'response'. In other words, one must observe, listen and think *before* responding/assisting, and even before checking for a response in those we hope to assist with (first) aid. Certainly, and at the very *least*, we need to regularly and seriously question how, why, what, where and when we should engage in service endeavour, especially as we enter into the lives of the complete stranger with the hope, aim and commendable dream of making things better for them.

And lastly, there's the issue of *returning*.

As hinted already, the enhancer for any leader, thinker and/or follower of authentic service within any community is, purely and simply, to understand the timely art of *returning*. It is an art form, which requires disciplined preparation and careful contemplation. It needs to be staged without creating a situation of dependence. For in order to truly grow past adversity, injustice or tragedy, a service relationship of longevity will only develop muscle through the eventual creation of independence. It is in some ways ironic that deep-rooted problems are rarely overcome by short-stay soothsayers and band-aid solutions, yet can be more effectively tackled by the very people involved, possibly suffering, at the heart of the matter.

I was recently inspired by a wise and pensive student of service learning who announced to me that she wished to study to become a doctor. This was a hard choice for her as it meant putting aside the upfront, rewarding, though nonetheless demanding, fieldwork that was nourishing that strong desire within her to effect positive change for those in her care. This tough decision was made so that she could one day *return* to the places where she once served (as a student) in order to make a *lasting and tangible* difference. She had recognised that service, like parenting, needed to be an *ongoing concern*, of serious interest, intent and respect for those we find ourselves working *alongside*.

Robert Hillman, when interviewing a passionate volunteer, similarly recognised that 'a lot of those with an urge to make some sort of contribution to the cause of Indigenous Australians' needed to ask themselves some fundamental and challenging questions:

> All well and good, but what contribution? Teaching, maybe? He had no qualification. He was forced to concede that good intentions alone wouldn't put him in a position to offer black Australians anything of value, and so went…with the idea of enrolling in a specialist course that would qualify him to teach Indigenous kids.[25]

With a maturity beyond her years, my Radford student realised that focusing her energies on collecting gifts, fund-raising cash and organising immediate return trips would not do sufficiently much to heal and tackle some of the root causes of the poverty experienced. If she were fair dinkum, she recognised, then she would have to do some more work away from the source of her immediate concern.

Service is not the same as a donation. *A caring donation does not necessarily require a relationship.* It can be executed through a generous tax-deductible offload across the internet; a rewarding feeling when flinging into and filling up charity bins with items we do (or do no longer) need; or a sneaky re-gifting of Christmas presents for the school, club or church's charitable hampers. (I am often bemused at how often cans of Spam appear in these.)

As insinuated, service also needs to be more than just raising awareness – along with those funds. We are too often easily satisfied, possibly proud, and consider it a job well done once we have made others *aware* of issues, injustices and injuries. Impassioned speeches at assemblies, conferences and conventions may stir the emotions (in the moment), and enlighten one to injustices that exist in the wider world (which remain hovering in the consciousness for about a week or two), but unless accompanied by real, regular and loving *action*, it's all just spiritual/intellectual spam. Like most of those funds raised, awareness will likely disappear down a big black hole.

I am often heard quoting from Dickens' *Bleak House*, where the narrator states,

> There were two classes of charitable people: one, the people who did a little and made a great deal of noise; the other, the people who did a great deal and made no noise at all.

Dickens, of all people, instinctively understood that charitable work required less fuss and greater action. (Ironically, a lot of his books take an average of 776 pages to suggest this.) And while speaking of nineteenth century classic literature that runs into 700 or so pages in length, this is where we also need to heed Uncle Derwent's treasured Dostoevsky. (See, there is method in Uncle Derwent's madness.) Oh, Fyodor, your calls – through the character of Father Zosima – for an 'active love' still resonate over 135 years or so since the many pages of *The Brothers Karamazov* first saw the light of day. In asking us to enter into a 'complete selflessness in the love of your neighbour', Zosima/Dostoevsky claims that the server's soul will consequently be cured of all niggling doubt. When you are on this good path, he advises, try not to leave it. (Surely that's worth an experiment.) But he is also quick to remind us that 'active love is labour and perseverance' and is equally quick to denounce that dreamy zeal which 'thirsts for immediate action, quickly performed, and with everyone watching'.

Fyodor would probably be increasingly uneasy about the growing number of poverty tourism bureaus providing packages, largely to high school and university students, offering experiences which have the potential, to use his phrase, 'to flit by like a phantom'. While those who participate in such tours would have the most noblest of intentions – and I have no wish to offend or unsettle these generous souls – it worries me a little that profit-oriented businesses are making money from seeking out and then organising tours/experiences/journeys of discovery amongst the underprivileged, dispossessed, powerless and desperately poor. While I applaud the outreach, I do hope the principles of the aid have been carefully formulated, considered and evaluated. I would also trust that the organisation *returns* any excessive profits back to the poor they are effectively using as a *raison d'être* for their tours (after costs, I would allow).

And what of the tourists themselves? For them I have a gentler critique, as I appreciate that at one stage in my own service journey, I too would have been attracted by such an opportunity. It could be that I just have a philosophical problem with the word 'immersion' which is often associated with these tours, and hopefully the less positive connotations do not underpin these tours' service practice. In my past life as an actor I used to be petrified of method actors who would 'immerse' themselves in their character. To clarify, if they were playing a homeless soul, they'd live like one for a week to see what is what like in order to make their acting more authentic. And then go straight to rehearsal. (God knows what they did if they were playing a cross-dressing, psychotic killer.) In any case, I worked out towards the end of my dramatic study that method actors tended to be a little obnoxious and sometimes smelly and/or dangerous to work with, as they not only lost their identity when 'in the zone' but also a sense that what they were doing on the stage was actually just make-believe. There are plenty of stories where actors playing a pugilistic character, for example, let loose of some actual aggro on some unfortunate co-star cast as their victim. Immersion needs to be approached with a degree of caution, control and plenty of self-awareness.

To 'immerse' oneself in another's poverty can undeniably lead to a rich experience through exposure to the daily plight of the unfortunate. This, in turn, can lead to greater empathy, future action and possibly life-changing revelation. But while this is all rich and rewarding *for the visitor*, what greater good will come to the people whose lives are being 'immersed' in? If I was living in quiet despair, or maybe even a state of being quite happy, despite being desperately poor, and someone was to say to me, 'H, I would like to immerse myself in your life,' I would probably reply 'Sure, go ahead' (and perhaps be cautiously grateful for the interest). But I would also quietly wonder how this other person's immersion in my poverty was going to make me actually *feel* at the end of it all. Their friendship and interest certainly would make me sense that I was loved and cared for *in the moment* but how would it make me feel in the lonely, hungry, colder and powerless months after they have gone home? Deserted possibly? Has immersion thus done anything to genuinely improve my situation, empower me and/or steer me towards independence? Hillman is even more direct in his description of the before-mentioned volunteer with an interest in Indigenous Australia:

> One thing he noticed about his departure…is that the kids he'd been teaching were not in the least surprised. A white bloke comes along, offers you a bit of this, a bit of that, then moves on. That's what some white blokes do – a bit of this, a bit of that, then move on.[26]

What is clear here is that some problems with the 'immersion approach' are that the experience 1) is sometimes brief and transitory, 2) might not be repeated more than once or twice, and 3) can be entered by the tourist in the knowledge that any discomfort, complexity or even tragedy shared by the said immersion *can eventually be left behind*. You could quite easily convince me that this is a sensible safety mechanism for the server. Yet for those being immersed upon, the best that such an experience will provide is some hope that there are people out in the wider world who actually care; who are interested sufficiently enough to travel from the other side of the world to immerse themselves in a contrasting reality. I repeat that this is noble in itself. In visiting East Timor with Radford students, Richard Browning points out this can be profoundly dignifying and 'empowering', for the Timorese can recognise themselves as one who possesses the dignity to give something to the foreigner in their midst. That is, we discover something of our own poverty and receive so much from those who apparently have little to give.

Another friend recently suggested to me that I am too intense and possibly unnecessarily negative about the concept of immersion. She argues that I should

> look at 'immersion' in a different, more positive, way. Immersion is about engaging as fully as possible in the lives of the poor and/or marginalised. It is neither pretentious nor presumptuous. It is as simple (and complex) as putting aside one's own ego, needs and wants for a time, and engaging with the reality of others' lives. The immersion experience is the reason for being in another culture. It does not involve having a few days 'helping' a community and then pursuing your own interests, such as a week or so sightseeing. Being immersed in another culture is about being entirely 'present'; it is about being there with others without agenda or expectations.

At the end of the day I find myself, once again, choosing a style of service experience not primarily concerned with losing oneself in an experience, but one which focuses on creating careful *relationships* through working thoughtfully *alongside* each other, and then *returning* if both parties agree that it is all heading towards empowerment and independence.

In having a relationship through service, you become less prone to glorifying and exploiting poverty when you carry your experience and its associated memories, reflections, slideshows, poems and other artistic responses back home to show your family, friends, workmates, schools, conferences and tour operator. You are also cautious with use of the first-person in your narrative; as Richard once emailed to me, 'the measure of worth of a work of service must not be our own good intentions, but the increase in those we seek to serve. That is, the worth of your work cannot be self-referencing.' As Pocock reflected on his own presentations on the work done with Eighty Twenty,

> I had talked about trying to speak in a way that presented our project in terms of the people in Nkayi, and how they were taking initiative rather than

presenting them as victims (as so much development and charity fundraising tends to do). We were conscious of not trying to emotionally manipulate the people at the dinner into giving money. In my speech I gave an overview of the work we are doing, as well as some personal stories of people I had met whose lives had been bettered. We also showed a video that showed what was happening on the ground and introduced the team at Nkayi.[27]

You are also less likely to glorify the self, the work and its worthiness, because, in having a relationship, you are careful with how you present the other's story, image, plight and poverty. You are sensitive with how you describe it, often in hushed tones, because you have put a name to the face that you may have seen in an advertising brochure or awareness campaign. And in *returning* to the relationship, perhaps you are stamping a metaphoric passport of service legitimacy and proving to the sceptics that it is not all about one's own personal, one-sided experience of poverty, but a mutual sharing of and then acting alongside someone else's.

As Richard pinpoints, 'do not glorify poverty or gloss over its profoundly dehumanising effects. By being in relationship, we also have to act. We cannot stand idly by.' He is certainly right here. Just don't rush in. His call to service arms, to engage in Dostoevsky's 'love in action', were similarly imprinted in the Redfern Address, with the added proviso that something tangible exists at the end of it all:

> Perhaps when we recognise what we have in common we will see the things which must be done – the practical things. We have to give meaning to 'justice' and 'equity' – and we will only give them meaning when we commit ourselves to achieving concrete results.[28]

In other words, after respect has been earned through common and careful listening and mutual imagination, what is left is the hard, cold, concrete and sweaty *work* required to give it all meaning.

One has to get off one's butt for that to happen.

When Phillip Heath asked me to speak at that 2012 AHISA conference, I was immensely uneasy about assuming any mantle of expertise when it comes to service learning. As is obvious from this chapter, I am more than comfortable with engaging in open-hearted debate about its essence and effectiveness. Valerie Browning unceremoniously reflects upon her own 'speaking out' for the rights of the Afar: 'They should be standing up and shouting and making a fuss. Someone has to do it, and, until they've been educated, that someone will have to be me.'[29] I feel the same way about my own possibly abrasive ideas about service endeavour under construction. I still need to wear a safety helmet on site.

So why work and play with all these words, ideas, philosophies and approaches you may ask? Why the need to self-righteously critique the good intention of others? Am I prepared and strong enough, as Clarice Sterling challenges Hannibal the Cannibal in *The Silence of the Lambs,* 'to point that high-powered perception at yourself'?[30] And why spend a chapter of a memoir checking these?

Because it is serious stuff, this service.

Because when dealing with the rights of others you have got to get it right.

Because, to quote the narrator of *Intimacy* by Hanif Kureishi, 'You can, of course, experiment with your own life. Maybe you shouldn't do it with other people's.'[31]

Or, as the emphatic and impressive Valerie Browning reminds us, when taking up the complex struggle of empowerment through service, you need to be fully and sensitively and completely aware that 'these were people's lives we were dealing with here'.[32]

I had hoped to find the first record my mother gave me – a 45rpm single of a cute *kinderljiede* called 'A Windmill in Old Amsterdam'.

Even then, I was exhibiting the alarmingly high levels of self-absorption necessary to become a successful lead singer.

Yet it wasn't the so-called headlining act which made the event so sunny and beautiful...

It was the BMS kids and their families.

The Lodge Gig was where a richer engagement with the real world was to start for me.

'I have gone from being a kid who was going down the wrong track, to someone who has a new and different perspective on life.'

Good people can, do and will come through for each other in the end, in various and unpredictable ways.

These amazing kids... Our future is secure with them.

The Warrumbungles and I go back a long way.

'I dream that in the future

programs that provide a way across this ever-growing divide

for those who have been left behind

will have their place cemented in our education system.'

Before we knew it, we were playing out at a spectacular sunset...

And so it happened. Six and a half gigs. Eight days.

Twenty-eight years thinking about it.

The Junkies and I had never played a concert through an open window before but were up for that challenge... Luckily, it was a big one.

There were the sculptors of junk behind me, sporting their 'Still Sorry' shirts, now a little faded and battle-worn,

creating raucous music from all that coloured plastic, lacquered wood and shining metal,

sweating on each and every note, chord and beat; massaging the song to travel smoothly, like lifeblood…

shimmering, shining, shouting and singing it sweetly into existence.

Track #4 Grow Anything In My Heart

Naturally, in 2009, my thoughts on service underwent a paradigm shift: I began to understand the necessity of avoiding the mantle of 'expert' in this field; of making hasty, life-affecting, possibly life-altering decisions and actions on behalf of those whose lives we had self-appointed ourselves to ameliorate; and to attempt to ignore easy preconceptions, unresearched assumptions, and the more subjective notions of what might be, for better or worse, 'the best' for those we should be working alongside. Instead, as Lilla Watson and her group had suggested, I needed to find a way to bind my own quest for liberation, empowerment and identity with those I sought to assist. And to do so after contemplative action, rather than premature or impulsive gong-clanging.

This was to trickle down to those in my charge. The teamSUPPORT boys, being a major focus of my service energies at the time, heard it like a worn out record. They always had to lead with a question: 'How best could we help alongside?' Thus, with the Lodge Gig, for example, the lads were careful to investigate, before any of our grandiose ideas were placed on the table, a couple of basic but essential questions. Did BMS actually require a fund-raiser and its associated publicity? Was the whole concert idea more about Radford than BMS? And, lastly, what is it that a school for students with disabilities might possibly *need*, if things were to go ahead? Thankfully at the time, Frank Fogliati was keen for things to proceed. He felt his existing school bus needed a drastic refashioning in order to more effectively transport his students with wheelchairs and other less conventional transport needs. (The concept of raising awareness and funds for issues of transport, notably buses, would also echo down the years into our association with the *Crossing the Divide* program at Bundarra Central School.)

In 2011, in the wake of the Lodge Gig's success in, at the very least, raising an awareness of the complex needs of young people with disabilities, Father Richard approached me with an idea of how Radford College might similarly engage in a less distant relationship with Indigenous Australia. It was hard not to feel compelled to do something in this regard, teaching at an affluent school with under 1% Aboriginal or Torres Strait Islanders in the cohort. As Ray Martin recently attested in promoting the SBS television series *First Contact*, in which he guided six Australians, with minimal experience of Indigenous Australia, across 15,000 kilometres of outback,

> I've seen with my own eyes shameful discrimination that persists today. Yet, the urban myths abound – about how 'those bloody Aborigines' get special treatment, with welfare served up on a silver platter. Forget the 'myths' – they're really urban lies.
>
> Everybody it seems has an opinion, formed from newspaper stories, talkback radio or the ignorance of latter-day Pauline Hansons. Yet, the truth is SIX OUT OF TEN Australians have never even met an Indigenous person. (At least not that they know of.) Never had a chance 'to walk in their shoes', for just a few steps.[1]

So it was that I became inspired to find a way to help Radford students 'meet' Indigenous people and hopefully, if trust developed, walk alongside them for a spell, and see and hear what it might be they have to show and tell. While such an enterprise may not be a musical journey, I figured it might be as close as I would ever get to following in Midnight Oil's *Blackfella/Whitefella* footsteps towards the dead heart.

Thomas Keneally once wrote,

> In Australia, movement is not westwards to the centre but eastwards to the coast. Australia is periphery. It dreams of and yet abandons the core.[2]

Well, here we go, I thought, once again characteristically working against the populist trend.

So what became known as the 'G-trips' began as an idea gently paid forward by none other than deputy principal John Leyshon, after being approached by the Gunawirra organisation to look at ways of doing something more substantial than the mere handing out of an annual donation. Richard Browning, shortly after his clothes had dried from all the vigorous dancing at the Lodge Gig, similarly saw some real and mutual promise in our school committing to a relationship with Gunawirra and Indigenous Australia. He then asked me whether I would be willing to explore things further. As our new principal evidently had a passionate interest in Indigenous education, the green light was not long coming.

Initially, the 'G' came to acknowledge this Gunawirra organisation, an inspiring group of people very much about sowing those seeds that grow good things in the heart. As their website indicates,

> Gunawirra is a not-for-profit, member-based organisation made up of Aboriginal and non-Aboriginal professionals and specialists working side by side for Aboriginal young women, men and their children from the ages of 0 to 5… Gunawirra offers projects and programs that encourage young Aboriginal mothers and fathers to avoid the dangers of alcohol, substance abuse, domestic violence and sexual abuse through every encouragement, self-empowerment in the community, group activities and individual psychotherapy.[3]

Their primary focus is to attempt all this mighty work through early intervention, prevention and mitigation. Quoting psychiatrist Frank W. Putnam on their webpage,

> A growing body of research links childhood experiences of abuse and neglect with serious life-long problems including depression, suicide, alcoholism and drug abuse, and major medical problems such as heart disease, cancer, and diabetes. Two basic processes, neurodevelopment and psychosocial development, are affected by early abuse and neglect. Scientists have begun to understand the mechanisms through which these adverse experiences alter child development and produce pernicious mental, medical, and social outcomes. These insights have opened opportunities to intervene, to prevent maltreatment and to mitigate its effects. Future success depends on the greater dissemination and refinement of these interventions.[4]

I was struck by an article I read in 2012 in *The Canberra Times* entitled 'The Lasting Impact of Early Stress'. It backed up Putnam's claims, reporting that neuroscientists were finding that

> there is a formative 'critical period' early in life when the brain – including the infrastructure for language and vision – is being moulded by experience, or by deprivation.

In an article that totally validates the central rationale behind visionary organisations such as Gunawirra, researchers continued to identify an emerging need to combat the insidious and long-lasting effects of social isolation and deprivation:

> Now, a growing cadre of scientists is trying to understand the connections among early social experience, biology and developmental problems that lead to long-lasting dysfunction. The hope is that the knowledge of what happens at the cellular and genetic level might help shape government child protection policies and social programs and point to behavioural interventions...[5]

The Gunawirra organisation's activities are many and are based on the premise of the importance of connecting with all stakeholders involved in a child's 'early social experience'. As a result, their links with preschools containing Aboriginal children are extensive. That said, their programs are also wider-reaching, dealing with holistic care for pregnant mothers; professional and emotional support for school directors and staff; development of projects which nurture relevant and strong Aboriginal role models and mentors; art therapy and other forms of therapeutic activity; the encouragement of social gatherings, home visits and camps to promote community well-being; and the development of DVDs, websites, booklets and other publications to assist families and their supporters with advice, help and information necessary and appropriate to their daily needs, to name a few.

Founder and board director Norma Tracey invited Radford College to play a more active role within Gunawirra, as the school had been supporting the organisation financially and through the advice and contributions to programs by interested Radford Junior School teachers.

Norma suggested that senior students spend time at Gunawirra-affiliated preschools, to witness first-hand the work being developed and completed there with Aboriginal children. This felt like an ideal opportunity for Radford students to leave the comfort zones of a cut-lunch lifestyle in order to experience life in real, rural, rustic Australia. For many, if not most, it would be the first time they set eyes on an Aboriginal child.

Norma provided me with a list of affiliated schools where Radford kids could settle in for a week to observe, learn, reflect, and assist where possible. I took the list to Richard, who was in the process of formulating and fine-tuning his ever-expanding ideas on service philosophy. (At the time, he was heavily influenced, like David Pocock, by Archbishop Desmond Tutu's promotion of the concept of Ubuntu. As outlined in my previous book, *Little Life*, Ubuntu seems to strike a chord with more than just rugby union enthusiasts. That said, Wallaby captain and ultimate service learner, David Pocock, refers to it frequently in his autobiography *Openside*: 'Tutu often talks about the African understanding of something called Ubuntu – Ubuntu is the essence of being human. Ubuntu speaks particularly about the fact that you can't exist as a human being in isolation. It speaks about our interconnectedness. You can't be human all by yourself. A person is a person through other persons.' NB: Pocock's songlines will once again cross with ours in this narrative.) Richard and I unequivocally felt that the Gunawirra proposal would be a wonderful way for us to test our evolving service philosophies with students in practical, challenging but safe spheres. At this stage, the school was also annually sending staff and students to work in Timor Leste, which similarly fell by chance at Richard's doorstep. With the Timor trips well under way, attempting and engaging in effective service learning on Australian soil seemed a logical, if not imperative step, one that would also silence those who were questioning why our service attentions had commenced overseas before our own backyard.

After carefully checking the suggested destinations from Norma's list on a map of New South Wales, we deduced that we could effectively place the Radford volunteers at most of her identified schools if we based ourselves in Tamworth, a country town with a population of just under 50,000. We were to find ourselves visiting terrific little preschools in nearby Gunnedah, Inverell, Kootingal, Quirindi and Werris Creek. Basing ourselves near the incongruous edifice that is the Golden Guitar, the only real stretch in terms of travel would be a small school submerged smack bang in the centre of Inverell (population of just under 12,000), two hundred kilometres away. After debating with myself whether to include this school or not, I decided in its favour after contacting its director, whose enthusiasm for us visiting and volunteering tipped the scales. She offered to also billet out (between herself and another staff member) the four students I would place there, and hence gave me the idea that the other schools' staff – as if they did not have enough on their plates – might be receptive to having decently mannered, well-intentioned city kids experiencing a bit of country life under the corrugated roofs of their family homes. Torn between pushing the limits of old-fashioned country hospitality and keeping the overall price of the trip down for my student volunteers, I accepted the billeting offers that were generously extended to us by each and every Gunawirran school.

I was, in time, to be particularly grateful to the preschool director at Inverell, not only for helping me find no-cost accommodation for the G1 guinea pigs, but also for drawing me to a place geographically close to the spot we would eventually identify as the spiritual centre of these trips.

I have established trust with most Radford students in just under three decades of teaching at the college, if not for anything but loyalty to the cause. I had become quite used to pitching extravagant ideas at teenagers who tend to nod and follow, as long as whatever I proposed did not involve too much required reading, opening emails, the consuming of vegetables or the necessity to put thought into packing suitcases. Because what I do is largely hair-brained, most know they are not likely to get overly bored by anything I might suggest. If they were uninspired, they always had their mobile phones.

In the past, I had taken to standing in the middle of a busy corridor and yelling out for volunteers for my schemes. You need to be specific and terse with this technique (which is where I fail). I would not encourage the following style of invitations: 'I need about twenty of you to help organise and promote a superhero-themed disco for people with disabilities' or 'I need half a dozen of you to give up a week of your holidays to help with bushfire remediation in the Warrumbungles' or 'I need a bunch of you to get dressed up as a singing and dancing fruit or vegetable of your choice in a promotional campaign for healthy eating at Black Mountain School.' Or finally, 'I need some guinea pigs to travel ten hours north to hang out with Indigenous preschoolers, ask their teachers how you can help, and assist me in the development of a program that bridges the gap between privileged urban kids and battling rural ones. As an important aside, being a fan of the album *Diesel and Dust* would certainly help.'

A student came up to me, a Matthew Reilly thriller under his arm, and said he would participate as long as he could read passages to fellow travellers from his favourite author on the trip up. I suggested he would have ample time to read all of it if he were to volunteer to be stationed at Inverell. (Max was to take this quite literally. He was to read all of the 770-ish pages of *Seven Ancient Wonders* throughout the journey, adding his own vocal characterisations and inflections and at times deciding to improve on the storyline by offering – without warning – his own improvisational plot additives to the narrative.) He then suggested in turn that maybe I could save time and my vocal cords if I stopped waving my arms around and just group-emailed all of Year 12 (he would show me how easy it is to do).

I thanked him and said I would buy him a Midnight Oil CD for Christmas.

'Who are they?' he asked.

I informed him that life existed outside of the fictional world of Matthew Reilly, but because he had so rapidly volunteered, I did not have the moral right to relieve him of and then *donk!* him across the head with his 770-page paperback. Yet I despaired in my heart of hearts that what

Michael Chabon once wrote about rock music was possibly very true: 'The length of time required to coat a hit song with a layer of oldie dust has always been breathtakingly short.'⁶

I hollered after the retreating lad, 'Oh and can you talk to any of your mates? Boys may evidently read Matthew Reilly, but they certainly don't read emails.'

'Especially if they are from over-enthusiastically verbose teachers...'

Touché.

Some girls then passed by and offered to be a trio of tap-dancing celery sticks. I told them they were just the sort of people I needed for the Gunawirra trip, and to augment whatever they thought they might be doing next holidays by signing up. As far as I was concerned, they could promote healthy eating and tap-dancing near Black Mountain, New South Wales,⁷ as well as Black Mountain, ACT.

'Say, have any of you girls heard of the Midnight Oil album *Diesel and Dust*?'

'Who are they?' they asked.

I told them not to worry and to go home and get their vegetable costumes sewn.⁸

G1 was not an overwhelming success. With the students billeted out, I effectively could not debrief them until the end of the week. In fact, I rarely saw them. When finally reconnecting during the day, they would be totally ensconced in activity with their preschool buddies. Accompanied by my own long-suffering buddy Rufus (who was still catching his breath from the Lodge Gig) and Jane Leyshon, a collegian/musician/teacher who had recently been working in Wyndham and the Kimberley in remote communities, the three of us decided to pass the hours looking for ways to enhance the trip with a more Indigenous flavour. While all the schools had a goodly percentage of Indigenous kids in their cohort, and most had children from families in desperate need, I was still unsure if what we were doing was what any of us had truly envisaged. We knew we could not realistically afford to transport ourselves into the dusty outback à la *Blackfella/Whitefella*, yet we still felt a need to outreach to somewhere a little more remote.

On the way home, as predetermined, we took our students to trek through the Warrumbungles, a destination with ample space and majesty, where we decided it would be appropriate to debrief the first G-journey and reflect on deeper matters of the heart. By the time we descended from Grand High Tops, we had mutually decided on a number of things: if possible, and keeping expense in mind, we wanted this new service venture to be affordable and not debilitating like some overseas trips.

Sitting at Ogma camp in the middle of the 'Bungles, the students expressed a desire to work in much smaller, remoter schools, and possibly schools with a higher if not fully Indigenous enrolment. I could certainly see the scientific argument for visiting more isolated places. In the 'Lasting Impact of Early Stress' article previously referred to, there existed a compelling argument to do so, as scientists and psychologists were proving more conclusively that 'neglect, isolation and abuse can have lingering negative effects, including difficulties with language, attention or social interactions'.[9] The Radford students certainly felt that they could do more to help, particularly in this final trio of identified difficulties.

I took this all back to Norma who suggested a new Gunawirra-affiliated preschool for G2, in a town just over twenty-five kilometres outside Inverell, called Tingha (which I often incorrectly pronounced as 'Tinger'). She also informed us that her organisation had strong connections with a school called Minimbah on the outskirts of Armidale, which was close to 100% Indigenous. The preschool director there, Ursula, was a real mover and shaker in her community and would be a person from whom we could learn a lot. Norma also alerted us to a school in Moree called Kiah, similarly requiring its students to be Indigenous in order to enrol, but she suggested that perhaps it would be a little outside of realistic travel distance for us.

These recommendations were, quite literally, to change everything.

All three preschools became regulars in what, by G5, had become known as the Gamilaraay trips – and their home towns are still on the G-itinerary today.[10] With our brief now expanding into the primary schools of these towns, we decided to change the name of the G-trips, so as to respectfully acknowledge *both* the Gunawirran organisation and its ideals, as well as the traditional culture and language of the region's Gamilaraay people. Alternative spellings include Comelroy, Gamilaroi, Gomeroi, Gumillaroy and Kamilaroi. Among the four largest Indigenous nations in Australia, the Gamilaraay of central/northern NSW inhabit an indeterminate area extending from Singleton in the Hunter Valley, across my beloved Warrumbungles in the west, progressing north to the centres of Quirindi, Tamworth, Narrabri, Walgett, Moree, Lightning Ridge and Mungindi, and even reaching into Nindigullu, Queensland.

By G5, the trips had become so popular amongst the Radford students that we now had a core group of staff attending in Mark Gannon, Dylan Mordike and Kim Stonham, with Collegian Andrew 'Apps' Letton[11] appearing frequently in a trio of the earlier G-trips. We also had regulars in the student population, with teamSUPPORTers Tom Earle, my godson Dougal Mordike, and Declan Pratt having attended at least three times.

The balance of personalities amongst the group would have done the Oils proud. Mark Gannon could best be described as Santa-on-a-Harley-Davidson, a hirsute and no-nonsense woodwork teacher with a heart of gold – or perhaps a less bling choice of metal. He is an unpredictable, outspoken but strangely cuddly grizzly bear, with arcane interests in many of the finer culinary arts, ranging from cheese and sausage-making to his famous G-nachos. He even scoops ice cream so that it tastes better on the cone. Of late, he has become indispensable to teamSUPPORT in his advice and assistance to the boys in the construction of everything from water-bomb catapults, towering sponge-throw boards, wooden jousting horses, loony obstacle courses and even fully functioning barnyard wagons and spaceships. I have never met a human being so capable in such a bizarre range of practical activities.

Assisting me with teamSUPPORT and G-campaigns, and equally

indispensable as she is practical, is the mercurial Super Mum, Kim Stonham. Accompanied by a maternal common sense, somewhat (and perhaps thankfully) absent in the three G-males, Kim's expertise in first aid – no matter how peculiar the ailment or injury, the less arcane culinary arts, *Game of Thrones*, social media and in deciphering the unpredictable baby-dragon behaviours of adolescents, have made her easily the most lovable of the G-staff. She is, in truth, Radford's answer to Daenery Targaryen. Everyone wants to be on her bus. Including the other drivers.

And last, but not least, comes Dylan Mordike, an unassuming fisherman with a soft spot for Oz Rock; he is himself equal parts Angus Young, Paul Kelly and Doc Neeson. Dylan was a final-year student when I was an in-service teacher at Radford in 1988. I suspect he would have bet his entire AC/DC and Angels record collection that the awkwardly dressed (and demeanoured) teacher with L plates was never going to get his licence to educate. A gifted man of all gadgets, especially the more intricate inner workings of pretty much any computer, Dylan scrolls a somewhat mighty mouse. Yet his greater strengths lie in an unassuming ability to read a myriad of situations, and armed with a vast and varied general knowledge, he often puts this sensibility to use for the greater good. It was Dylan who first introduced the daily reading of portions of Paul Keating's timeless Redfern Park speech on the G-trips, which became an excellent springboard during reflections at the end of each day and a point from which to positively jump into the next.

Yes, if I was thrown into that testing, unforgiving, unrelenting, crude and somewhat violently unpredictable world of *Game of Thrones*, I would certainly want this loyal team of able and uniquely-gifted individuals at my side. Accompanied perhaps by Tyrion Lannister to keep us all honest.

Both Minimbah and Tingha preschools were feeders to their own primary schools, which essentially existed on the same campus, within walking distance, and through or over a few gates. Kiah, we were to later learn, was a feeder to Moree East Public, although it was not until G8 and the efforts of Mark Gannon, that we finally got around to negotiating for Radford students to work there alongside its staff and students. If and when Radford numbers permitted, we also periodically sent our students to the serenely secluded smaller schools in the villages of Gilgai and Gum Flat, and during G2 extended an offer for regular visitation to Bundarra Central School, a small K–12 school with 160 pupils, forty minutes drive from Tingha, and nestled beside and often reflected across the surface of the nearby Gwydir River.

I am reminded here of a passage Dylan once chose for reflection from the Redfern address that underpinned our humble aims: 'If we improve the living conditions in one town, they will improve in another. And another.' I remembered stating to the G-kids that this was a good principle from which to commence and expand our own thinking and actions. While improving another's living conditions might, for now, be a little too lofty a goal, we could certainly improve those smaller 'conditions' of life: such as bettering an uninspired or unnoticed child's day at school by chipping away at whatever stones might be weighing down that precious little person's rucksack. As Keating reminded us, 'When we see more dignity, more confidence, more happiness, we will know we are going to win… If we open one door others will follow.'[12]

Taking out a map once again after G1, it was decided that centring operations at one of these new schools, preferably whichever one existed closest to the middle, would be the ideal way to minimise transport costs (which the Radford Collegians Inc. has annually helped to offset) and allow us to bring all the kids together at the end of the long day, rather than the less-preferred option of billeting out. Tingha was thus the centrifugal spot when the curvy line was drawn and all dots were joined, although it did mean a little over an hour down the Guyra Road to get to Armidale, and a little over two hours westward along the Gwydir Highway to get to Moree, meaning a four to four and a half hour commute for any students going in to Kiah. When I pointed this out to the first batch of students who had nominated to go there, I was warmed by their response. Lachie, Sarah and Jack looked me in the eye and simply replied, 'If they could use our help there, then four and a half hour hours on the bus it is, H.' The three of them should be knighted. I wanted to hug them on the spot.

My friend Jenny Bell at Radford, mother of G4 wonder-girl Nicole and teen prodigy and former Junk Sculpture guitarist Michael (now the drummer of up and coming Canberra band Safia[13]), went trawling through the internet and came up with a uniquely situated and niftily constructed place called Green Valley Farm and suggested that it felt like just the sort of accommodation I was after.

'What do you mean by that, Jen?'

'Well, they have a website framed with cartoon sheep. It appears to have water slides and lots of other fun things, on top of ample accommodation to suit our needs. It's family-owned too.'

I told her I was already sold at the cartooned sheep and asked her to secure a booking. Again, I had no idea that this would be the start of a relationship, both for Radford and for me personally, that is still growing exponentially to this day. More on this later.

In time, we discovered those surrounding places of interest that Rufus, Jane and I had originally envisaged would enhance the trips by showing our participants various historical, man-made and natural landmarks that existed around their trajectory. Notable stops along the way now included Myall Creek, the Stonewoman Aboriginal site, Cranky Rock Nature Reserve, Mount Yarrowyck Aboriginal cave paintings, Copeton Dam, Molong junkyard and the bizarre Animals on Bikes,[14] in which participating farms along a stretch of road between Molong, Cumnock, Yeovil and Dubbo – among others – display their junk sculptures created on that there very theme.

For me, service and natural wonders have always been linked. Perhaps because both encourage a CAT scan of the soul in the observer, revealing the more profound and sometimes more uncomfortable of truths, not only about that said individual's inner workings, but also about the grander human condition. Maybe, as the preacher in Geraldine Brooks' *March* esoterically reflected on the linkage, 'the divine is that immanence which is apparent in the great glories of Nature and in the small kindnesses of the human heart'.[15]

So, at the close of their week at the schools, the groups were to continue in G1's footsteps and retreat to the strangely shaped mountains of Warrumbungle National Park to reflect on their experience, what they had learned, and where their next footsteps might lead them. And perhaps expanding their outreach to matters even more divine, immanent and transcending, whatever their bent. Since the bushfires in the national park and surrounding areas in January 2013, I had taken an assortment of students to Coonabarabran in the subsequent Easter school holidays to undertake remediation work in and around the Warrumbungle Mountain Hotel, run by Dick and Sally Perram. Again, this was to become a burgeoning relationship, with songlines extending throughout the ensuing narrative and into its final chapters.

'I think we are beginning to see how much we owe the Indigenous Australian and how much we have lost by living apart…'

Many passages of the Redfern Park speech have left G-participants stunned by what was written in 1992, back before they were even a twinkle in their parents' eyes. They are also often disappointed that seemingly little reconciliation appears to have occurred since then. Before setting out on a G-trip, I often ask the volunteers to utilise their imagination, as Keating had suggested, so that they can come to listen more effectively and respect the people they are likely to meet, in a myriad of contexts, across the week ahead.

> We cannot imagine that the descendants of people whose genius and resilience maintained a culture here through fifty thousand years or more, through cataclysmic changes to the climate and environment, and who then survived two centuries of dispossession and abuse, will be denied their place in the modern Australian nation… And with the spirit that is here today I am confident that we won't.[16]

It was almost as if Keating was speaking across two decades, directly to the G-kids; now at the start of their week of living not quite so far apart from an ancient culture that existed only a little beyond their own metaphoric back fences. Yet in my heart, I was still struggling with the students' preparation for the trips. I felt something potent was still absent in the manner I was waving the starting flag at the expanding convoy of Radford minibuses.

Then, on G4, a worker at Kiah Preschool named Rosie – who became enamoured with the Radford kids' willingness to dress up as reindeer and dance awkwardly yet with unabashed jollity during Christmas carols – asked me if I would take this, the third group of volunteers from Radford at Kiah, to a place called Myall Creek. Knowing that the site now contained a walk and monument dedicated to the 1838 massacre, in which a gang of eleven stockman brutally and systematically slaughtered twenty-eight defenceless Aboriginal elders, women and children, it suddenly seemed to be a destination we should have always included in our itinerary. Although the number of people killed is tragically higher at nearby Slaughterhouse Creek,[17] the Myall Creek massacre was unique in that the perpetrators were brought to trial and seven were subsequently found guilty and executed. Given that each day we passed the turn-off to Myall Creek at Denulgra, en route to and from Moree, there was really no excuse to not visit the site one afternoon on the way home. With Andrew 'Apps' Letton in tow, Morgan, Natasha, David and I became the first of many G-trippers to walk the rainbow-serpentine track out and into this dark chapter of Australian history.

The effect that the visit had on the five of us was deep. We were immediately stunned into silence at the first information tablet. And by the last, the students and I were adamant that every G-volunteer needed to come to this place to be exposed to a part of Australian history which inexplicably took over a century to appear in some history books. Also, in spite of some folk more recently questioning why we would see the need to take young people to such a despairing, depressing place. Those voices perhaps echoed the resistance experienced by the likes of Apex member Len Payne, when he attempted to establish a monument at Myall Creek: 'The whole idea is ill-conceived, unconsidered and mischievous and an insult to the Bingara people,'[18] complained a property owner in the

Bingara Advocate. Sorrowfully, by the time of his death in 1994, Payne was still six years short of seeing his vision of a memorial realised. (The Myall Creek Memorial Committee officially opened the memorial on 10 June 2000.)

All I could do in response to his/my detractors is to simply point to the Redfern address:

> We simply cannot sweep justice aside…any more than we can hide behind the contemporary version of social Darwinism which says that to reach back for the poor and dispossessed is to risk being dragged down. That seems to me not only morally indefensible, but bad history.[19]

Or as Henry Reynolds emphatically reminds us, 'What happened to the commitment to healing the wounds of the past when they could not be referred to?'[20] And lastly, David Pocock incorporates and sums up a great deal of what has been covered here already in challenging us all to re-imagine the 'bad history' and consider an alternative retelling of it from the perspective of those who have seen little recompense since its initial recording:

> History is usually written by the victor and when you are part of that victorious race or group of people, considering an alternative story challenges the paradigms through which you see the world. It challenges the stability of the world you live in… If we are going to work for peace, we need to begin to see history from the position of the marginalised, the minorities, and importantly, the women, to hear their stories and work for true reconciliation, not just offer apologies.[21]

Perhaps this is what created our initial quiet, or disquiet: a small but significant cornerstone of what constituted our country had been chipped at, and that rock had not been quite as noble, egalitarian, upright and solid as we had always been led to believe. Yet surely this silence that enveloped us should not last forever if we are to heal?

Neil Murray, a member of the Warumpi Band who had been on the *Blackfella Whitefella* tour, wrote a song called 'Myall Creek' after attending the opening of this monument. He voiced a need for this historical muting to be addressed when he sang, 'this beautiful land don't want no bad thing in here / Break open all the silence…' He was to then be struck by a startling moment of reconciliation, when

> A descendant of the murderers,
> a descendent of the slain,
> met at Myall Creek
> and sisters they became.

In an addendum in the final pages of his fictionalised account of the Myall Creek Massacre entitled *Demons at Dusk*,[22] Peter Stewart writes about these sisters at the opening of the Myall Creek Memorial:

> Among those attending the opening of the memorial were Des Blake, the great godson of John Blake, and Beaulah Adams, the great-great niece of Edward Foley. In an unprecedented act of reconciliation, they stood with and were embraced by Lyall Munro and Sue Blacklock, a descendant of one of the Weraerai boys who had escaped the massacre by hiding in Myall Creek. There is a rainbow.

This rainbow of reconciliation similarly appears to arch over and shine upon Murray's song, which became a call for unity and a literal and metaphoric joining of hands and hearts:

> …to show what you can do
> when you forgive what's been done
> turn darkness into light,
> fear into love.[23]

In many ways, in visiting Myall, we were hoping to be offered a revealing glimpse, amidst all that 'bad history', of how we ourselves could effectively respond in an act of fair dinkum reconciliation. Yet it took many weeks in the surrounding schools, as well a number of return visits to Myall with entire G-groups, before we could fully come to grips with what that response might be. It was certainly one that required further researching, reading and reflecting. It had a *leitmotif* about weeping then healing, sighing then singing, despairing then dreaming together. And it required a deep, proactive approach to reconciliation *through* service, one that both embodied Keating's call for concrete action and heeded Rudd's warning to achieve something more substantial than the mere clanging of gongs.

Between trips, I diligently read the work of those who had not remained silent about Myall Creek, which ultimately led me to Neil Murray's song. I explored the stunning and unsettling studies of Australian frontier warfare by historian Henry Reynolds; a play by John Summons called *Massacre at Myall Creek*; and the fictionalised account *Demons at Dusk*, which contained a short but striking introduction by (another Wallaby!) Peter FitzSimons which went as follows,

> if we are to celebrate Australian history in the courage and heroism Australians displayed at Gallipoli, Kokoda, Tobruk and Long Tan; if we are to glory in our achievements in so many fields from sport to agriculture to literature and the arts, then we must also remember and acknowledge Myall Creek and other stains on our national soul as a crucial part of our past. This, too, is a part of the Australian mosaic; this, too, was a part of our journey as a people through the good, the bad and beyond ugly to bring us where we are today, and we cannot pretend otherwise – as much as we like to, and mostly have to this point. Surely as a nation, there can be no 'reconciliation' if we do not acknowledge just what horrors we are reconciling from.[24]

As Henry Reynolds reminds us,

> Reconciliation means the reconciling of two stories about what happened when pioneer settlers met the Indigenous people all around a vast, moving, ragged frontier… They want us to take it seriously and treat it with gravity, to recognise that violence was not just an aberration or an accident but rather that it was central to modern Australia.[25]

And punctuated with Pocock's reflection on Tutu's Ubuntu:

> Surely the only way forward is the way of heroes like Desmond Tutu, who advocate reconciliation. Not a reconciliation that simply forgives and forgets, but a reconciliation that rights wrongs and allows all parties to begin sharing a common ground, realising their common humanity and making reparations for past damages.[26]

Stirred by Pocock's previous point about consulting the women of damaged communities, I recalled how DBC Pierre once observed about Australia that

> The men have gone to great lengths over the years to spread an image of rugged independence, but the place is run by women, as the same lengths would suggest.[27]

Around this time, in an informal discussion with environmentalist/lawyer Phillip Toyne, it was recommended to me that speaking to the women of the G-communities was a must for their traits of balance, resilience, wisdom and insight. This was finally punctuated by Robert Hillman, who wrote that

> The feminine force is invariably more active, the more creative… There are contradictions but, overwhelmingly, life unfolds at the bidding of women, or through the agency of feminine spirits.[28]

Thus I chatted further with Rosie the next day and thanked her for inviting us to visit Myall and to 'take it seriously'; we assured her that the Radford quartet at Kiah had certainly treated their walk at the monument with the utmost gravity. The students had indicated at reflection time the previous evening how much they had wanted to do more, to act, to right wrongs, to make reparations, and to scrub at that 'stain on our national soul'. I suggested to Rosie that maybe we should both ask the students how they might 'show what can be done' in their own ways. But Rosie simply pointed out towards the multi-coloured playground equipment, being played upon by people of multicolours themselves.

There, the Radford and Kiah kids were playing, building, creating, celebrating, singing, dancing and laughing together in a delightfully authentic and unaffected way, and in a manner that might assure any neutral observer that the country's future was in safe hands. I listened to Tash emphasising the importance of reading and taking her collection of kids inside to do just that; I watched David gently nurturing and patiently understanding a volatile but lovable child; and dear old Morgan, a gentle giant himself, enticing Andrew to don some antlers and do a Christmas dance of joyous abandon with a posse of preschool children, who would receive comparatively less under their trees on 25 December. (We had brought our own Christmas gifts for them, but when the music started they had been left, discarded, where they had been opened.) The joy of the dance in that crystallised moment seemed to transcend everything else going on in the universe. Kiah – what a great place to liberate yourself for a day.

Rosie turned to me and, emphasising my earlier messages of returning, almost begged of me, 'Just keep coming back, won't you.'

'That's what we intend to do,' I assured her. 'Probably without the presents…'

Upon saying our goodbyes, David's little mate unceremoniously gave him 'the bird'. As golden as their week together had been, this child had grown too accustomed to males in his life providing only brief bursts of transitory interest. To quote Pete Townshend, he was not getting fooled again. When Davo expressed to me his disappointment in the child's blunt, single-digit au revoir, I could see in his teary eyes that he knew – the second that that he had expressed it – that his own tears could ultimately only do so much. I felt for him and his big, thumping heart. I hoped in my own that David's sadness might one day ignite within him a desire to ultimately return and do something that might gnaw away at whatever it is that makes these little lives so hardened to emotion and sometimes resistant to these short, finite bursts of attention and love. Like that fellow student who vowed to become a doctor in order to return one day to effect some measurable and lasting change, I hoped for some resolve in Davo. In any case, putting on the antlers and jigging did the right thing by Andrew 'Apps' Letton; he was to eventually use them to prod and promote the Collegians to continue sponsorship of the G-trips and in doing so allow handfuls of future Radfordians/Australians to have a similarly transformative experience.

I was fortunate to be at Kiah with these wonderful kids on the last day of G4. As we left for the car park, there were tears streaming down all of our cheeks, not helped by the staff providing us with a farewell party and an accompanying lunch, possibly well beyond their means. Or by them following up on all of this, by forming a line and vigorously waving, in over forty-degree heat, at the exit gate as we drove the bus out. I remember as we disappeared into suburban Moree, turning to the kids and suggesting that I had better pull over to 'get something out of my eye'.

When the road eventually rolled on by beneath us en route to Coonabarabran, we began to discuss the need to perhaps do more, now that the silence had been broken and the pools of tears were drying up. We commenced plotting future ways of augmenting this experience through joint art projects; awareness and fund-raising campaigns; exploring the possibilities of exchanges – or at least the sponsorship of study costs – in order to open educational doors that may be jammed; and even the possibility of return visits as Collegians.

We spoke again about Myall Creek and the guilt and shame we felt there. But it was handy to have Keating's words still ringing in our ears: 'Down the years, there has been no shortage of guilt, but it has not produced the responses we need. Guilt is not a very constructive emotion.'[29] We all recognised the need to shape and produce a response that was constructive rather than self-indulgent or guilt-inducing. And upon returning to Radford, this quartet of students was particularly vocal and adamant about not only the Kiah experience, but their visit to Myall Creek; they would highlight the need for our school to now show some leadership by learning more from those atrocities and similarly hidden or untold histories. Constructive and concrete outcomes transpired: from G5 on, all G-trippers would now go to Myall Creek at the outset of their journey and reflect on its significance. For Year 11 General Studies, I would be available to lecture on the events and ramifications of Myall Creek to the entire cohort, not just the G-trippers. In early 2014, Radford's new principal, Fiona Godfrey, also accompanied me there to pay our respects.

In preparing for the General Studies lecture, I came across Henry Reynolds' words from his most recent tome *Forgotten War* (2013) where he repeats, pointedly, where reconciliation has failed: 'If we continue to have two quite different stories about the past our paths will never converge.'[30] Whenever I stand with the G-kids and G-staff at the tablets and monuments above Myall, and overlook the plains and homesteads and silos of opulence below, I hope that in providing others with the understanding that there actually are 'two stories' that exist, it might hasten a way toward the convergence that Reynolds and all those who share his views, and in fact the nation entire, urgently require.

Speaking of convergence, it did not escape my attention that the Myall Creek Massacre site had been included on the National Heritage list through the urging and support of a 'Minister Garrett' in 2008, at the 170th anniversary of the atrocities. And while on the topic of converging songlines, perhaps it is best to close this section on Myall Creek by returning to Neil Murray, Garrett's *Blackefella Whitefella* tour mate, and his grim reminder in song that despite all this advancement…

> There are many other places still to go
> where the killing times
> have left their bitter bones,
> where haunting sadness
> lingers poison in our towns.
> Smoke each place for peace,
> consecrate the ground.[31]

I am often asked how we ultimately ended up over twelve hours north of Canberra working alongside the Gamilaraay. Without wishing to sound like a Maharishi, my glib reply is often that sometimes service finds you. As rock poet Patti Smith once wrote,

> it is a service one enters without expectation or design. Where one, lost in thought, may feel a tap upon the shoulder and find oneself far flung, in a swirl of dust, swung about…[32]

So in time, the G-trips were flung and swung into three dusty areas of operation, with three regular staff assuming responsibility for the ongoing relationship in each: Kim embraced Armidale (Minimbah) under her large and protective wing; Mark gripped the steering wheel for the many miles of travel to and from Moree (Kiah and more recently Moree East Public); and Dylan's understanding gaze encompassed the Tingha/

Bundarra region (Tingha Public and Bundarra Central). This allowed me, as an overseer of sorts, to begin investigating *where* the children we worked with in these pre and primary schools might eventually be ending up, and if we should be forging links there as well.

As our friendship with Green Valley Farm deepened (which is to be outlined in the next chapter), we were alerted by its owners' children, who attended Bundarra Central School, to a program existing there called Crossing the Divide (CTD) and run by an experienced and visionary teacher by the name of Matt Pye. We understood CTD to be a program offering trade pathways for young students who had become disengaged with traditional educational ones, but soon came to realise that its scope was broader and more complex than this (and this will also be explored in the following chapter). It was the straight-shooting Matt who first alerted me that a high percentage of his 'clientele' were either former students or current residents of that tiny tin town that I was growing particularly fond of: Tingha (population 887 people, 888 cows). Oh, and you'd better pronounce it properly, as the locals mock you if you do not.

He also brought to my attention a national research study prepared by Dr Tony Vinson in 2007 on behalf of Jesuit Social Services and Catholic Social Services. Entitled 'Dropping Off the Edge', it identified Tingha as one of the most disadvantaged communities in the region, for reasons outlined below. As Matt highlighted at a recent conference utilising statistical data from the report,[33]

> disadvantage was assessed by consolidating a range of items such as criminal conviction rates, unemployment rates, education attainment, income levels, child mistreatment and disability/sickness levels. SIEFA also ranks Tingha as being the most socially disadvantaged community in the Northern Inland NSW region. Tingha has a recorded Indigenous population of 32.7% compared to 2.3% nationally (2006 Census). Of these residents only 4% had finished Year 12 and 47.2% of adult Aboriginals were recorded as unemployed. The median gross weekly household income was in the $500–$649 bracket.
>
> Sadly, there isn't much around in the way of support to address these alarming statistics. My team and I hope we are playing some small part in

effecting change in Tingha in what is effectively our backyard but there is much to be done still there and across the country.

When I told the Radford students attending Bundarra about the CTD program, and the people it was attempting to target, they were all genuinely keen to learn more about it and the lives of its participants. They correctly imagined these lives would be in stark contrast to their own. And so it was on G4, towards the end of 2012, that Isaac and Meg became the first of many Radfordians to put down their pens and pencils, turn off their computers, and pick up a monkey wrench and put on a welding helmet. When they initially ambled across the street to where the workshops were housed, I remember watching them and sensing a metaphoric power in the sight before me.

The G-trips were beginning to cross divides and to help the young towards a realisation that life was bigger and more complex than they may have originally perceived it to be. There was no doubt about that.

I wished that Peter Garrett and Neil Murray, possibly even Paul Keating and a couple other prime ministers, were sitting in the Radford bus with me looking through the insect-spattered windscreen at the road ahead. 'Look,' I would say to them, pointing forward. 'You see that city boy and urban girl crossing the street? They're winning back a little of what's been lost in living apart from what is happening in their own backyard. This, too, is worthy of a speech or a burst of song, surely…'

The building of a beautiful bridge at Bundarra that is still being wandered over today.

'What's the name of that place you take the kids to again, H?' Brownie the bass guitarist asked me around this time.

'You mean Green Valley Farm?' I asked back.

'No, a town where one of the schools you place kids in is situated. Tinger, I think you call it?'

'Oh, Tingha.' (I pronounce 'Tin-ger'.[34]) Beautiful place. Great people. Many cows.'

'Ever swum in the pool?'

I never had. It is not of the usual, concreted Olympic-variety found in the centre of towns. It is an unassuming swimming hole, built at a former mining excavation site. It has always invitingly glistened across its pristine, smooth, blue-green surface, despite being man-made, in the many times I had passed by it. But being an unsupervised venue and unpredictable in depth, I had risk-assessed it out of the water, so to speak.

'Hang on – how do you know about the Tingha' (I pronounced 'Tinger') 'pool?' I asked.

'Because I swum in it as a boy.'

'What are you talking about? You grew up in Tingha?' (I pronounced 'Tin-ger'.)

'Went to school there for six years between 1967 and 1973. We lived next door to it. My dad was the principal.'

'What the – ?'

'Pretty coincidental, hey.'

'Brownie, that is unbelievable. I've been heading up there all this time. We centre operations for the G-trips in that place. And across the decades, all those songs, all those gigs, all the while, the bloke standing behind me plucking a bass was actually a local of that very town.'

'You never asked.'

'I never knew. I cannot believe it.'

Brownie started riffing, 'My brother used to work for the Chinese family that ran the local grocery store.'

'No way.'

'Got face-planted by an Aboriginal kid in my class playing rugby once on the school ovals. There's a cricket pitch there in the middle. That's where it happened.'

I was incredulous.

'Dad built a tennis wall there too,' he continued. 'He wanted to produce the next Evonne Goolagong.'[35]

(I bet he could have too. That school is full of kids with natural athleticism.)

'I planted a tree down where the cricket nets are. Is it still there, do you know? Has the tree grown?'

I was still a little speechless. I suggested we had some things to catch up on. I also knew in my heart of hearts, the best and only way to answer a lot of these questions. But before I could suggest my idea, Brownie halted my thoughts by adding,

'Oh, and by the way, the reason I didn't make any connection was that you pronounce Tingha incorrectly. Bloody hell, H. You go there so often and you can't even say the town name properly. It's Tin-gha. Not Tin-ger...'

I was ashamed. Getting the pronunciation wrong was fundamentally inexcusable.

'...you idiot!'

Track #5 Drive That Mystery Road

As songlines began to criss-cross along the G-journey, my fellow travellers and I discovered doors less cautiously opening. Hotspots on the G-GPS started to pulse, as worn soles trod alongside the pin-straight highways of northern New South Wales, sometimes spiralling off into those more mysterious, cratered, corrugated roads inland; through the gaps between mountains; in between the cracks of scattered boulders; and extending out closer to the heart of the country and its people, there where the bush becomes the back of beyond.

As always, that band's music, that man's voice:

> Where is the ground, the beloved country?
> Women and men who have fallen silent.
> Where are the words that can speak forgiveness?
> Now is the time,
> Now is the time,
> Now is the time to heal.[1]

Driving the G2 bus in pitch-black darkness along the mysterious New Valley Road, on heightened roo-alert, I occasionally checked through the rear-view mirror on the fourteen bodies who had well and truly succumbed to a bumpy slumber. I had no idea that the new day would witness the start of so many beautiful and complex relationships that would widen our definition of 'family' to a more entwining and encompassing sense of the word. These would stretch over many years into the present. And be stronger for each of those years. Due to the late evening gloom, pressing fatigue and a case of severe destination-syndrome, we were all about to fail to spot the distinctive skeletal outline of the surrounding fun park on the rolling hills, and so many attractions that provide wonder and delight in that bush oasis that is Green Valley Farm.

Walking into the kiosk to announce our arrival and pick up the keys to our cabins, I could have sworn I had walked under the bulk of what seemed to be a World War II fighter airplane.[2] Had my torchlight picked up the outline of what appeared to be a mechanical giraffe? And further up the hill what might be the base of a baby roller coaster? I must be more deliriously fatigued than I thought. Surely that couldn't be the sound of crazy monkeys chattering from over a line of hedges? Hey, I was tired. (Later I would discover that every single one of these nocturnal visions and sounds was in fact *exactly* what I saw and heard.)

I was immediately struck by the warmth of Kathy Vickery and her daughter Monique, who were both waiting at the door to greet us. I'm not sure what they thought as the dishevelled leader of the walking dead, uncertain over what he had just stumbled under and into, said 'G'day' (I resort to tourist mode as the best approach when in the bush) and announced the bleeding obvious – that Radford had finally arrived. Despite their long wait for us, a real effervescence emanated from Kathy and off the fireworks of her abundant, tangly hair, giving off a bounce befitting her personality. Being a mother of eight, she evidently had some notion of the cantankerousness associated with escorting minors on over twelve hours of road. She handed me the keys and said that she would catch up with us in the morning once we had settled in. I thanked her and facetiously said to Monique, by her side, that we would all be friends by the end of the week. Even after this brief exchange, I was struck by this young girl's air of competence *sans* arrogance, and a remarkable ease in the presence of people. My first impressions would prove to be correct. Monique Vickery was exactly the sort of 'good country folk' the G2 kids needed to be around.

Kathy's slightly more elusive mum, Beryl, a sage of sorts, often spruiked and acted on the wacky notion that giving kids a rural retreat, every now and then, would serve as a timely antidote to oppressive city life. Yes, it was the wholesome thing to do when trapped in a high-rise existence. She had constantly received this wise message from her own mother, Thelma Asquith. Thelma would take snooty city kids to her Blue Mountains farm in the first half of the 1900s and reveal to them the myriad aspects and curious delights of daily country life. They would share experiences which urban visitors may not have had from living in or near Australia's largest city. Thelma must have instilled this concept within her daughter Beryl, who reconfirmed for me recently that it is 'vital that children see the basics of life'. She looked at me with that stern, school-matronly knowingness and footnoted that 'often the basics are camouflaged in the city'. I nodded, agreed that they certainly were hidden there. I further reassured her that she was preaching to the converted here. (I was scared she might make me write lines otherwise.) 'This was a major reason for why we were bringing Radford to Tingha,' I stated. 'That's nice,' she laconically replied.

Beryl married Patrick Stewart in April 1964, the year the Beatles toured Australia.[3] If photographs are to be believed, Pat was similarly still clean-cut, trim and tailored – a far cry from the Pat Stewart I first met as he sauntered into the dining area during G2 and asked me if I was Chinese. (Initially taken aback, I came to discover that in the early 1880s, Tingha had a population of up to 5000 people, a quarter of which were Chinese. It was, at the time, the largest tin-producing region in new South Wales. In 1900, the famous Wing Hing Long General Store, run by Chinese herbalist, John Joe Lowe who hailed from the Guandong province, first opened its doors. It is still doing so – as a museum – today. More on this later.[4])

'Who let grandpa out?' I remember hearing one of the Vickery hobbits exclaim. At it turns out, we were lucky in fact to see him at all. In late 2010, he had been thrown over 10 metres from the back of his son's ute on the way to shearing. At first sights, Pat could not be further from his namesake: the actor who plays that bald-headed, straight-laced, humourless, fastidiously tidy captain of the Starship Enterprise – or even the wheel-chaired leader of that gang of Marvel Comics' misunderstood, mighty and sometime maverick mutants. (For those not savvy in sci-fi comic movie adaptations, I am referring to Marvel's X-Men here.) That said, he does immediately strike one as a battle-weary yet benign man who reveals himself slowly – but more than willingly – across many an impromptu cabin visit. Often as the sun descends on a long day, with a quartet of loyal sheepdogs – Buddy, Cocoa, Jess and Joe – encircling him with the frenzy of blowflies, I'd hear a voice announce at the flyscreen, 'Ah, George, me favourite Chinaman, thought I'd pop in and see if you were lonely.' As you penetrate his leathery exterior, toughened by almost three-quarters of a century before political correctness, you will find beneath it a horse-sized heart. You marvel at his dry wit and mocking self-deprecation and acceptance of whatever trials and tribulations have befallen him. And some, as time revealed, were not slight. You also get a sense of his cheeky wiliness, and a feeling that he is keeping something back from you, a small pocket of knowledge that he'll only open up if in dire straits or when the listener has earned the right to its bounty.

After living at a property named 'Hilton' for a short period – without electricity and with fourteen gates to negotiate – the realisation hit both Beryl and Pat that a fifty-kilometre return trip, needed for transporting their kids to and from school, was not ideal for farming life or raising a young family. So they bought Green Valley Farm (Beryl: 'Not sure why they ever called it that. I mean look at it! Nothing all that green around here!') and were now much closer to Tingha Central School (as it was called at the time, being a K–12 school). It was 1973 and the asking price was the tidy sum of $18 000. (Junk Sculpture's Bassman Chris Brown was in his final year at the school at the time with his father, Peter, the principal.) By the end of their first decade there, the Stewarts were already thinking about emulating Thelma's vision, with the enthusiastic encouragement of their daughter, Irene, in providing city kids with a holiday experience that removed camouflage and helped young people get back to them basics.

'How are we going to entertain kids who have everything?' Pat pondered as groups of up to twelve kids, mostly girls, began arriving at their doorstep. He answered his own question as thoroughly as any human being possibly could. With family and friends rounded up to help, Pat and Beryl began to build an enticing and somewhat bizarre museum;[5] a welcoming and inexpensive kiosk; a gift shop attached chock-a-block with knick-knacks and collectibles to brighten your dull home from pantry to pool room; a mini-golf course; mini roller coaster; mini botanical gardens around which peacocks and snow-white geese waddle; a still, reflecting pool which often captured the golden sunset, a boon for the pensive navel-gazer; huge tin slippery slides; an array of creatively assembled, concocted and welded (largely by Pat and his son, Michael) playground equipment ranging from rustic see-saws, rollicking roundabouts to the before-mentioned giant 'giraffe' which tips the rider perilously forward (as if the mechanical animal has decided to take a break from munching the leaves of tall trees and resorted to good ol' fashioned, low-levelled grass);[6] and uniquely designed rural experiences including everything from bush cooking, sheep-shearing to camel rides (and eventually waterslides after a nifty suggestion from 'a little girl from Narranderra'). They even built a zoo, equipped with animals such as highland cattle, wild pigs, alpacas, kangaroos, emus, dingo, duck, deer, wombats, monkeys (Crab-eating Macaques whose names are Bushy, Fred, Simba, Tar and Timone, if that matters to anyone), a six-legged sheep, goats, deer, turkey, guinea pigs, chickens, rabbits, and even a cantankerous ostrich. This long-necked Ebenezer Scrooge of the animal kingdom I believed had been specifically programmed with an in-built private-school-kid detection device, which ignited within the burly bird an unnaturally huge urge to kick at an intended victim's backside, usually with a force strong enough to return the child back to the gates of the austere, marbled establishment from which they originated.

But as Beryl pointed out, all of these man-made distractions are nowhere near as appealing as the everyday attractions of the farm. The more 'basic' delights such as getting up with the sun, trapping rabbits, the arcane arts such as shearing and even skinning sheep (Pat: 'Liver. Brains. Stuff opening up. The girls loved it!'), and the even more dubious visual ascetic of animals urinating, tended to leave the more lasting impressions. When early visitors were asked what the best part of their stay was, one dainty girl's highlight was 'watching a calf do a wee'. On a recent perambulation of the Green Valley fields, I decided to analyse the degree of joy associated with the bizarre past-time of viewing farm animals relieving themselves. I can emphatically report I could not for the life of me see any attraction in it.

As time passed by, the grandeur of the fun park increased, expanding to essentially become an attraction for day-trippers or families simply passing through, perhaps en route to those glitzy, soulless and expensive theme parks on the Gold Coast. 'It was all free at this stage,' explains Pat. 'We were getting good money from wool. We just charged for the museum.' As far as authentic holidaying goes, few could argue the place does not give tremendous value for money.

When I first arrived with G2 in 2011, I noticed a photo collage on the wall of the eating area in the kiosk which showed what appeared to be thousands of people sitting on the slopes amidst and above the playground equipment and various slides. Pat revealed that the picture was taken in 1993 when Slim Dusty first performed at Green Valley Farm on a wooden stage attached to their wool shed, which Pat and the family built especially for the Australian country music icon.

'Slim Dusty performed here?' I said incredulously. This person and this place were so full of surprises.

'Three times. In '93, '95 and '97.'

'You're kidding me, Pat. On that stage, near the water slide?'

'Had to build a stage 'cos you couldn't put him on the back of a truck.'

'I guess you couldn't. He must have liked it if he came back three times.'

'He said it was the best privately run concert venue he had played at.'

'Have you had any other acts here?'

'Sure. We had Stan Coster. Gina Jeffreys – she was big back then. Graham Connors. Pixie Jenkins. Chad Morgan. Troy Cassar-Daley. The McKean Sisters. John Berry – nothin' much came of him...'

I nodded. Pat may well have been listing the names of stars in the Coma Berenices constellation for all I knew.

'Oh, and the Wheel – that was Lee Kernaghan's band – you know, with the McCormack Boys?'[7]

I didn't. But nodded some more. They were possibly asterisms. (While I suspected some of these acts could possible induce me into a coma, on researching them I discovered some formidable country-music resumes. I was particularly touched by John Berry's numerous charitable endeavours.) I began to wonder if Sandi Farina had ever considered performing here.

'Slim charged me $12,000 back then, so we needed a big crowd. They came. That was way back before you needed security guards and fences and the like. They got value for money. He played for three or four hours.'

I made a mental note that one day I would play Pat Stewart a Slim Dusty song there on that very stage, and for well under $12. While the thought of listening to Slim for more than twelve minutes would probably result in me gnawing my arms off, I did realise that despite it being the twilight (if you pardon the further astrological imagery) of his career, it was an immensely impressive feat to have Mr Dusty's austere presence and dulcet tones echoing across the not-as-green-as-it-could-be valley. From the photograph in the kiosk, you might not have been able to see the colour of the not-quite-greenish-grass in any case, such was the massive size of the crowd. I hoped the pub had stocked up on beer.

I looked up at the stage while listening to Pat's stories about Slim and wondered if I would ever get the chance to play up there on that amazing stage. What an honour! But then, I was not a shining star in the music world by any stretch of the imagination, albeit in country or western spheres. Yup, both kinds.

From G2 onwards, Radford stayed at Green Valley Farm for all future G-trips. It is our acknowledged home base and the Radford staff and students have developed many deep and blossoming friendships with the Stewart, Vickery, Hickman, Little and Stewart-Little (I kid you not) families over the ensuing years. Monique broke even more new ground in becoming the first student from the region to travel south and spend time with her new friends *at* Radford *in* Canberra. (She even invited my easygoing godson, Dougal, to travel twelve hours north to accompany her to her Year 12 formal.) Yet during those early trips I had felt, like Pat's secret pocket of knowledge, that there was something stored away at the centre of these open-hearted families; something tough, raw and unflinching, possibly sad and tragic; perhaps a hovering loss there in the hidden tracks along the Green Valley songline. As relationships became more entwined and complex, it was not until a couple of years into my own friendship with not only these families, but the region as a whole, that I was to uncover the exact nature of the loss.

In escaping to Green Valley in 2013, it was only when attempting to recover from a sense of defeat and deflation, with my own pack of black dogs yelping and growling around me, and that all-pervading fear that the only music on rotation was being played in the pathos of a minor key, that I could truly listen to the poignant lyrics of their sad song which said so very much.

Then share my own.

I had to be somewhat pushy in order to get Ryan to take the final step and put his name down to attend G4. I highlighted to him that it was in his best interests and would help restore trust and credibility that might have been lost by recent indiscretions. To say he had been in a spot of trouble at school would be a reasonable description of the state of things. (His assessment, not mine.)

As always, I was not immediately convinced of his bad boy image or by any hastily proffered opinions on and solutions to reputed actions. Since his suspension and as part of his reinstatement, I had regularly seen him at RAID basketball, where he had 'volunteered' to work with the teamSUPPORTers. He appeared to enjoy spectating and eventually coaching from the sideline, and spending quality time alongside his little brother, Joel, who was a participant. I had worked RAID into Ryan's rehab, without trying to force it upon him, as I suspected he possessed an empathy for people with disabilities, given his wonderful fraternal relationship with Joel. Ryan often exhibited unflappable patience with his team while speaking to them in that gruff, earthy, cheeky, worldly-wise-and-occasionally-weary manner that we had all had grown somewhat accustomed to. What was striking, however, was his uncanny ability to diffuse, ease and often dissipate tension and stress whenever participants, lost in a moment of injustice due to a bad call or scoreline, would subsequently erupt. It was a calming gift I wished I had possessed myself. You would often see him talking, with a mischievous smile, to any miscreant, one-on-one, providing the necessary balance of respect, listening, empathy and wisdom needed to get the player, and inevitably his team, back on an even keel.

All that fluffy stuff aside, when I eventually got him on the bus to G4, he did spend most of the four-hour trip to the Molong Junkyard with a scowl on his face that suggested maybe I was taking him to Siberia for incarceration. It was at the junkyard, in fact, that I offered to turn the bus around and take him back home if he didn't put a smile back on that dial. He gave me a look that made me feel like a dag/dad who was still using phraseology carbon-dated back to the 50s.

As we walked into the junkyard, most G4 students ogled at the multitude of literal junk sculptures housed there – plenty of animals on bikes, oversized motorbikes, dinosaur bones, robots playing pianos and all the intriguing detritus of human existence which owner Ben returns to the curious collector for a fee. This amazing place always acts as a reminder to me that immense value can be found in discards or in the discarded; the beautiful and bizarre amidst the abandoned; and that at second glances, something rough and rusty can truly be a diamond in disguise. The Radford kids are always instantly attracted to the place, and we traditionally take a group photo in amongst the abandoned cars and farm machinery. Most are equally unable to resist the urge to pick up cool relics: an old road sign; a tie even our great-grandfathers would consider old-fashioned; illustrated cigar boxes; rare LPs and cassettes; marvellous money boxes; strangely shaped and discoloured tools; all too terrifically tacky figurines; and broken but beautiful toys – dolls and bikes that once brought smiles to the children of yesteryear. Then I'd see Ryan, wired to his device, wandering unimpressed past an ancient U-turn sign. Yet by Monday and Minimbah, an about face was certainly about to occur.

Always taciturn at reflection time, he offered one sentence of hope after that first day at his school placement: 'That was all right.' (I decided not to push it.) And then by the second: 'That was better than I thought it would be.' Then the third: 'That place really is amazing.' The fourth: 'That place is going to be hard to say goodbye to tomorrow, to be perfectly honest.' Last day, through tears: 'I've got to go back. You wouldn't believe what that place has done to me, H.'

I would believe. I believe so much it hurts at times. I believe that something on G-trips can really shoot arrows (foam and blunt-tipped) straight at the server's heart and kick-start it once again. When I visited Minimbah during the week of G4, I could see for myself that this was the case. Here was a lad who was becoming increasingly disengaged, hanging around with the wrong crowd, and delving deeper into the darker distractions rather than the stuff of life that really mattered. What he found that truly counted was what he saw in others, and eventually himself, at Minimbah.

Minimbah Aboriginal Preschool and Primary School is an independent establishment with eighty-five students enrolled in each section, largely from families living on an income well below the national average. Approximately 95% of these students identify as being Aboriginal. At the time of writing, it was in its fifty-second year of operation since the preschool opened in 1963. Preschool director Ursula Kim and primary school principal Jenny Brown have been there since the early 90s and are as experienced as any teacher gets. As the school website pointed out about its origins, following talks between the aboriginal community of Armidale and representatives from the Save the Children Fund, a need was identified for an appropriate educational facility for young Aboriginal Children:

> In 1970, a basic pre-school was built on the corner of Cooks and Long Swamp Road. In 1971, Mrs Dianne Roberts, OAM, became the first Aboriginal Director/Principal appointed to Minimbah Pre-school. During the early 1990s, Minimbah expanded its horizons and developed into a primary school. Currently, Minimbah continues to provide an education for the surrounding Armidale Community including Narwan Aboriginal Village, which is located within close proximity to the school.

Over and beyond their focus on literacy support and Indigenous language workshops (in Anaiwan, Dunghutti, Gamilaraay and Gumbaynggir in the past), other specialist programs that have existed include early intervention, family support, nutritional programs, health services and environmental preservation. As with a lot of the G-schools, the school is about more than just what occurs in the classroom, with various support structures in place aimed at strengthening the family unit. As former principal, Dianne Roberts, wrote on the 'Dare To Speak' website:

> Every child's parent or parents is encouraged to participate in the education of their child. The school also visits the homes of participants to encourage and advise on patterns of care that best support early learning, and to build the capacity for the mother/caregiver in that task. Twice weekly there are playgroup sessions for mothers and their children aged from newborn to three years old. During this time mothers come together and support each other though discussion and group activities. A team of staff, the head of which is a fully-trained midwife, offers advice and support and if necessary referral to other community services available in Armidale. Another objective of the playgroup is to take the opportunity to recognise any childhood illnesses among the children…
>
> Minimbah staff sit down with students who have been behaving in a negative way (and often their family members) and try to find creative solutions to what is going wrong in the classroom. The school has student groups which perform at community and civic functions. Students also visit local aged care homes about twice a year to perform… Singing and performing encourages Aboriginal children who have hearing deficits to listen carefully and they listen and perform better.[8]

Current primary school Principal, Jenny Brown, also tells me about their wonderful relationship with nearby private school TAS (The Armidale School), where coincidentally Richard Browning also went to school:

> Our partnership with TAS involves the TAS boys (Years 9 and 11) coming over every Tuesday to play sport and read with our kids. It's part of their Community Service and Pastoral Care programs. We also do our Athletics Carnival with them and various other cultural things – NAIDOC week,

Musica Viva etc. They also allocate one or two scholarships to our Year 6 boys every year.

To hear this warmed me considerably. Not only to share TAS's genuine interest in a small aboriginal school on the edges of its own environs, but to read of its incorporation of sport and music as unifying activities between its students, was encouraging indeed. Jenny proceeded to inform me about increasing government and media attention in the small school. While I was there during G8, the ABC visited to prepare a story for Radio National[9] on the friendship between Minimbah and Radford, also focusing on its connection through art as our G8 visitors were initiating the shared creation of banners for NAIDOC (National Aborigines and Islanders Day Observance Committee) week. At the time of writing, SBS were also compiling a story on Minimbah's Birth Certificate program, a project based on the students' family tree, while the school was also preparing for a visit from the South Sydney Rabbitohs and the Governor General. Kudos to all.

It was amidst this atmosphere of playing, caring, creativity and even song, that I walked in on Ryan during G4 and could not believe what I saw. There he was, helping a Mini with his maths, teaching numeracy intuitively with a count-your-finger method and with just the right quantity of firmness to keep the boy friendly, focussed and fascinated. You would often find him counselling the post-tantrumers in the sulky corners of the classroom, playground or car park, and with a success ratio of tears-to-smile that left Jenny, Ursula and me shaking our heads in admiration. At lunch and recess, he would always have his minions around him, jostling for attention by leaping on his back, questioning him about girlfriends, pulling at his arms or playing chase. Watching him often flash past with a childish glee that I had rarely seen before, except maybe at RAID basketball, it provided me with considerable hope that this bounce, silliness and drive would not disappear in a blink the second we headed back south.

The entire Minimbah school farewelled Ryan on the last day of his first visit on G4. It was 'the Dreaded Friday' that he had not been looking forward to primarily because his G-experience was soon to be ending. He had to give a speech as well. ('I'm not much of a public speaker, to be perfectly honest.') He was given a precious and eye-catching Indigenous necklace to wear and remember the school by. I imagine he stumbled through some heartfelt words of gratitude, encouragement and farewell. ('It was pretty hard to not cry while I was speaking, to be perfectly honest.') To quote Kim Stonham, who had been fortuitously present during it all,

> They never had done anything like this before for volunteers. There were tears in his eyes as well as the kids and staff. He was quiet for most of the way home, but then began talking and reflecting and opening up. He went from being so introspective and closed up at the start of G4, to turning into someone who now felt wanted and valuable. And who had stars in his eyes…

I stood there in awe, wishing there were television monitors that might beam these stellar images back to educators worldwide. They would serve as a reminder to any who work with youth of the dangers of limiting and labelling those perceived to be 'at risk', and of simplistically boxing and branding teens as 'bad' boys or girls. (I have always been uneasy with any educative institution making a somewhat less than angelic child someone else's problem through suspension or expulsion without exploring the many alternative routes. It is understood that it is never simple, especially when you take the perspective of any child, teacher or parent who is incessantly bearing the brunt of another student's negative behaviour, especially with no end or relief or redemption in sight. Yet I am still to be convinced that banishing the problem out of sight is the answer. Giving up on someone does ultimately mean we are confirming – or at the very least recognising as insurmountable – the very flaws in our own approaches and systems, if not society's, as we fail to counter the 'badness' perceived in those lost souls who we are to cast out to the wolves. Granted, it may not be quite as simple as shipping wayward kids to jackeroo in the Warrumbungles, or to regularly visit schools like Minimbah or Tingha or Kiah, or even spending reflective time in the classrooms of kids with disabilities; but imagining alternative methods and providing more government funding to explore strategies such as these would be a start. It may be my next project.)

It was a lesson I was about to learn even more acutely at Crossing the Divide. As the unforgettably roguish character of Boris in Donna Finch's *The Goldfinch* laments, 'What if our badness and mistakes are the very thing that set our fate and bring us round to good? What if, for some of us, we can't get there any other way?'[10] What if, indeed. As I saw nothing but the profoundly 'good' happening there in the many visitors to magical Minimbah over the years, all I could end up feeling was strangely grateful that this particular lad's apparent past indiscretions and missteps were that 'very thing' that led him to be closer to his brother on a RAID basketball court at Radford; and to many of the Mini-kids, in a classroom carefully wrapped in Indigenous paintings, totems, craftwork and whispers from the Dreamtime, holding up fingers so that the maths added up just right.

While the transformation in Ryan was gigantic, the effect on some of the kids he was working alongside was similarly palpable. Perhaps Jenny Brown was less staggered by the change in him, being blissfully unaware of any past reputation which had never even been slightly manifest while at Minimbah. Her face glows whenever she speaks about his time there.

But perhaps the most telling evaluation of Ryan's experience, if not the entire G-experience, was that within half a year he was returning to Minimbah and to his beloved Mini-kids. When I told other Radford staff, many were pleasantly surprised, particularly those who may have found themselves on the receiving end of any surliness or in the unfortunate position of having to discipline, reprimand or inevitably suspend him. At Foundation Day 2013, when I asked him if he would speak at the service, in Richard's 'open space' and in front of 1,700 students, he told me that the thought terrified him.

'Besides, aren't you always on about keeping the good stuff we do quiet, H?'

I nodded. He had me there.

He pressed his advantage. 'We don't want people thinking we're up ourselves just because we do service.'

'Just sometimes, Ry,' I replied, 'sometimes you have to remind people that you're still around. There may be other rough nuts like you that will sign up for a G-trip and have a similar experience if a rough nut like you, got up and said what they thought about this whole service thing.'

He looked at me with that look he fires off whenever I use phrases like 'rough nut'. 'I'm no public speaker, to be perfectly honest, H.'

'You told me that once before. That's why whatever you say will come across as perfectly honest.'

'You don't want to check up on what I have to say?'

I had to fight every cautious, once-bitten-twice-shy, risk-averse cell in my teacherly body. And said, 'I trust you, mate. Tell it how it is.'

He started to walk away and I pushed my luck.

'I'll book a spot for you.'

He didn't look back as he sauntered off like Jimmy Dean. Out into a silence that lasted for all the weeks preceding Foundation Day. He had probably taken his fears of failing out on pretty much everyone except me.

In the week of Foundation Day, I had still received no word, even in passing through corridors of the senior block or via text. Nothing to give me any peace of mind that he had the speech down. But with my own health starting to deteriorate, I didn't have the energy at this stage to hunt him in any of his school cubbyholes, or go through his mates who he may not have told about his recent membership application to the public speaking team. I feared excessive, in fact any interest, might sway him the other way. And by April 2013, I was in bad shape myself. To be perfectly honest, to use Ryan's catchphrase, I was being battered with a strange and yet-undiagnosed fatigue and a side order of influenza, which on any other day would have seen me call in sick. Yet I knew I had to go in on that Foundation Day, on the possible chance that Ryan would get the heebie-jeebies and consider doing a runner.

But this was a different kid now. I saw him, hanging near the entrance, surveying the 1,600+ in attendance and looking as edgy as I'd ever seen him. I sidled up next to him, excused myself as I stopped to fill my hanky, then had the following conversation. (Our conversations are rarely wordy. So what is recorded below may be somewhat tidier and longer than it actually was; but this was the spirit of our dialogue, given a playwright's treatment for dramatic effect.)

'How do you feel, dude?'

'Shit-scared, to tell you the truth.'

'You'll be OK. And don't swear, 'cos there are little kids around.' (Snort of the nose.) 'If you are really shit-scared, just think of all the Minimbah kids. All the faces that you've helped over that last visit and will in the next. How any single one of them would love the opportunity to go to a school like this and get the start that you've had and mustn't throw away.'

'I guess.'

'So if you've got fears, maybe put them aside, use a little of your tough-nut swagger and deliver a speech that will stir others to go to Minimbah and places like it and do some real good for a change – working alongside inspiring teachers like Miss Jenny and Miss Ursula. Remember how you felt when you saw all those mini-Mes starting to sense a future opening up for them if they started to learn stuff, play fair, do the right thing. 'Scuse me, mate. (Another snort, another tissue.) Besides, if you want to become a teacher one day you might need to stand and deliver in front of a similar number of kids. So stop being a chicken.'

'There are not close to two thousand kids at a school assembly at Minimbah, H. Look, if I become a teacher – which I'm not sure is what I want to become to be perfectly honest – it would be at Minimbah.'

It was lucky I was so bloody sick that he could not see how emotional I was getting. He was probably thinking his teacher was in dire need of a course of antibiotics and a new hanky. I said to him the same words I've said to so many students before they entered the wonderful world of service. 'I believe in you, mate. Just go do it.'

He did. What he said went something like this:[11]

> I'm no public speaker, but here goes… Last year I found myself in serious trouble at school, and as part of the consequences, I had to undertake a certain amount of community service. I thought that might all be a waste of time to be perfectly honest.
>
> But I started going to RAID and the fun everyone was having there opened my eyes a little. Not really sure why it took me so long to get there. With the gentle encouragement of several teachers – and perhaps the not-so-gentle encouragement by Mr H – I found myself heading out on Gamilaraay

4. I thought the entire experience was going to be terrible to be perfectly honest, but actually those nine days were the best of my life and completely changed me in so many ways…

I have gone from being a kid who was going down the wrong track, to someone who has a new and different perspective on life. If you're thinking of going on one of these, you should stop thinking about it and just go. It might change your perspective on stuff. Might change someone else's life for the better. Thanks for listening.

As Ryan finished, I was literally sliding down the wall of the sports centre. Yes, I was overcome by emotion, but equally so by a tsunami of nausea that had become very apparent as Ryan was getting over the line. A teacher next to me expressed concern and suggested there was no way that I was in any state to continue at school that day. I told him I couldn't go home because I was in charge of touch footy and deeply essential to its smooth running. (That was how delirious I was.) It was arranged for me to go home. The touch footy ran as smoothly as it has ever done.

I stumbled to my office to get my car keys, to find it filled to the brim with balloons for my birthday from the irrepressible and warm-hearted Celia Lindsay and the teamSUPPORT boys, RAID staff and the glorious participants – God bless their cotton socks – the night before. It was almost submersion by coloured inflatables in there, as I struggled through the cheerful balloons to retrieve my keys. Yet even feeling at death's door, I found myself needing to engage in a symbolic act (like an obsessive-compulsive hand washer), and regardless of there being no audience. I grabbed a red, yellow and black balloon and liberated them to the winds en route to the car park. I whispered, 'There's a few saved that might not've been' and watched them hover for a moment above the sports centre, before bobbling off in their own separate trajectories, up along the Barton Highway north, and maybe on to Gamilaraay country.

When I drove slowly home that Foundation Day, I did not realise it was to be my last full day of teaching for some time. The fatigue was to be more serious and deeply rooted than I initially thought. Before a sleep that lasted three days, I texted Ryan to thank him for one of the most wonderful days of my teaching career.

Around the middle of 2014, an article on the Crossing the Divide (CTD) initiative with the byline 'A unique program in Bundarra that targets youth who have disengaged from mainstream education' appeared in the glossy New England edition of *Country Living*.[12] The article featured the 'indefatigable' program founder, Matt Pye; the omnipresent and effervescent Monique Vickery of Green Valley Farm fame; the varied personalities of the CTD students; and even mentioned a May visit by Radford's new principal, Fiona Godfrey, and my humble self on the day the magazine visited Bundarra.

I have previously and superficially described the socio-economic background of the students who are part of this program and its basic curriculum design. It is perhaps best to leave a fuller description of CTD's origins to Matt Pye, its tough, unwavering, headstrong and huge-hearted engineer. It should be stated for the record that he is a personal hero of mine. The CTD program is such an organic entity that when describing it to people, I have often been left with an uneasy feeling that I have neglected or omitted something salient about its ever-evolving make-up.

> Our program started quite accidentally as a four month, two day a week proposition to effectively burn some money a service organisation had left over. I was approached with this funding and subsequently targeted a group of five Indigenous youths who had been sitting around for four or so years having left school in Year 9. In discussion first with the Elders and then the boys themselves, it emerged that they liked to tinker with bikes so we got a few old bikes donated to work on. New faces would show up in the old shed we were using, asking to join the course. At that stage, in late 2011, there actually was no course but they didn't disappear and it was then we began to realise that we had to do something in a meaningful way to help these guys. They had excellent self-taught automotive skills and this was a great launching pad for us to try and formalise somehow.
>
> In 2014, there are thirty-five participants in the program ranging in age from 16 to 47 years of age. 80% are Indigenous and 40% of our boys have been involved with the NSW Juvenile Justice Service or NSW Correctional Services.[13]

In short, CTD has created an educational rarity that would be the envy of most schools in the country: a hands-on, functioning, relevant, adaptive and alternative curriculum, based and built almost entirely on its participants' needs. After only three short years, it now has interested students (or their families, guardians, counsellors and even past detractors) knocking at the garage doors to get in. The attendance rates of those already enrolled appear to show significant levels of re-engagement.

In many ways, this is as unfamiliar a terrain as any on our Gamilaraay radar, to take students from an affluent, conservative and traditional school such as Radford College to walk through and alongside. Yet I have been constantly amazed, over a similar three-year period since inception, how effortlessly and almost comfortably the Radford students connect with the CTD participants and have developed significant empathy with their plight. At nights during the debrief, I have listened to many express, often with tears rolling down their cheeks, nothing short of outrage at the injustice most of the CTD boys have experienced and partly overcome in their lives.

'How can we work with them to make things better?' ask my indoctrinated service learners.

'Good question,' I reply. 'Spend some time with them. Get to know them. Get to know the place. Then we'll come back to it...'

As the CTD boys can be distrustful of strangers and are tricky to connect with as a result, it is a little bewildering how they almost immediately cottoned on to the fact that the Radford visitors were not interested in being judgemental of their past transgressions or family histories, of their often somewhat scruffy appearance and sometimes surly demeanour, or of their poor academic standing. Having been burnt by life, their bullshit detectors were evidently hypersensitive. But as one of the CTD lads said to me while reconstituting a buggy, 'These Canberra kids seemed to be interested in us as people.' I came very close to responding with a lame platitude but was thankfully asked to pass a wrench.

I am reminded here of Valerie Browning's frustration with the superficial assessment by other Ethiopians and western onlookers of the Afar work ethic. Due to their nomadic lifestyle, no one is 'employed' in the traditional, Western sense of the word, and much of the day is spent tending to the animals which are extremely vital to their livelihood. But while they give the appearance of being ambivalent to work, Valerie tells how she has witnessed them

> literally breaking up a hillside to make a road, led by the Sheik chanting for them, while the women at the bottom of the hill were keeping them supplied with water and shahi. They work together fantastically if they have to get something done, but they're not good at turning up at the office at nine sharp.[14]

So when Matt described to me how his boys – sometimes similarly maligned as the Afar – recently helped a local MS sufferer remodel her house in Bundarra so that she could move inside it more freely, the boys, commissioned with what Adam Cox[15] would term as 'purposeful work', laboured skilfully and selflessly. And were any of the critics of their appearance, punctuality and work ethic there to see, or at least imagine these boys in this different light? I am reminded of a character in Philip McLaren's often brutal novel *Sweet Water... Stolen Land*[16] reflecting on White Australia's haste to prejudge the indigenous in their population: 'We draw conclusions with limited information about these people.'

So, spend some time alongside, we did. Drawing hasty conclusions, we did not. I could walk past a CTD workshop at any time of the day and observe the Radford students, easy in their own vulnerability, asking for or receiving advice on welding, woodworking, motor maintenance, panel beating/spraying, and even the finer art of junk-sculpting from staff and more importantly, the CTD students. To see them hurling a footy around during recess and lunch breaks (albeit getting massively skinned throughout) only added to my relief. Any divide that needed to be crossed between our kids who come from a privileged world of shiny cars, massive homes, pay TV, reliable phone and internet connections, regular health care checks and relatively tiny amounts of adversity – and those who ride rusty bikes because they cannot afford petrol, live in garage lofts or tin shacks or under the Tingha bridge, have had electricity disconnected, have never seen a dentist's chair or doctor's waiting room, and live with regular, incessant and often violent adversity – had almost been done by secret handshake.

I would often challenge G-trippers at the start and close of their G-journey to ponder the question 'Why exactly are you here?' and have noted the unique poignancy of response coming from those who have wended, welded and worked alongside those of CTD. One G7 student, Henry, was rendered speechless when I put this very question to him: 'I don't really how to answer that yet,' he confided in me. It was clear that I had quite perplexed Henry. I didn't push him, expecting that this would be the end of it. But I am ashamed to admit that I had not given the boy enough credit, as stirring inside that head of his was a contemplative, meticulous and unhurried response that took well past the close of G7 for him to emphatically deliver. After Ryan's speech about Minimbah at the 2013 Foundation Day service, I did not anticipate that I would ever experience anything quite that moving from a student for many years to come. But wow, was I wrong, and boy, did Henry ever deliver. More later.

Not that I needed further convincing, but the final proof of the pudding came when a reserved but immensely artistically gifted senior CTD student announced that he would not attend the Bundarra speech night – at which he was to receive an award – unless the Radford students from G7 came along and accompanied him. 'H, will you just get him there,' instructed a frustrated Matt. I took the mission seriously and yes, we got him there on time, but not before searching the bushland surrounding Tingha calling out his name for twenty minutes trying to locate him. It was worth it. Watching him walk across the stage to receive his award found us applauding rapturously and without an ounce of decorum, as if we were now well and truly a part of the CTD community. That Monique Vickery had to give a plethora of characteristically crystallised speeches, and that a healthy number of Vickerys and Hickmans were also receiving academic and sporting commendations, made us feel even more a part of some extended family. We gave them unrestrained applause as well! Yup, we were definitely at the right place at the right time.

'I wish our awards nights were like that,' came a voice from the back of the Radford bus on the return trip.

'In what way?' I queried.

'Smaller. Realer.'

Another voice suddenly piped up, 'Like every person who walks across that stage matters, has a distinct identity…and is valued for it. We could learn from that.'

'Someone has issues,' volunteered a fourth.

(Short pause.)

'There are certainly some things you miss out on in the big city, aren't there?' murmured the fifth and final contributor, slightly more deadpan than the rest.

There followed an unmistakable staccato slap of a high five which I assumed (as I diligently had my driver's eyes scanning Thunderbolt's Way for rogue roos and wandering wombats) was between a wide-eyed kid from the city and his newly found buddy from the bush. That sound, so sharp and unambiguously positive, was all that was really needed to punctuate a perfect evening.

Monique Vickery was now the school captain of Bundarra Central School and in her final year. (She was in fact the only Year 12 student in 2014. But she would have been school captain if there were 4 million enrolled.) She often voiced her warmth and unreserved admiration for the CTD boys. It is always touching to hear her speak in this way. During both her visits to Radford in 2013 and 2014, she mentioned in formal speeches and at informal gatherings the importance – for both advantaged and disadvantaged youth – to look positively into their own future. Irrespective of background and circumstance, every individual should have the right and the resources to establish, define, attempt to act upon and ultimately (and hopefully) achieve some of their more realistic and attainable goals for life. As she said to *Country Living*, 'I went to primary school with a lot of these boys and the transformation they have made is truly amazing. They now have dreams.'[17] That these dreams have taken significant steps towards fruition at CTD is a credit to all concerned.

The CTD program provides a workshop, both literally and figuratively, where its students can access the equipment and facilities necessary to begin forging a reality out of the stuff of dreams. These boys, mostly in their late teens, finally have the chance to start believing that they just might have it within themselves to overcome and leap over those barriers, obstacles and divides that do so much to diminish them. Yet while it is easy to blame socio-economic hurdles, educational conservatism or especially the toxic pessimism often voiced through the irrational fears, dismissals and inaction of naysayers – who always seem to be disinterested in finding or working towards a solution – the CTD participants, staff and supporters are learning to say phooey to any finger-pointing and backstabbing. But it is the participants who must now recognise, three years in, that the program's lifespan rests on them to assume a greater responsibility; they now have to take those challenging but emphatic final steps towards the workforce and the independent future that Matt and his team have brought within their reach. And then, *perhaps it is up to us,* dear reader, to challenge the workforce to provide them with a job-opening that is not token or tick-a-box. The likes of Matt Pye cannot do everything, heroic as they are.

While on the topic of 'chance', it is similarly important to add that second chances are imperative for these boys who have perhaps taken a catastrophic misstep in early youth, a misstep which may have stained, strained and maybe even disintegrated all hopes for future prosperity. Matt often challenges us to consider where we would in fact be in life, had we had not been lucky to be born with a silver spoon in our mouths, and how do we think we might fare if our own lives had started in the same socio-economic reality as his CTD boys? An unsettling question indeed. As he challenges us,

> They are the youth who simply are not catered for in our education system and who will not fill the university spots or the job advertisements. Their pathway is pre-determined at birth. They will be the statistically uneducated and unemployed. They are constantly ground down by an inflexible and impersonal system that doesn't acknowledge the many barriers they will face nor the lack of opportunities presented for them. They will be labelled as dole bludgers, drugos and no hopers... There are probably hundreds of similar

communities to theirs across the country. Society can be quick to judge and condemn them without exploring the underlying root of their issues and problems and this is understandable. We all lead busy lives and have jobs to do. I have been guilty of this perception myself in the past.[18]

It is hard not be ashamed when those of us born into privileged society appear unwilling to imagine 'the shoe being on the other foot'. As Keating reminded us, we often fail

> to make the most basic human response and enter their hearts and minds. We failed to ask – how would I feel if this were done to me? As a consequence, we failed to see that what we were doing degraded all of us.[19]

Occasionally, I would play in classrooms or perform at smaller gigs, Ron Sexsmith's highly empathetic song 'For the Driver', which asks us to place ourselves squarely in the shoes of those whom we might too quickly judge or malign at the centre of extreme and tragic situations. Like the driver who collides 'with a child who chased a ball across his path' or 'the soldier in the throes of war' or 'the lady in the crimson light with demand on the left and judgement on the right'.[20]

As an extension of this empathetic ideal, Matt himself implores us to *imagine* a little harder what lies behind the actions of his charges, if not people in general; how we all need to develop more finely-tuned skills of empathy if we are ever to effectively work with those who do not *appear* to fit in; and ultimately spark in them a desire to help themselves and make the most of the opportunities in front of them. He recounts an incident which occurred to him years ago where one of his junior high students swore profusely at a maths teacher who had admonished him for not completing homework:

> This young man subsequently fled the school and hours later I finally tracked him down and we sat in the gutter to talk it through. When he was sufficiently calm, he broke down in tears and revealed that his dad had spent the night with a shotgun pointed at his mother's head the evening prior. Having witnessed and endured this, this young man was then expected to front up to class as per normal. Funnily enough, algebraic factorisations were not high on his agenda on that particular day.

I tell this story because too often we get so caught up in everyday machinations that we forget that there are many significant undercurrents going on in the lives of those around us. As a society, we can be quick to judge behaviours and actions with little knowledge of the complex subsurface and this can be extremely damaging.[21]

Those in privileged circles can quite casually dismiss their own great adolescent missteps as merely being 'a part of growing up', 'the sowing of wild oats' or 'something from which to learn'. But for the CTD boys, brought up and often smothered by the realities of financial hardship, racial prejudice and social degradation, an incident such as the one outlined above can often become an imprisoning moment – one as hard to escape from as Alcatraz. That simile was chosen to be deliberately provocative; as Richard, 16, stated in the *Country Living* article, 'I didn't believe in a second chance until I met Matty. If this hadn't happened I may now be in prison.'[22]

For Neville, after two years in the program and now formidably equipped with a potential royal flush of tickets in welding, bobcat, excavator, front-end loader and forklift, he can start to realistically consider, alongside his mate Richard, making inroads into the mining industry. Neville also acknowledges that his busy CTD experience has provided useful distraction from his own self-destructive tendencies: 'This place has stopped me from doing stupid stuff.'[23]

And then there is the mischievous and ebullient break-dancer, Jamahl, nineteen, who is a year into the program after a battle with crowded classrooms, stultifying curriculum and his own personal demons. Suddenly, like a bolt from the blue, he found himself with more room to move:

> I was kicked out of a number of local schools and I thought I should give this program a crack. I have never liked crowded areas and here [at CTD] you can get better attention. Drugs messed me up and I needed to complete Year 12 again. I have a passion for dancing and my aim, with support from Matt, family and friends is to audition at the Sydney Dance School. I don't want to let Matt down.[24]

Revealed here is the importance of educating and embedding in participants the arts of self-belief and well-being, which have been nurtured through health classes, fitness regimes and hygiene practices not previously taught in either the classroom or family home. The recent introduction of a fully equipped gym, which the entire CTD cohort voluntarily attends, must also help in this regard. And not to mention other salient life skills covered in the CTD curriculum, such as anger management; the development of (and in some cases an introduction to) social skills; and vitally, with over 80% of the participants being Indigenous, the exploration of cultural identity. As Matt elaborated in his Dirrum Dirrum speech,

> Students connect back to their traditional culture by partnering with the local Aboriginal Land Council and the local Aboriginal Health Service. Outside agencies are invited in to deliver a variety of services from dental check-ups to cultural workshops. We regularly go out to see the Elders and we invite them into the program for meals and fellowship.[25]

Perhaps the most telling self-evaluation CTD has had proffered was in a Facebook post by one of its participants, confirming that his well-being had been, for the time being, well and truly recovered:

> I used to look in the mirror and hate myself. But now I feel good about myself and nobody will ever take that away from me again.

I hear Bruce Springsteen singing how 'at the end of every hard earned day people find some reason to believe'.[26]

While quietly proud that for the past two years Radford College has chosen to focus on (and return to) CTD as its national charity; while Collegians continue to astound me with their own considerable generosity and interest; and while Junk Sculpture continues to periodically donate performance payments toward the program, the bottom line is that regular, committed, informed and high-profile financial, spiritual and professional support is still needed to keep stories like those above being told. But as already indicated, for all the good work that CTD undertakes, in order for the program to become fully accountable in terms of getting participants into the workforce, a societal shift needs to simultaneously occur. As Matt indicated in the *Country Living* article,

> we need to develop employment pathways to funnel students into once they are workplace ready. Local workplace experience partners are vital, so the students can consolidate their new skills.[27]

Will you be one? A month after this article hit the newsagents, Matt was even more explicit at the 2014 Dirrum Dirrum Conference:

> For our older boys, we have looked to offer qualifications that might enable them to transition into work pathways. It was recognised that this group needed help in a range of areas outside of our expertise. For the past 24 months we have been approaching, accosting and harassing a variety of different organisations to try and put services and support in at ground level for our students. This is not always easy given our size, our location and our relative obscurity as a program.
>
> There appears to be a window of opportunity that exists at 18–25 years of age where these young men realise that they want to effect change in their lives. Typically at this stage they have been out of the system for a number of years. They have very low literacy and numeracy levels, poor communication skills and poor self-discipline. By this stage, their opportunities are extremely limited particularly in the rural areas where facilities are few and far between.
>
> If opportunities and work placements cannot be found for our students to transition into, then my biggest fear is my boys will be thrown back on the scrapheap. Their two-year turnaround and all their qualifications will amount to nothing. We are currently trying to make contact with political figures and mining corporations to see what may be available. Many of the boys are willing to move but they will continue to require an ongoing strong and supportive network behind them.[28]

So far it would appear, in truth, Matt's call for developmental pathways has fallen on deaf ears. Exposure through this book, between songs at GHJS gigs, at enlightened bookshops/venues such as Beyond Q[29] and Teatro Vivaldi, through the awareness and fund-raising of schools like Radford, and in the pages of the inspiring *Country Living* article (and kudos to them for finding CTD, researching, beautifully photographing and writing it[30]), is definitely an encouraging *start* – but it is nowhere near enough.

My hope for CTD, as with all authentic service endeavour, is that a significant shift will occur in the minds and hearts of future generations by those understanding souls (such as my own teamSUPPORTers and G-trippers) in better-off schools. It is this cohort that will statistically *become* the leaders of governments, commerce, industry and social reform, as well as in the areas of arts, sports and other educational institutions of the rapidly approaching future. (There is room for optimism here as Matt Pye's assessment of the G-trip students was publicly offered at the 2014 Dirrum Dirrum Conference as follows: 'The depth of maturity, empathy and insight shown by your (Radford) students is both heart-warming and inspiring for me and obviously a credit to this community of family, friends and school. If what I have encountered is representative of the wider community here in the nation's capital, we are in good hands.')

Perhaps these G-trippers are the ones who, at the end of their own hard-earned days, diplomas, degrees and possible promotions to positions of real power in the community, if not the nation, need to provide others in their backyard with a reason to believe.

Had Radford not continually returned to Bundarra and Tingha to spend time alongside the CTD students and people of the Gamilaraay region, the *depth* of their understanding and the ensuing response to their service experience would probably be as fleeting as any other tick-a-box community service visitation or requirement. To engage in service in such an anonymous and distant manner feels as empty to me as sending a donation by mail overseas; while the parting with cash is a generous gesture in itself, it is a faceless one that no amount of compensating photos on a fridge or on Facebook will ever hope to nullify.

In convincing the likes of Richard, Neville and Jamahl – and even the tiring, embattled staff of CTD (who I suspect have rarely heard a word of gratitude for the costs to themselves and their families for their selfless work) – that they matter enough for an individual, group or organisation to travel for over twelve hours, check in regularly between visits, and then return every few months: herein lies perhaps the most valid and viable model I can glean to produce more authentic service experiences for our more privileged youth. This is particularly pertinent as private industry, particularly in the field of travel, becomes increasingly interested in the money-making and profile-raising opportunities surrounding charitable endeavour.

It is through commitment to creating a real relationship with 'the other' which I believe draws out heart-wrenching responses such as what follows by G-tripper and future PM, Henry. This inquiring service learner spent a rich week laughing, learning and living – and being perplexed and puzzled by – his own whole CTD experience. As he eloquently stated at the Foundation Day service[31] as well as the launch of the Dirrum Dirrum Conference in 2014 (with David Pocock sitting in front of him),

> There exists a divide in this country – a divide that leaves hundreds of thousands of people of our generation facing the world with no hope for a better future – a divide that has become increasingly impossible to cross.
>
> Behind this divide, there exist immensely complex problems that we cannot pretend to fully understand. Not understanding is no excuse for not trying. I dream of a straight-forward fix. Unfortunately, it is far too late to be so simple.
>
> It is easy for us, in our position of relative privilege and good fortune, to turn a blind eye and plead ignorance to the injustice which does not directly affect us. It is easy for us to judge others, when we have no concept of the harsh realities that dictate their lives. I dream of a world where we do not.
>
> Most importantly I dream of a future where opportunity and choice in the life you lead are not governed by your place in society which you had no say over. I dream that in the future, programs that provide a way across this ever-growing divide for those who have been left behind, will have their place cemented in our education system.
>
> A future within OUR lifetime, where EVERYONE is at least given the CHANCE, to Cross the Divide.

I remember gazing across at Pocock and wondering if he recognised something of himself in this no-frilled, idealistic and intelligent young man. I suspected so. I wished I could have similarly and personally identified, but knew the seventeen-year-old I had once been lived in a world too insulated, sugar-coated and self-centred to ever be able to articulate anything this profoundly empathetic and informed. My dreams were about being a rock star loved by all, and perhaps could and should have been more about being a rock, or a provider of light, that radiates love outwardly rather than expecting or desiring it aimed at himself alone.

My hope was now that Henry's Dream[32] would not only be fully realised one day, but that he may play an active and loving part in its realisation. I suspect then, and only then, will the true worth of the G-program and service endeavour like it, be appropriately measured. But for now, his inspirational words, informed by experience, spoke volumes about the potential for service learning to effect deep and lasting change in people and places. I believe Henry will one day return to Bundarra. (He did in fact do so on G10, his last school excursion with Radford College. I also feel certain he'll return in the future as a collegian.)

In the Midnight Oil song 'Star of Hope',[33] Peter Garrett implores that its subject might 'shine upon this half-made man, blinded by a new tomorrow'. He goes on to imply that 'the light on the hill is so far away' and perhaps that the star of hope 'won't be seeing him again'. Somewhat bleak, I hear you say. So, as a rebuttal of sorts, perhaps the final words in this chapter should come from CTD's Lex, who hails from Tingha and who at the age of twenty wants to do a 'returning' of sorts; one that might send out benevolent ripples, if not towering waves, towards the shores of even the most desolate, dispirited and despairing of inner landscapes. As Lex relayed to *Country Living*, 'I would love to go back to Tingha, feeling like a "star" to guide the other kids.'[34]

In returning whence he came, in such a shining way, 'stars' like Lex would have a gravitational pull far greater than any well-intentioned do-gooder. With guidance, Lex could effectively and more profoundly begin, for those smaller stars in his orb, to seal up the black hole which very nearly sucked them all in. It would be a beautiful thing, wouldn't it, to see Lex at Tingha Public, with Henry there *alongside*, setting a stellar example, to anyone who might care to observe, of how to successfully negotiate and ultimately cross an ever-growing divide.

If I was Matt Pye, or a member of his intrepid CTD staff, I would find not only vindication, but some solace and solution from that shimmering light, showing us the way through even the most darkest, foggiest and bleakest of nights.

Despite what anyone might say, or sing, to the contrary.

Track #6 Shifting Sands and Broken Plans

I was stopped in my tracks by a passage in Judy Atkinson's *Trauma Trails* which described the healing capacity of community life in some aboriginal tribes. She writes,

> Relationships, at the individual level and between groups, were negotiated, redefined and healed on an ongoing basis, in ceremonial pursuits and day-to-day activities… Men and women came together in ceremony both in gender groups and as community, through dance, art, music, theatre, crafts and storytelling, used and acted out in day-to-day secular and sacred ritual. Thus relationships and interconnections were established, maintained, strengthened and healed.[1]

One can only get the impression of a respectful, functioning and curative existence from descriptions such as these. While sporting ridiculous hats and awful, impractical, frilly clothing, what exactly was it that most of the early Europeans visiting Australian shores actually imagined they were seeing at Indigenous ceremonies or in their observation of daily activity? Were they truly only capable of witnessing then reporting on such industry and interaction as being merely 'excessive leisure, social entertaining'?[2] (Then again one should not be mystified by interpretations of 'the new world' by men too long at sea. This includes the inept naming of its landforms; when Cook saw Pigeon House Mountain and decided it reminded him of an abode for feral, feathered creatures he certainly didn't see what most other people saw. The Aboriginal name for the mountain is Didthul, which means 'woman's breast'.)

Atkinson's passage reminded me of how integral the arts can be in the building of community and in the healing of its members. For me, a performance, or in fact any type of artistic gathering, is augmented when linked by such a purpose – leisure or frivolous entertainment notwithstanding. I have always felt that the power of the arts is apparent *after* the event: through the sharing of stories, experiences, opinions and reflections which shoot out like inspired saplings from the central stem of experience. When this occurs, it is art at its best; it can establish, maintain, strengthen, reconcile, inspire, cajole, challenge, connect and heal those receptive to its orb.

It is no small wonder that I was attracted to *Diesel and Dust* all those years ago, as it does all of these things. This relatively restrained album found Midnight Oil finally putting its abrasive personality, forceful social conscience and unflappable self-confidence to some very constructive social use. I was certainly reminded of its music, messages and strengths when reading *Trauma Trails*, as both works were concerned with exploring and repairing connections severed by traumatic pasts, both personal and historical. Both seemed to promote and desire, in the words of anthropologist Bill Stanner, more

> activities of relationship, of making connections, of creating, maintaining and healing relationships, in which the primary virtues were 'generosity and fair dealing', working to 'unite hearts and establish order'. (Stanner 1963)[3]

Bill Stanner's words echo in the lyrics of both 'Beds are Burning' and 'The Dead Heart'. And surely a successful rock gathering, or even a thoughtfully curated music festival can quite powerfully do this. It perhaps also explains why I could never fully comprehend the boorish, self-indulgent abandon of the moshpit, or the no-holds barred self-appointed permission of those lost in the frenzy of alcohol and other substances to willingly or unwittingly stand in front of, punch or swear at, spill liquids on or be inexplicably rude to a fellow fan of rock 'n' roll. Surely we had come united in a desire to forget our woes and have a good time *with* others? I do have to concede that the muscle and agro of some of Midnight Oil's more incendiary performances could often incite and feed this boorishness in the intoxicated and/or over-excited. Luckily, Peter Garrett seemed always prepared to take on such behaviour from the stage.

Atkinson and Stanner both struck a chord in me, musical pun perhaps intended. As a result, I was not immediately certain why it took me so long to get onto creating a Midnight Oil tribute show to raise awareness and funds for Indigenous people, especially as I had given time and money to some worthy yet relatively obscure tribute acts, themes, charities and beneficiaries in the past. Perhaps the show itself was patiently waiting for the right time to be played and its messages revisited? Or maybe I needed to wait for just the right fit of musicians to come along?

But by 2013, the time had indeed come. And it equally came as no surprise that I felt its calling just as the G-trips were finding their feet.

In a Junk Sculpture hiatus, Chris Brown, Rob Marshall and I – with newcomer Joel Copeland occasionally backing us on drums – had begun playing periodic, smaller gigs at my dwelling. (This unit eventually became known as 'the Unified Theory of Everything' or 'UTE'.) The idea was to share, on a more intimate level amidst my slightly nerdy Beatles, KISS and Dr Who paraphernalia,[4] a diverse, unpredictable and heartfelt interpretation of a dozen or so songs, ideas and images that were exciting or exigent to the band. (Although the truth is I tended to hog the set list.) And have every member of the similarly diverse and unpredictable audience feel that we were relating, playing and performing directly *with* them in community. Not to, not for, but with. Entry was by way of some food or drink to share with others.

I appropriated the private home 'performance' concept from American playwright Wallace Shawn, who occasionally chose to perform his plays in intimate venues outside of theatres. In a recent *Paris Review* interview, he explains,

> I'm not just trying to entertain somebody, I'm trying to tell somebody something that I mean. And you can't do that in a theatre, because if you put a person on a stage in a theatre, that person will be interpreted as a character in a story. No matter what happens on that stage, it will be interpreted by everybody as a form of entertainment... I was trying to speak as a friend to a friend, from one human being to another.[5]

Former Yes drummer, Bill Bruford, understood the power of this intimacy. As he states in his autobiography,

> It may be a distinction between affecting a lot of people superficially (perhaps with a disposable single with a shelf-life of about ten minutes) and giving a small group of people (perhaps your colleagues or other taste-makers) the experience of a lifetime that they will never forget and that will cause them to alter their perspectives, in turn causing others to alter their perspectives, like ripples on a pond.[6]

This was entirely what I desired if not needed to do: break away from the central mimicry and mere entertainment elements inherent in tribute shows and get back to being and performing as the Real Me. But stepping away from Shawn and Bruford, I realised this could still be achieved while playing other people's music; that I could 'tell something' and 'alter perspectives' even when using somebody else's words and music. This would mean prioritising interpretation above characterisation with an audience, and attempting something a lot closer to authentic conversation, albeit a musical one, between friends. (Or any strangers who just happened to show up.) Thus, the home gigs were to be unapologetically interactive, under-rehearsed and spontaneous. Usually with a glass of raspberry or lemon cordial in their hand, people could share ideas, opinions and experiences about the work on offer, contribute vocally or percussively, and even, if space and self-confidence allowed, express themselves through dance or less-refined bodily movement. I should invite Judy Atkinson, Bill Bruford, Bill Stanner's ghost and Wallace Shawn to one of these gigs as I think they would appreciate the community building, the sharing of song and the revelation through stories about who it is we actually are.

Some serendipitous moments would often occur at these intimate mini-gigs. Reinterpreting 70s and 80s numbers, such as Glen Campbell's 'Rhinestone Cowboy', Mike Oldfield's 'Moonlight Shadow', Roxy Music's 'More Than This', Midge Ure's 'If I Was' or even Cold Chisel's 'Ita' as bruising, brooding, existential statements was of particular joy to me. Attempting bizarre requests or at least sending them back as improvised rap became another trademark, as did singing some of the more self-serious numbers of the set list in an Elvis voice. (I was accused of heresy when I did this to one of Springsteen's bleaker numbers from *Nebraska*. To this day I still can't help singing the third verse of the gritty album closer 'Reason to Believe' with Presleyesque persuasion.) We would then greedily belt out songs which maybe should never have been unearthed in rap or blue suede formats, such as the Seekers' dreamy 'Morningtown Ride' (yup, we went there). That said, these numbers often had the most self-serious audience member gaily clapping along and unashamedly blaming their mother's record collections for their near word-perfect recall.

I also started to incorporate some of my photography into precisely timed slide shows projected onto a screen behind. I remember a particularly poignant example when I selected a striking set of images of ancient rock formations from the Lakes Walk in Kosciuszko National Park to accompany a version of Tom Petty's 'I Won't Back Down' – in respectful memory of a friend of Rob's in the UK who had recently passed away. *Thus relationships and interconnections were established, maintained, strengthened and healed.* I hoped for healing. I prayed for strength and reason.

But perhaps, for me, one of the most resonating moments occurred when I segued together three Australian classics which I did not consciously recognise were related in spirit, lyric and decade. 'Under the Milky Way' by the Church rolled beautifully into 'Solid Rock' by Goanna[7] (which happened to be in the same key) before a brief transitional passage modulated neatly into the Oils' 'The Dead Heart'. The effect was that of a mini rock operetta of searching, longing and dispossession with a distinctly dusty, antipodean feel. A beautiful accident.

It was at these gatherings that I finally started playing my own compositions. It was no small coincidence that most, including a song called 'No Way Nadir' (which used the flooding across a causeway on the Bundarra Road into Tingha as a metaphor about those obstacles in life which block our way to a better place) and 'Circle of Surrender' (about the circuitous, if not closed, pathways to a better place for many of the young in the Gamilaraay region) were first aired. Again, photographic images complemented and transformed the music.

As the new songs started to flow, the final pieces of the Midnight Oil tribute show were being put into place. I wish I had seen an interview/documentary on Peter Garrett on SBS's *Living Black* conversations before doing the first of these shows. At one point, the inspirationally self-deprecating head Oilman stated,

> I think we all change the world in our own ways if we're alive to what's happening around us. For me, it was very much a case of wanting to work with other people to try and make things improve...[8]

It sure was reassuring for me to hear a hero from my youth state that Option B from my childhood wish list was still very attainable even though Option A's Rock Star Status may now be lost. (I had totally given up on Option C by now.) For someone who has achieved so much, to state that we all have the capacity to effect positive change in our worlds, if we retrieve our heads from out of the proverbial sand, was nothing short of timely, and motivated me once more to fight against the forces inside and outside my own body that suggested otherwise.

Despite being diagnosed with excessively high iron, chronic fatigue and a complex case of the (almost paradoxically labelled) non-melancholic depression, I had every intention of continuing to attempt positive change in the world through my newly found service learning responsibilities. This was particularly in conjunction with those with disabilities and through the growing relationship with the rural folk of Gamilaraay country described in previous chapters. Yet I also had never let go of the hope that my musical endeavours might somehow follow suit into these service fields. Until it did, I am not sure I would ever feel fulfilled. So at the start of 2013, as I dusted off another heartfelt rendition of 'The Dead Heart' with UTE, I began to consider more seriously whether the most appropriate and appealing way to connect my service and music activity, might actually be through the words and music of Midnight Oil.

If indeed so, it all needed an audacious, brash, loud, emotionally mature, musically masterful and huge-hearted band to do it. So I called on a new-look Junk Sculpture to rise to a challenge set by Kevin Rudd in 2008 and echoed by Phillip Heath a year later. I wanted the band to do more than gong-clanging, but figured if we were ever going to bang any spherical, metallic, percussive instrumentation, we'd certainly be doing so bloody hard. And as unsubtly as Rob Hirst attacked those water tanks decades ago.

The new show was to be smarmily called 'Burning the Midnight Oil'. This was because late and last-minute sculpting and eventual delivery of product was the same with all permutations of the band as it had been with the teamSUPPORT boys: do it at the death and don't kill the fireworks of spontaneity. Having lost Swainy to the tyranny of distance, and Michael and Dan to the growing momentum of their own aspiring bands, loves and lives, Brownie and I, once again, had to recreate the beast from the possibilities around us.

We did not need to look too far. Rob slotted in easily from the trio on guitar, bringing with him his friend Tim Kuschel,[9] a gifted audio engineer (not without virtuosic piano skills himself) who seemed to effortlessly and instantly relate and relax into the groove, grunt and gifts of the band. At Radford at the time, were two slick, hip, happening, young-gun muzos on staff: Joel Copeland and Matt Heinrich. Both were incredibly gifted multi-instrumentalists who had been won over when playing with the band at a charity evening at the school in 2012. (Junk Sculpture, never afraid to improvise or willing to be tied down by the rigidity of charts, predictable song-structures and/or inflexible set lists, played an evening of songs by artists with names or hits that started with the letter B. Naturally and thematically, all proceeds went to Barnardo's.) Lastly, a much-needed brass player was an initial stumbling block, until we realised that there is usually a teamSUPPORT lad around expert in even the most arcane of skills – and ready and willing to help: thus entered Callum Sambridge stage right with a shiny trumpet protruding from behind a lush mop of spinifex.

I had organised two gigs at Teatro Vivaldi's, our regular haunt for many a tribute show or New Year's bash. Teatro Vivaldi, a theatre restaurant at the heart of the Australian National University, is an utter joy to perform in.[10] Always sympathetic and amenable to my unpredictable list of tribute shows, owners Anthony Hill and Mark Santos did not bat an eyelid when I said I'd like to entertain the regulars with a revisiting of the works of one of Australia's iconic bands. I knew that in their heart of hearts, the owners would have been more keen for an ABBA, Boney M or possibly even Celine Dion show, but they had never stood in the way of my artistic whimsy, despite me never really accommodating theirs. I will pitch my Sandy Farina show to them next.

I had selected Crossing the Divide as the relevant organisation for which to raise awareness and funds. The idea was that after the Vivaldi's shows had generated sufficient interest, we would play for donations at Beyond Q Bookstore and then at Radford College, both extremely dependable in their generosity as well as love of retro-rock.

Jim Moginie had stated in a wonderful reflective interview on the Identity Theory literary website[11] that 'Beds are Burning' was a 'heartfelt more than incendiary statement'. (This was where he famously stated that he felt as if the band had been 'screaming into a fog of indifference'.) So I demanded of Junk Sculpture to do all of these things: to scream from the heart, yes, but maybe without starting a bushfire. The Teatro Vivaldi gigs' set lists were full of fireworks, if the truth be told, but not at the expense of emotional fragility, vulnerability and maturity. They contained a healthy sprinkling of tunes from *Diesel and Dust*. My increasing fatigue, iron and non-melancholic depressive levels had reached worrying heights in the lead-up to the gig and were eventually to mean the postponement of the Radford performance, after I had unwisely chosen to burn out rather than fade away at Vivaldi's. But as far as meeting childhood dreams head on, this was as close and precise a shave across the thin scalp of dream-realisation that I was ever going to get.

One of my gifted and artistic students, Riley Krewaz – a teamSUPPORTer who had attended a G-trip in the previous year and understood the gist of what I was trying to do – designed, at my request, a collection of white T-shirts with the in-yer-face style of the cover of the Oils' 1997 Greatest Hits package, *20 000 Watt RSL*. I proudly brandished Garrett's signature 'What's Your Excuse' lettering while the rest of the band sported '(Still) Sorry' on theirs, as a nod to the Oils' Sydney Olympic Games performance in 2000 where they hit the stage with jumpsuits offering the apology that (up until then) the Australian government had not been able to give to its Aboriginal nations. Riley designed a nifty series of images as a nod to the album covers: the loaded roo of *Redneck Wonderland*, the anorexic chicken of *Bird Noises*, Uluru from *The Dead Heart* EP, *Blue Sky Mining's* lightning strike, Ken Duncan's shotgun shack (South Australia) from *Diesel and Dust* and the splayed Garrett-hand adorned our backs, so that we certainly looked the part (from behind).

We opened both of the initial Vivaldi's sets with 'The Dead Heart', whipping the audience into an early sing-along frenzy with the doo-doo-doo-doos and catchy chorus, propelled by Brownie's pounding, dirt road bass. By the time we got to 'Put Down That Weapon', the atmosphere all fogged up by Matt's haunting synth, I knew things were more than just talk and that we were in a very mystical place somewhere above the waterline. I started to riff Garrettesque between and during songs, exhorting people to read Xavier Herbert and join the Jindyworobak movement, before Rob's mellifluous jingle-jangling propelled us into the heart of 'Capricornia'. I also managed my trademark rap, utilising the lyrics of 'Kosciusko' amidst an extended jam during 'King of the Mountain', where Joel's fervent and athletic drumming performance gave no sign of abating as he scaled his own dizzying heights.

During 'Tin Legs and Tin Mines', a musical prayer to Tingha, I sang for the kids and staff whose friendship with my school was disarming in its authenticity; 'In the Valley' found me crooning out to our hosts at Green Valley Farm and their unbridled, daily celebration of the importance and longevity of family and friends; in 'Hercules' I decried – while flailing my sweaty arms recklessly in a way that would do Peter Garrett or even Richard Browning proud – the utter stupidity of sinking so much money into arms when so many people in our own country require more than a brief shotgun blast of education, medication, sanitation, commiseration and reconciliation. See! I do sound like 80s Garrett! Oh for sure: 'The rich get richer, the poor get the picture. The bombs never hit ya when you're down so low.'[12] Yee-ha.

The band sizzled, particularly in the quieter, more intense moments: 'One Country', 'Wedding Cake Island' and 'Shakers and Movers' did not allow places to hide and each musician's 'voice' was heard (thanks to Tim's perfect mix) in an appropriately democratic way. It was also intuitive to what Oils drummer Rob Hirst described as a musical necessity, inspired by their experience in the desert, 'to slow down and turn down' and enabling the band 'for the first time to put space in our music'.[13]

It was great to look out into audiences and see the Radford staff and students of past Gamilaraay trips with their families, adding to my conviction that the seeds of this communal gig were all correctly sown. I even pulled an unlucky member of my Year 7 Drama class, Harry, onto the stage along with Joel Copeland's mum, Maryanne, and instructed them both on the fine art of high-voltage hand gesturing, before refereeing a Garrett-off to the delight of the punters. And to have a teamSUPPORT representative onstage in Callum trumpeting his wares – his face toreador-red from blowing and singing his guts out, as demanded by songs such as 'Forgotten Years' – was just the icing on the cake of connectivity and inclusivity.

However, it was in the final trio of songs from *Diesel and Dust* that the proverbial roof was raised and the music permitted to soar towards the celestial fireworks above, somewhere out beyond the wondrous stars of Warburton. 'Warakurna', 'Beds are Burning', then into my beloved 'Sometimes'. What a way to finish…

I finally understood 'Warakurna'; its unexpected time signature potholes, its insistent campfire chord changes, a subtly morphing mantra and unromanticised scribble of images drenched with the sweat of Australiana. It all found me desiring to write a letter of apology there and then to Jim Moginie for ever questioning its beauty. As the Junkies and I sang that 'there is enough for everyone' I could feel the music suggesting just that very sentiment as the room seemingly opened out towards the vast expanse.

Our penultimate number and highly anticipated show stopper 'Beds are Burning' followed and – an improvised and teasing introductory rant aside – remained faithful to the original. I remember climbing onto someone's table and stretching my arms out à la Garrett in the 'One Country' video clip, worshipping the light from a neon shroud and allowing the Good News from this midnight mass in the Church of Oiliness to transport the converted towards a place where rent was fair, paid on time and people could once again dance on an undisturbed and unmoving earth.

And then came 'Sometimes'. I precariously climbed monitors and then deliberately fell off them, limbs flying everywhere, in honour of Garrett's graceless Exxon Building tumble – the hardcore fans in the audience understanding my clumsy homage, the rest asking if anyone knew first aid. As outlined in Mark Dodshon's biography of the band,[14]

> during 'Sometimes' Pete fell a couple of metres from the top of one of the big speaker boxes. He managed to climb back up in time to deliver the next line and in doing so inadvertently illustrated the 'never say die' theme of the song.

And just for a moment, as the band rocketed towards the final chorus, my thoughts returned to that gig at the University of Canberra, to Dorothea Brooke and stolen hubcaps. Here I was, twenty-six years down the Gunbarrel Highway of life and finally playing that triumphant song. But for all its long and lengthy lead-up, it did not seem like the ultimate rendition of the song in my soul. In truth, I was starting to quite literally feel that I had been beaten to the call, taken to the wall and my face was starting to fall in the wake of my persistent, nagging maladies and my own mother's slowly-failing health. 'But you don't give in...'

Many of the photographs taken during the evening, particularly a beauty by Matt's father snapped as the band was taking a delirious bow, exhibit the joy and satisfaction of a job well done but possibly unfinished. Brownie looked rapturously ecstatic. Any fears I had of being unable to successfully hide my unwanted fatigue were knocked on the head by Richard Browning who reviewed the gig as follows:

> It lit a fire deep within me for lots of reasons; some of it was just about going back to bouncing in the boarding house with a sense of pride in an Aussie rock band that lets the dust/country/story of our land sing through its music... I do remember looking at you and realising that although you were putting on the moves and character of Garrett, it was you; it was not just a gig, that the music, the politics of the songs and the soul of the lyrics reverberated deeply within you. That is, you weren't bunging nuffink on, it was real, and the sweat and strain of it all came from your heart. Singing 'Let's give it back' was not a lyric but a heartfelt protest.

The unplugged gig at Beyond Q bookstore a few days later attracted a small crowd, as gigs often do when the ACT Brumbies are playing on the same night and when having an annoyingly winner season under their new (and soon to be old) coach, South African legend Jake White. I had to do the gig seated – albeit nearly breaking the stool I was rocking on throughout – but by the time we got to 'Sometimes', I was starting to feel that I had been now well and truly taken to the wall and was starting to unceremoniously slide down it like the executed in a Tarantino back alley.

I was starting to feel exactly the same way I felt on the day Ryan gave his Foundation Day speech. I had now hit the point of total exhaustion and had to subsequently cancel the much-anticipated Radford gig. I desperately hoped that at some future point the band could return and perform not only to fulfil the promise made to Matt Pye and the Crossing the Divide lads, but to finish the job that had been started. Yet at the time I could not see past lengthy visits to the family doctor, school counsellor, dietician and masseuse. Even so, the words of the previously and unfairly maligned 'Warakurna' were still ringing in the skull; I hoped they could equally apply to me:

> Some people leave, always return.

As already indicated, after my twin capitulations before the amazing

Foundation Day service and the Radford Oils gig for Crossing the Divide, little did I know that I would not return to the school or play music with my band for the remainder of 2013. Between these events, I perhaps unwisely took a bunch of rough nuts up to the Warrumbungles in the Easter holidays, honouring my commitment to assist Dick and Sally Perram with bushfire remediation around their hotel, ignoring the fairly obvious signs my body was giving me that it needed to rest.

The trip was immensely successful, as an energetic bunch of lads (hats off to Adam, Baily, Declan, Mitchell, Ned, Rowan and Tom) appreciated the joy of labouring for others, punctuated with the joy of seeing one of the best sunsets in the solar system at the end of each day. But the rock removal, entrance gateway and gutter painting, and the replanting of gardens took its toll. The sands began to well and truly shift as my plans for the year seemed to be broken and scattering before me like piles of unsorted scrap at the Molong junkyard.

Then in August, Mum passed away just after celebrating her ninetieth birthday, as a wild, stormy night opened up into a day of cloudless blue skies and sunshine. As always, alongside the kindness of friends, it was music and the miles that provided an initial source of comfort as I came to terms with a grief which I thought I had been, in so many ways, well prepared for.

I had received a call from Mum's GP, Dr Kate, to return home quickly and pay my last respects. I was, once more, creeping up the Newell and was actually at the edge of the Warrumbungles. I was heading back to Green Valley, where I had decided to go to commence an earnest fight against the stultifying effects of the Three Stooges – my personification of my high-iron level, chronic fatigue and non-melancholic depression. The previous day, I spent a beautiful afternoon walking around Mount Canobolas, near Orange. I recall sitting at the base of the formidable Federal Falls thinking about Mum. I had just taken that call from Dr Kate the previous evening, when she had suggested that I might have to return quickly. A small rainbow appeared at the base of the falls and glistened like an illustration out of a children's picture book. It fuelled my spirits and I decided to press on to the Warrumbungles hoping that, as had happened in the past, Mum's decline was a storm in a teacup. I was in denial. While leaving the mural-covered town of Mendooran, I noticed another message from Dr Kate, more strongly suggesting that I should immediately turn back, as my mother may not see the day out. I travelled west towards the Newell Highway when, of course, I discovered I had a flat. I will certainly never forget Dick and Sally Perram helping me out of that pickle, as it was not only the tyre that was deflated. After Sally made the best chicken sandwich I have ever had, and Dick helped me with the seemingly impossible task of finding a replacement tyre in Coonabarabran, I was back on the southbound road.

I doubt I will ever forget the next seven or so hours spent rushing back down the Newell Highway to be by Jeane's side, wondering if a kangaroo or sundry other species of wildlife might be waiting to spring out from behind nearly every single bloody tree from Gilgandra to Yass. While Dylan Mordike kept checking in on me hourly on the hands-free, Richard Browning was dependably there by Jeane's side, gently whispering in her ear that I was coming home and to hang in there just that little bit longer. The silence in the car was oppressive. I remembered deciding that it really wasn't the time to turn on Garrett and the boys. I found myself steadied by the tunes and words of *The Joshua Tree*, *Retriever* and *Ghost on the Canvas* in equal doses while desperately hoping that this would be one of those 'sometimes' when Mum, veritably taken to the wall, would not give in.

When my father lost his fight with lung cancer on my first day at Radford College in 1989, I recall taking a road trip to Sydney with friends. We had *The Joshua Tree* on constant rotation and I recall on the return leg, near Lake George, the thunderclouds open in my heart as the soaring melody and stormy imagery of the majestic 'One Tree Hill' seemed to rise up and over the water:

> I'll see you again
> When the stars fall from the sky
> And the moon has turned red

> Over One Tree Hill
> We run like a river
> Runs to the sea
>
> We run like a river to the sea
> And when it's raining
> Raining hard
> That's when the rain will
> Break the heart[15]

Now twenty-five years later in August 2014, with my mother dying, it was comforting to return to a collection of songs I had often played when suffering any kind of profound loss and sense of purposelessness: *The Joshua Tree* lent itself to this mood, from its bleak, black and white cover to those songs which yearn for hope amidst disorientation in nameless streets, against the spiritual vacuum of modern life, and across endless depths of those holes found in long-abandoned mining towns.

When I arrived at her retirement home, the deputy principal, Allan Shaw, greeted me in the car park and we went in to join Richard. Although breathing with considerable difficulty, Mum was still thankfully with us. I was so proud of her, of the fact that she loved life so fully and completely and so desperately that she was clinging on to it with all her remaining might. In her final hours, a savage, knock 'em down storm continued to rage outside as the day begged the night for mercy. And it was not until I left her bedside, as the stars fell from the sky with the arrival of dawn, that little Jeane finally chose, once again, to leave her hometown to be with her beloved Jan in that undiscover'd country.

> Oh great ocean
> Oh great sea
> Run to the ocean
> Run to the sea

Almost immediately I felt the urge to run. As more and more of our beautiful friends arrived to farewell her, including my most long-standing one, Justin De Marco, I became irrationally scared that I would say thoughtless things in my sadness, or not properly thank those who had done so much for us over time, or not do whatever the proper thing is when one's mother passes. Even at this point, a need to respond perfectly to the situation began to overwhelm me to the point of being destructive to my own mental and physical health.

Mum's service was near perfect and punctuated with so many people who have lined this narrative and many unwritten others. So many who, for both Jeane and me, were the perfect image of those cherished friends Ulysses S. Grant found in adversity: 'I can better trust those who helped to relieve the gloom of my dark hours than those who are so ready to enjoy with me the sunshine of my prosperity.'[16] Richard was the celebrant; Phillip Heath read from Luke; Vikki spoke bravely and beautifully about her best friend; Ryan reminisced about his adopted 'grandmother'; Mark spoke about Jeane's Sideline Café[17] and of his football team, many of whom also acted as pallbearers; Dylan produced the service booklet and seamless slide shows of celebration; my schoolyard ally Justin was there, as always, a silently hovering presence, ready to catch me when I might fall; Brownie was sitting just to the left and slightly behind me, where he always positions himself during gigs; Ned and Rowan, two brave teamSUPPORTers, tentatively slipped me a home-made card with the Warrumbungle skyline on it; loyal players from a myriad of my soccer teams lined up, one more time, to carry Jeane out, past a display at the back of the Radford Chapel encouraging folk to support Crossing the Divide, set up by my dedicated Bundarran G-trippers, led by my godson, Dougal Mordike.

Travelling home to the wake, I decided to fill the silence with music and turn on the car stereo. Not without some gentle irony in itself, *Ghost on the Canvas* had been sitting inside it, and after some gentle finger-picking of strings, Glen Campbell sang,

> I've lived and I've loved, oh
> Such times at such a cost
> One thing I know
> The world is good to me
> A better place awaits you, you see[18]

Wakes are always a blur to me and mum's was no exception. But I do recall Richard approaching me before he left, and in that knowing chaplainesque way he looked me in the eye and asked if I was heading north any time soon. I found myself saying to him that I hoped that Mum was in 'a better place', catching up with Jan, and was being wisely directed to God's pantry – if the afterlife knew what was good for it. I told that dear, perspiring priest that I did not want to waste too much time holding off attempts to get my heart and body to 'a better place' myself.

Immodestly, I hoped that I had given some compassion, energy and inspiration to my relatively new friends up in Gamilaraay country, even in a small way, in the six visits to date. Knowing it was perhaps very selfish, I was hoping to get any one of those three qualities cycling back to me in return. God knows I needed it. There was really nowhere else for me to be now except twelve hours north and up the Newell, there amidst the tiny tin town that is simply just what it is. Strangely, I now unequivocally needed to be back with a people and region I had chosen to enter a service relationship with. Wounded by fear and injured by doubts, I needed somewhere to lose myself. As Bono sings,

> I'm hanging on. You're all that's left to hold on to.[19]

With its green valleys, deep waterholes, cantankerous rocks, give-a-shit cows and cheeky, scallywag kids playing chicken with trucks – Tingha was to be the perfect spot to become a ghost on a canvas for a spell. And for me to discover the incredible two-way exchange that can exist when one returns to an authentic service relationship.

Tingha was to be the perfect spot to become a ghost on a canvas for a spell.

'I planted a tree down where the cricket nets are. Is it still there, do you know?'

After some singing and percussive instruction and improvisation, we played 'Beds Are Burning'...

...as a teaser for the evening's concert for the entire school community.

You could be certain that nobody behind me on stage that evening,

or hopefully in front of it, felt anything less powerful or poignant

than the joy one feels when being reunited with a best mate from childhood.

The Minor League fundraiser was indeed a tiger burning bright.

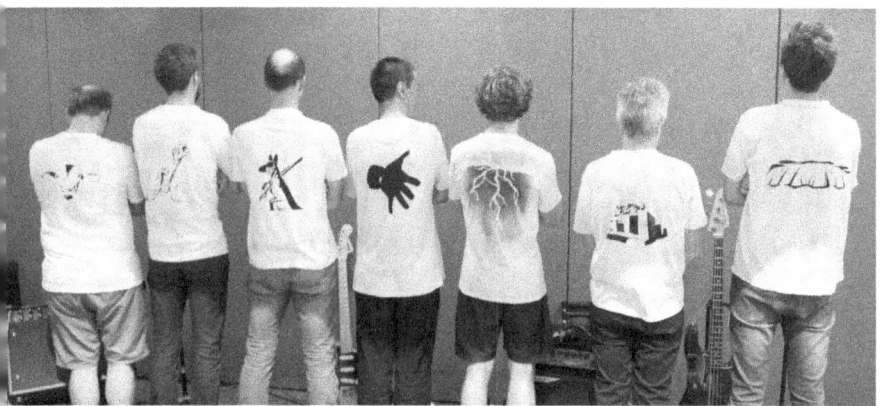

As eight blokes harmoniously played out of a woolshed in the afternoon sun to a motley collection of folk

who understood the importance of connections, of family, of working the land, of striving to get beyond the pain of the past,

this gig was a mini, but mighty, musical version of reconciliation.

'...you're born into a family, your family of origin, and you're stuck with it.

Once I recognised that, it freed me up to have a different kind of family: a family of choice.

The people I surround myself with, spend holidays with, look to for support

and comfort and validation – that's my family of choice.' – Bob Mould

The all-Oils setlist was a bare, bald, bold, no-holds-barred, no-BS, ballistic, stand-and-deliver statement of truth.

Here, where I have brought everyone from footy players to service learners to lost souls to immediate family – all to feel the healing power of this incredible spot under the Milky Way.

Track #7 You Don't Give In

'I'm sorry about your mum,' he said, grabbing both my hands in his and looking me straight in the eye.

Never had a student done this before, quite that directly. I was caught off guard, used to most Indigenous kids hanging their arms and eyes downward, almost parallel, when addressing a stranger. They often seemed to be burdened with an almost adult heaviness and shame. I had often marvelled at how Tingha Public School embodied their motto, 'Totally Proud and Strong' into the physicality as well as spirituality of its students. The staff always seemed to be actively encouraging the kids to stop and look people respectfully in the eye, and take care in listening to them. And to then, quite literally, shake or even take them by the hand. It had certainly rubbed off on Malcolm.

Mal had been sad the day before. For whatever reason, he had pulled himself away from the main group and was sitting with a small squadron of his mates, with his head down, in the middle of a smoking-hot playground. I knew his family life wasn't straightforward and wondered if something had happened there to upset him. I thought of going over to check on him, but figured friends might be a better source of comfort than awkward adult advances and clumsy use of cliché.

I recalled a conversation I had with Phillip Toyne where he advised me, when working with Indigenous communities, to help them with the three Rs, deeply listen to what they had do say, and then talk to the mothers and grandmothers – the veritable pillars of communities. This had all made extreme sense to me, so I decided to help Mal with his long division after lunch, ask him what was up, and then maybe speak with his kin when next walking down Ruby Street, Tingha's straight and central spine.

It was a day when I was actually feeling far from heavy-hearted. In fact, I was in extrovert mode, highly energised from too much toffee-flavoured ice cream the night before at Green Valley Farm. I was leading a game of Bullrush with a playground full of TPS kids but, being in the mood to entertain, was hardly taking the game as seriously as some of the children. Instead of identifying a victim or calling out Bullrush (which means all participants had to negotiate getting past those who were 'it', without being tagged, to the safety of a set point beyond), I improvised on the rules by yelling out, 'Anyone not called Linda or Frank! Anyone who was not born on earth or anyone with tentacles.' (The TPS kids are great big fibbers and would all run anyway when any of these were called out.) They found this quite silly. I also pretended that I had forgotten the aggressive-sounding word Bullrush and would shout 'Bullfrog!' or 'Gold rush!' before eventually settling on the somewhat meek 'Goldfish'! I hope I left a moronic legacy and that my little TPS Bullrushers are still calling out for glistening *cyprinidae* and then giggling profusely when it is 'game on'.

It was the following, stinking-hot day, when the kids thankfully were not in the mood for playing Bullrush/Goldfish, that a snake had been sighted near the playing areas. (Some boys got into big trouble for chasing it.) The buzzer had sounded and the TPS kids were hardly rushing back to class. I was momentarily alone and wondering which year group I was going to disrupt next, when I was grabbed by Malcolm.

'I'm sorry about your ma.'

'You heard, did you?'

'I was in the principal's office. Saw your card sitting there on the desk. I read it.'

It was a 'thank you' card I had made for staff and students, that commendable habit I had picked up from Mum as a child. In it I had expressed my gratitude to TPS for letting me volunteer at the school while I was working through my grief. Mal had asked the principal why I was unhappy and she told him straight out the reason why. Which was good. I love the lack of BS in this place.

I ruffled his hair to break the mood. (It was all over the shop so I couldn't really do any stylistic damage in rearranging it.) I remember that Julian Barnes once wrote how grief can sort and challenge those caught in the orb of the grief-stricken: 'The young do better than the middle-aged…'[1] In Malcolm, the description had certainly hit the mark. I thought about asking the boy about his own sadness the previous lunchtime, but as with a lot of kids, when a conversation with an adult helicopters anywhere above the small village of Seriousville, they look for ways to parachute off.

'I hope you don't mind that I did that. Took a look at the card and all.'

'Not at all. In fact, thank you, Malcolm. Thank you so much.'

He gave me a look of puzzlement, probably that I was expressing gratitude for something that would usually have put him in Time Out. Like most adults, I assumed that the uncomfortable silence needed words blurted into it – as opposed to simply leaving it be, to tail off in the crunching sound of feet on gravel.

I hollered out after him, 'I'm not sure you could understand how much that meant to me, mate.'

I had a feeling we'd talk again.

My feelings after Mum's passing were still very raw and grief was as unpredictable and inconsistent as the Canberra Raiders. At least in the city, I had developed a tendency to withdraw into myself and shun any lengthy attention to it. I was mindful of poet Les Murray describing depression as

> apt to make you into a bore. I had to beware of telling people about my condition, and I especially had to beware of talking about it in its own ghastly demeaning style.[2]

Not wishing to ever be perceived as a bore, I somewhat ironically lost myself in books and travel. I would take joy in wallowing in unsettling passages of literature that I was supposedly seeking comfort and refuge in, such as the following from Uncle Dostoevsky. Despite its call to arms against compartmentalising the soul, Fyodor's words failed to light a candle in the nether regions of my deep, dark cave:

> For all men in our age are separated into units, each seeks seclusion in his own hole, each withdraws from the others, hides himself, and hides what he has, and ends by pushing himself away from people and pushing people away from himself… For he has accustomed his soul to not believing in people's help, in people or in mankind, and now only trembles lest his money and his acquired privileges perish. Everywhere now the human mind has begun laughably not to understand that a man's true security lies not in his own solitary effort, but in the general wholeness of humanity.³

Even a seemingly direct warning from a hundred years down the road by Cormac McCarthy, especially for *huerfano* (orphans) like me, remained largely unheeded:

> he must cease his wanderings and make for himself some place in the world because to wander in this way would become for him a passion and by this passion he would become estranged from men and so ultimately from himself.⁴

After all this time preaching about the power of Ubuntu and the need for the individual to act, work, live and dance in community, when the chips were down, I seemed unable to do that myself. Instead, I tried to vindicate my hermit-like existence by purchasing books entitled *I Want To be Alone – Solitary Lives: Salvation Seekers, Celebrity Recluses, Hermit Poets and Survivalists from the Buddha to Great Garbo.*⁵

Being a non-melancholic depressive, I would then chirpily berate myself for being hypocritical, not only about my own personal life approach, but all of my goals as Radford's appointed service learning guru. There is a danger rarely stated in the (non-existent) service textbooks, that the costs associated with the largely unseen 'solitary efforts' needed in making community endeavour work, both effectively and authentically, can be far greater than they seem.

Matt Pye and I have often spoken about the 'under-toll' paid at the pearly gates of service leadership, both by the leader and those deeply cared about immediately surrounding him/her. Coping with the constant questioning of your own and your program's motives, aims and interests; the incessant need to continually justify both; the unrelenting investigation of everything from risk assessment forms to detailed documentation to your daily accounting/reporting; the intense scrutiny given to the wording in your program's official publicity, external publications, media articles and electronic presence; and the disproportionate need to hyper-evaluate nearly every single outcome – all of these weigh heavily on the compassionate heart.

Matt clearly articulated to me once the added frustration associated with 'the imposition of tangible targets and measures with little regard for the intrinsic non-measurables'. (My God, if the CTD boys were anything like me, it may not be until they are forty-seven years of age that the indications of just how positively and deeply they have been influenced, affected and inspired will become evident.) And while all of the above are quite clearly logical, if not essential processes, due to inevitably strained resources, their responsibility generally falls upon *one person* and is often overshadowed with a tendency to accentuate the negative rather than celebrate the positive. As a result, that one person becomes typically defensive under all the associated pressure; how s/he reacts tends to be, in my experience, polar in extremes: either they throw in the towel, or they wipe their face with it and progress – often to the detriment of their physical and mental health.

I had become blind in the haze of grief, fatigue, depression and sundry other deficiencies, especially to the goodwill of friends and family reaching out through it. I began to forget my more virtuous goals and my more admirable qualities. I ignored that imploring voice of one of McCarthy's seer-like characters in *Cities of the Plain* suggesting that

> one must live with men and not simply pass among them. He said that while the huerfano might feel that he no longer belonged among men he must set this feeling aside for he contained within him a largeness of spirit which men could see and that men would wish to know him and that the world would need him even as he needed the world for they were one.[6]

Belligerently, I would skim over similar passages of Dostoevsky that could have served as hopeful balance, had I paid closer attention to the text:

I predict that even in that very moment when you see with horror that despite all your effort, you not only have not come nearer your goal but seem farther from it, at that very moment, I predict this to you – you will suddenly reach your goal.[7]

In an almost desperate need for validation of my own 'largeness of spirit' – apparently visible even to the eyes of strangers – I found myself fleeing towards where I felt both my personal and professional (and possibly also artistic) goals had happily collided – and also where I could perhaps be useful in my uselessness: Gamilaraay country.

Miles and miles on the road drew me closer to the music on the iPhone. I recall almost stopping the car to hear Johnny Marr sing the following:

> Left home a mystery
> Leave school for poetry
> I say goodbye to them and me
> Mission velocity
> It's made me just run faster now
> I'm gonna take it all
> Drive around
> Make up my mind
> With the windows down[8]

Radford kids on the most recent G-trip (when Mum was gravely ill) had asked me to play something on guitar and sing for them. It's not my chosen instrument, but I played U2's 'Running to a Standstill', the title of which perfectly described my fatigued stasis at the time. Yet it was the first single from *The Joshua Tree*, 'With or Without You', that I found resonating more deeply within me as I drove into Tingha a short while later, dodging all those plump cows of grief, after her passing. I had occasionally and inexplicably pulled the song out when playing with UTE, so it was fresh in my head. The title, again, seemed somewhat timely and poignant when slightly reinterpreted as living life with a loved one suffering from dementia. I do not know how many times I had seen the storm set in my mother's eyes as she got all lost in its cloudiness.

I know 'Standstill' is about drug addiction, and 'Without You' about a distressing break-up, but we all appropriate meaning to lyrics of the tunes we adore. As we also do with the memories involving those we love. I began, once more, to seriously wonder if I should be opening up my musical expression beyond these Radford kids and out to those I had entered a service relationship with.

I spent, on and off, three months in and around Tingha with the car windows down. I did not take the unlimited speed sign outside of town too literally and actually did the complete opposite. I would be often caught engaged in one of my favourite pastimes: ambling down Ruby Street *sans* vehicle. It is an impossible stroll to take without being barked at by one of sixty-three dogs, mostly bossy little ones, or being stopped by friendly or curious locals desiring a chat. Perambulating down Ruby is one of the delights all G-trippers working at Tingha Public get to experience. In fact to me, it is one of my favourite things in life. The walker is often joined by a procession of kids from the school, happy just to chat, but also deviously shortening the odds on the possibility of a free milkshake or $2.50 worth of delectable chips and/or wedges – quite possibly the best in the world – from the Red Rose Café. I have often arrived there at the end of the day to see the Radford lads swarmed by adoring fans.

It was on one such afternoon that one of my favourite photographs of the Ruby Street Rovers was taken:[9] as James, Rowan and Matt – with Meison and Ned squeezing their Smeagol-like faces in between the trio in front of them – carry their mischievous burden of three TPS Hobbits on their shoulders for a feed and water. It is a picture of warmth and friendship and connection and silliness; about walking down roads, caring and carrying on despite whatever differences usually keep buddies such as these just under a thousand kilometres apart. This was the first of many taken of the Ruby Street Rovers on this theme, culminating in the photograph captured on the cover of this book. More on this later.

At nights before bed, I decided to desist with the reading of books based on the Walden theme. I discovered a disproportionately large collection of short films made in the region including *Danny's Egg*,

Brother Boys, The History of Tingha and even was a bystander at some of the filming of Bernie and Colleen Graham's locally-produced *Barni... The Dreamer*, which featured the entire TPS school in a charming, smaller-scale reworking of *Bran Nue Day*. (I kept some of the less focused extras occupied between shoots with a footy.) I worked my way through as many town histories as I could get my hands on, including Helen Brown's *Tin at Tingha*, Doreen Dean's *Well Well! Goanna Oil and Other Tingha Tales* – which Julie Terrific 'loaned' me from the TPS library – and the locally bound (well stapled and taped) *Tingha Topics*. Jean Symes, one of the co-authors, was a volunteer guide through the amazing Wing Hing Long, a Chinese-Australian general store that operated between 1881 and 1998 and is now a nifty museum.

I spent more than a couple of hours wandering, photographing and exploring goods from the 90s (there was still an ad for KISS ice blocks in the freezer), accounting books, dioramas, dredging machinery, dental/torture equipment, fading black and white photographs, mummified corpses and newspaper articles on items of interest, such as the local schools or those notable Tingha Tigers, Nathan Blacklock and Preston Campbell;[10] past workers' lodgings, and a rusty collection of musical instruments, to name but a few curios, dating back to the previous century. (I have lied about some of the attractions.)

I tried desperately to find photographs of Brownie in school and football team photographs (I looked for sepia ones) but alas there was nothing on a former TPS principal's son or an article about any savage junior football injury. The vigilant volunteer ladies were sensationally well informed – particularly of pre-war events – and thrilled to have an interested visitor under ninety-three perusing their museum. I certainly enjoyed smashing down buckets full of ye olde tea and scones and having all my bizarre questions answered in precise and intricate detail, and even with a twinkle in their eye if it involved a scandal. I am sure that if I had warned them I was coming, they would have got a perm the night before.

From Wing Hing Long, and after a quick hoi to the kids on the playground near the bridge, I would cross the street and sit in the Red

Rose for a coffee and await my own burgeoning TPS posse to arrive. As mentioned before, TPS kids have a natural, in-built sensor that pulses and glows whenever a generous, wallet-wielding Canberran was in town. Those kids can really eat chips and wedges by the truckful and, quite literally, until the cows come home. (In Tingha, as already indicated, this is with great regularity and volume. Brownie told me whenever he needed the grass to be mowed back in the seventies, he just left the front gate open.)

TPS's irrepressibly life-affirming front office lady, Julie Terrific (whose real name is Trevithick – although this one is more apt), along with her full-of-facts husband John, ran me to Paradise in an effort to show me some of the surrounding sights. (I am quite glad they did not literally make me run there as this small, charming but ghostly collection of farmhouses is 32.9 kilometres outside of Tingha.) The Terrifics similarly live just outside town in Old Mill, named funnily enough, after the old mill which once stood there before it was probably replaced by a younger one.[11] Julie, as already hinted, is like all of the front office ladies species in any school, any galaxy, any universe: a sheer Wonder Woman in everything from first aid to school counselling to suddenly producing baked goods for the teary and misunderstood, to being an expert computer technician ('I just switch it on and off and that appears to fix it'), and she welcomes any newcomer to the school as if they were a long-lost relative or someone bearing a mango cheesecake. John works in an abattoir and hence the Terrifics are not short on a meat-rich meal. My iron levels probably went through the roof after coming over for a pork (that is, sharing a roast pork dinner) at their home.

Bob 'Beaster' Mould wrote in his autobiography,[12]

> you're born into a family, your family of origin, and you're stuck with it. Once I recognized that, it freed me up to have a different kind of family: a family of choice. The people I surround myself with, spend holidays with, look to for support and comfort and validation – that's my family of choice.

His words nicely conveyed the feeling I had whilst staying in my newly adopted hometown and with every passing day I was getting to know the Pyes – whom I affectionately called the "Pyeklets" (Jen, Jack, Camo, Maddie, Will and Bruiser), the Hickman kids (Shannon, Jarred, Brad and Irene), the Vickeries (Kath, Adrian, Brayden, Erica, Monique, Breony, Tory, Shanae, Paige and Dakota), the Stewarts (Beryl, Pat and son, Michael), the Littles (Matt, Connor, Olivia and baby Gavin), a Stewart-Little (Steph!) and family-friend Jodie, the undisputed peg-toss champion, so much better. (Peg-toss is a highly competitive Green Valley Farm sport where one tosses clothes pegs into a bucket from a distance. City folk are rarely deft at this. It is often a GVF whitewash when Radford steps up to challenge.) I gave them all nicknames as otherwise I had a snowflake's hope in hell of remembering all their names.

I was also beginning to deepen my relationship with the Gamilaraay people though my friendship with the Munro family: particularly Paul (still pleasingly chuffed in recollection of the carnage he once created on Brownie's face), sister Ella and didge-wielding brother, Alex. Both Munro boys had been officially welcoming to country the G-trippers, with Alex introducing a smoking ceremony to proceedings with G7. The Radford kids were respectfully moved by it all. Although our friendship had still not developed to the point where I was brave enough to share an echidna or a goanna with Paul at recess – he didn't seem convinced when I told him they were high in iron so I couldn't eat them – as time progressed, I had hoped to share a tune or two with him on guitar or learn the finer art of dot painting in which he was very proficient. (I hope he never found out that I had a pork at Julie's.)

Beryl Stewart had passed on to me a book on post-death experience, which I struggled with in truth, but I was struck by a passage which resonated with me as I strolled down many a bovine-filled Tinghan road: 'how we spend our time on earth, the kind of relationships we build, is vastly, infinitely more important than we can ever know'.[13] As already hinted, it was thrilling for me to sense that import in what had begun as a service relationship between my school and the region and its families – such as those at Green Valley Farm, the Pye Shop and Old Mill – as well as through our ongoing presence at, and encouragement of, programs such as Crossing the Divide. Things were now steering perilously towards what I might even dare call friendship.

Also, what had not escaped me was this most beautiful realisation: that the people I had chosen to and/or accidentally come to serve alongside, were now throwing me a sturdy rope and pulling me out of that old, dark mineshaft that I had tumbled into.

With that realisation, it suddenly felt that everything I had been viewing and reading was now informing me on how to climb out of the hole/cave. I had been viewing *Beasts of the Southern Wild* while reading Lionel Shriver's disturbing novel *We Need to Talk About Kevin*. Moments in each reassured me further, after Malcolm's spontaneous condolences.

There is a scene near the end of *Beasts of the Southern Wild* where the central character, a hyper-imaginative little girl with the unfortunate name of Hushpuppy, looks an equally imaginative and primitive beast that's been chasing her straight in the eye. The monster suddenly does not look quite so fierce any more and literally bows then lays down before her, like a contrite puppy or humble acolyte. It reminds me of Desmond Tutu's words, 'Look the beast in the eye, it has an uncanny habit of returning to hold us hostage.'[14] Her taming of the beast, which to me was an imaginative manifestation of her confrontation with the inevitability of her father's impending passing, shows how death's effects can similarly be tamed when not feared and when confronted, quite literally, head-on.

In *We Need to Talk About Kevin*,[15] the book's less-than-savoury title character bemoans, 'People who actually do anything are a goddamned endangered species.' His mother, the narrator, identifies that a lot of his brooding anger was directed at 'the passive spectating of modern life'. Although the context in the novel is deeply tragic, I found myself drawn to this provocative and challenging phrase. Along with the image of a retreating beast, it was a central motif in some pensive reflection over a trio of hours and coffees when writing at the start of each day.

I also began to admire even more the likes of Matt Pye et al., who continue on their service journey essentially with little thanks or accolade. It made me (less aggressively at last) question my own need to be constantly patted on the back. Uncle Dostoevsky had been there himself in *The Brothers Karamazov*:

> And if the sick man whose sores you are cleansing does not respond immediately with gratitude but, on the contrary, begins tormenting you with his whims, not appreciating and not noticing your philanthropic ministry, if he begins to shout at you, to make rude demands, even to complain to some sort of superiors (as often happens when people are in pain) – what then? Will you go on loving or not? And imagine, the answer already came to me with a shudder: if there's anything that would immediately cool my 'active' love for mankind, that one thing is ingratitude.[16]

Fyodor reminds us all that in striving for gratitude and praise, 'then of course you will get nowhere with your efforts at active love'.

After three months existing, reading, researching, rejuvenating, re-evaluating and rewriting around a small rural school, I came to the conclusion that I would now more readily salute those compassionate, frequently unthanked souls who actually *do something*; who act bravely, maybe spontaneously, looking any beast/adversity squarely (yet lovingly) in the eye, where many others choose to passively spectate. It had become abundantly clear to me that we can sometimes undervalue our capacity for spontaneous goodwill, as well as smother our more altruistic tendencies, in a risk-averse world. (This ironically creates even more passive spectating.)

I am glad that an *idea* of active love – which got me here in the first place – did not remain an intellectual exercise or mere philosophically sound intention. After all, an empathetic twelve-year-old boy decided to act on a respectful, compassionate and big-hearted idea that he had: to approach and reach out to a quietly grieving but otherwise loud and exuberant man he did not know all that well. And express his sadness and concern about that man's loss. It all happened quickly and simply without adornment or sentimentality. The cameras weren't rolling. But the world shook. Surely.

I know that happy-sad, soft-and-loud man learnt something at the school that day. I know that man was glad that this kid didn't passively spectate. I know that man was appreciative, stirred and soothed by the boy's *action*. I know that man intensely hoped that kids like these are not an endangered species and vowed to find ways to nurture more of them.

And I know that man will tell a few others about it, in the hope that maybe they might similarly reach out to someone in need, look someone in the eye – totally proud and strong – and say compassionate things which they *really mean*.

Often, at dusk, I would hear the sound of amplified music coming from the Green Valley Farm kiosk. It was often the same sequence of tunes, played at a similar time of day and there was something far from random in their choice and amplification. It was music that was meant to be heard – by someone? Something? Me?

I once asked Pat about it, during a spontaneous cabin call and he enigmatically replied, 'She plays it loud so Gavin can hear it.' I didn't push for further explanation. The time did not feel right. But assuming that the 'she' was Beryl, I made a mental note to ask her when an appropriate time presented itself. So instead, I returned to my cabin to recommence work on this book.

But then, in starting out on this work, I found myself strangely drawn to thoughts on the nature and power of song. I began to wonder about those that recur and resound across one's lifetime, periodically returning to the ears and hearts of the people that love them. Such tunes are so often bestowed with a great and personal significance, and become a soundtrack of sorts to precious memories of time, place and people; all this, while also providing solace as the memories fling back into the present and, in doing so, perhaps offering those deeper four-part harmonies of wisdom, courage, joy and truth with which to hum the melodies into the future.

My thoughts would often sweetly drift away from the laptop and out towards those songs dutifully played in the late afternoon at Green Valley Farm, and I suddenly could not wait to speak to Beryl, as elusive as she can be in her role of headmistress of the school of back-to-basics that is GVF High. When I announced to her, through Monique, that I wanted to talk to her about stuff beyond the mere history of the place, I expected Beryl to be even more reserved. But the opposite was the truth, as it so often can be. She did not waltz around any subjects, as difficult as they might have been. I will try to take a leaf out of her book.

'My children's death increased my faith,' she began, and proceeded to tell me the stories of the inspirational Irene, who died in 1982, and then the headstrong and gregarious Gavin who recently passed in 2009, just two years before the first Radfordians arrived between the twin lions that adorn, possibly safeguard, all beyond the gates at the GVF entrance. Quoting everyone from Plato to former Monkee, Michael Nesmith, Beryl slowly opened up directly to the middle pages of her own story. They were pages as poignant and potent as any I have read.

Beryl explained to me how particular songs are linked with her own memories of the moments before the passing of both Irene and Gavin: Jon and Vangelis' 'Somehow I'll Find My Way Home', Weissberg and Mandell's 'Duelling Banjos', John Fogerty's 'Sail Away', Charley Pride's 'Missin' You' and Mike Nesmith's 'Rio'. The first and last of these were vital and sorrowful soundtracks to Beryl's life, having been heard on the very days that Irene and Gavin respectively passed.

In 1982, as the GVF dream was slowly taking off with the scaffolding around a future museum, budding buildings and exciting enclosures, it was Irene who was a persistent, youthful voice making darn sure nobody would slack off or let the vision slip away. Beryl speaks about Irene's premonition of things to come and how she would point at all that had been done, and all that was still to be done, and implore her, 'Whatever you do, keep on with it.' And earlier on the day that she died (from an enlarged heart), Beryl tells how the Jon and Vangelis tune had been playing from her bedroom:

> My sun shall rise in the east
> So shall my heart be at peace
> And if you're asking me when

> I'll say it starts at the end
> You know your will to be free
> Is matched with love secretly[17]

There, momentarily lost in an overwhelming grief, she told me of how she held her dying daughter's hand inside her own at the turn-off to Gilgai, en route to the hospital in Inverell.

> Just hold my hand and we're there
> Somehow we're going somewhere

Were I not lost myself in the sadness she described, I would have liked to have told Beryl, there and then, that this was exactly how I had felt too, not so long ago at the bedside of my mother, clasping her hand in mine as she fought for every last breath. And how I told her that I loved her, that I was proud of her, that all was forgiven and I would remain, in all ways, *close by her side*.

But instead, I told Beryl – and Pat and Shannon Hickman who had joined us – something a little easier, yet still concerned with the strange music of 'coincidence'. How I was a big fan of a band called Yes, particularly when I was Irene's age. How their former singer is the 'Jon' who sings the song. How only a few months earlier I had even seen and heard him sing, acoustically and raw, and metres away, this very song.[18] How it had not lost its beauty over time. And how maybe that this was the ultimate test of these things.

Thus, in much the same way, when life dealt her a second devastating blow, Beryl spoke of Mike Nesmith's 'Rio', a tune that so deeply resonated with Gavin, before he took off on a final bike ride to the coast to 'clear the cobwebs from his mind'. It too, reverberated almost prophetically across the years:

> I'm hearing a light from the window
> I'm seeing the sound of the sea
> My feet have come loose from their moorings
> I'm feeling quite wonderfully free[19]

Once more, lyrics about flight and freedom.

'And is that why you play these songs so regularly, Beryl?' I asked. So dutifully. So lovingly...?'

Beryl paused, and at this point began to denounce the unnecessarily exorbitant costs of modern funerals – and didn't I know it – especially as you carry the dead with you, in your heart, like a song that does not leave the rotation of the sound system in your soul, in your memories. There were no cobwebs in this certain and stoic woman's mind when it came to honouring both music and memory, and all those trifling matters of life and death. 'Nothing happens for nothing,' she reminded me. Like the regular rotation of visitors to both Thelma's Blue Mountains Retreat and now this 'Piece of God's Earth Put to Some Wholesome Pleasure' that is GVF, there is no equivocation as Beryl calls back together, each and every member of the family, to her home for a feast and reflection at least once a month: 'so that the children can know the basics'. Of her beliefs. Of her values. Of the importance of family. And how these all can diminish, if not destroy, the doubts that become so debilitating in our fragile lives when death comes a-knocking.

No questions I'm not alone.

Walking back to my cabin – Thelma's Retreat, it is serendipitously called – I noticed three things.

Firstly, upon looking back, my eyes were captured by the Slim Dusty stage in afternoon light and behind it the wool shed in which, Beryl reliably informed me, Irene would so freely and fearlessly roller-skate. I can imagine her doing so, perhaps while singing any one of those wonderful songs from her tasteful music collection.

Then in the distance, I could hear the sound of a Vickery or Hickman child, rapping out a quad whilst herding stray sheep. Thus I pictured Gavin, soaring on his own motorbike, 'using the music for flight', and understanding that there's 'wings to the thought behind fancy'[20] of even the most whimsical notions of the heart. He must have known that these served, like a broom in the brain, as an effective cobweb-remover of doubt.

And then thirdly, I passed a gigantic tree near the kitchen shed, under which over two hundred and fifty G-trippers have now prepared their meals for a day of joy and discovery alongside the people they are to serve and spend unforgettable times with. Standing almost chubbily, there in the centre of things, its many branches stretch out randomly in so many directions, a myriad of pointing arms. Suggesting, as much as a tree can, the multitude of possible adventures which could occur if you wander this way, or that way, or over there perhaps. A magpie takes off from somewhere inside its foliage, flying off gracefully but definite in its business. A peacock caw-caws out for attention. As I sat, for a short while, under the protective shade of this ancient mother, I decided that I should sprinkle some of another old gal's ashes around here too.

Somewhere close to where young people gather. Near where children play and chase and smile. And sometimes fall. It is then, I found myself singing along to the music wafting from the kiosk below…

Somehow I'll find my way home.

The weekend before I returned home for Christmas, I sat myself in the Inverell Library and finally got to viewing the Karla Black SBS *Living Black* interview with Peter Garrett, without the Red Rose kids crawling all over me or sitting on my shoulders asking me if my laptop had any games on it while tapping the keys with their feet.

When Garrett was asked to reflect on his reasons for undertaking the *Blackfella/Whitefella* tour he indicated how he always

> knew it was something that was embedded in our consciousness… To go into the heart of the continent we had to go into our history…and inhabit that space for a while.[21]

I was reminded then and there of Neil Gaiman's exhortation to seek out and 'find the spaces between fences'. This got me thinking not so much about inhabiting a space – I had certainly been doing that these past few months – but about what had actually been learnt in doing so in all this endeavour in Gamilaraay country. I had been certainly feeding (a possibly selfish) hunger to be useful and purposeful and significant through service engagement with the people of the region, and in doing so perhaps augmenting the (predominantly young) lives that I brought along with me. Yet my experiences with Paul Munro strumming his guitar, and Beryl Stewart playing the songs of her soul, taught me that this journey was not only about authentic service and expanding teenagers' world views. Music had always been hovering around, playing an intrinsic, but up until now, ambient part. I marvelled at how, sometimes unexpectedly, those albums and songs described in the first chapter often reappeared, like Pat Stewart, at my cabin door. Providing a new way in not only hearing their content, but reviewing the life that had been lived since they were first heard.

And what of my own desire to emulate *Blackfella/Whitefella,* that inspiring idea embedded in my consciousness over two decades ago by Midnight Oil? Were the G-trips enough to satiate that hunger? I was not sure that they had been.

I had been reading another Gaiman work, *Anansi Boys*, at nights when I stumbled across the following passage:

> Each person who ever was or will be has a song. It isn't a song that everybody else wrote. It has its own melody, it has its own words. Very few people get to sing their own song. Most of us fear that we cannot do it justice without voices or that our words are too foolish or too honest, or too odd. So people live their songs instead.[22]

Yet I could never be content to merely live rather than sing my songs, even within such a beautiful definition. I knew that the time was closing in for me to start appeasing Matthew Sweet by writing my very own songs and combating any fear that might consequently manifest itself. In an interview in the late 1970s, Brian Eno tells how he read

> a science fiction story a long time ago where these people are exploring space and they finally find this habitable planet – and it turns out to be identical to Earth in every detail. And I thought that was the supreme irony: that they'd originally left to find something better and arrived in the end (to somewhere) which was actually the same place.[23]

With tribute shows, I knew I would always be arriving on the same, identical artistic 'planet', no matter how far or how thrillingly I had travelled. And as music and service were evidently so strangely linked, I would eventually have to find a way to fuel the rocket with some high-octane creative juice, and take off on a mission that would encompass both.

Yet before all the wheels coming off in 2013, the Midnight Oil tribute show still had one unfinished gig promised to Crossing the Divide that steadfastly beckoned. The occasional and unlikely sage, Keith Richards, once slurred, 'The first forty years of life give us the text; the next thirty supply the commentary on it.'[24] So, expanding on Keef's metaphor, I decided that there was at least one set list of tributary 'text' left to recite – one more thematic tour to honour, to play out, to learn from – before a possibly thirty-year 'commentary on it' could commence. What was irrefutably fastened in my consciousness was that George Huitker and Junk Sculpture had to return (to use my own buzzword) – like the Radford kids, Father Richard Browning and even my band's bass-playing old boy – to Tingha, to play some music. To answer a calling and inhabit an expansive space we were somehow strangely linked with. And while there, to find a distinct voice with which to truly, finally and beautifully sing. To test its mettle in community with others. If we were ever to sing those Oils tracks with a living, beating heart which carried the true country along its ridgelines, bloodlines and songlines, we would have to play them, for at least once in this life, far from the creature comforts of home.

> This land must change or land must burn.[25]

So, at the start of 2014, I informed the band we were going to tiny Tingha town, to visit Brownie's old stomping ground, to burn some more midnight oil and to play some rollicking tunes.

Then waited to see what they had to say.

The day after the Year 6 graduation, I was having a milkshake and a water tank full of chips with Malcolm at the Red Rose. I had felt honoured to be the official photographer at this auspicious event and tried my best to get 6x8 shots of all the graduates and their families developed and distributed before I was to return home for Christmas.

I wished Mal all the best with his future life, in some high school somewhere else. He responded with a series of massive slurps of the straw, mining the last morsels of chocolate syrup from the bottom of his tin cup. I told him he had it within him to make his mark in the world.

'I'm a little scared about what's to come,' he confided, wiping his mouth.

'Me too, Malcolm,' I responded. 'Me too.'

I felt a little hopeful that day, like Alyosha at the end of *The Brothers Karamazov*, talking to the precocious Kolya and the other schoolchildren and imploring them to keep precious memories, particularly of those who have passed or those of your childhood, as an energy source for the future when you may feel depleted or defeated:

> You must know that there is nothing higher, or stronger, or sounder, of more useful afterwards in life, than some good memory, especially a memory from childhood… You hear a lot said about your education, yet some such beautiful, sacred memory, preserved from childhood, is perhaps the best education. If a man stores up many such memories to take into life, then he is saved for his whole life.[26]

So I ended up telling Malcolm to remember the good times he had had in beautiful Tingha, as at the core of these memories pulses a lifelong power-reserve that one can unleash in the seemingly distant, fearful future.

I then added that sometimes you have just got to call out 'Bullrush!' and race into the next stage of your journey. With friends and family around to quite literally catch you, life becomes considerably less scary.

Track #8 The Dreaming Never Ends

> I know that the sunset empire shudders and shakes
> I know there's a floodgate and a raging river…[1]

And so it happened. Six and a half gigs. Eight days. Twenty-eight years thinking about it. Then suddenly in sharp and shimmering real time, you find yourself ticking off a forty-year-old musical bucket list, one item after another. With each gig up in Gamilaraay country, golden moments would sparkle in rapid succession. And like those iridescent flares of white across the surface of Tingha Pool on a crystal-clear day, it was all over in a twinkle.

We left rainy Canberra with a vanload packed to the brim, sound man Tim Kuschel characteristically not leaving anything to chance. Knowing that the gear in the bus would take up more cubic space than any of our audience might, we set out along our own version of the Gunbarrel Highway – that unbending road between Mendooran and Coonabarabran – travelling cautiously along the slippery byways towards northern New South Wales. Rain had no chance of dampening our spirits. Radford had kindly loaned us the school's minibus, and with the back seats taken out, the 'silver spaceship' (as it had once been labelled by an elder) served as an excellent teleporter of Tim's stacks of sound gear, industrial-sized fridge units, a nuclear reactor and three satellite dishes to make us sound/look like we knew what we were doing. I desperately hoped that some of our intended venues would have enough power points, double adaptors or hamster-powered windmills to light up the extravagant Oil Change circus. We packed Rob in the back and not only because he was a lead guitarist; he has a low tolerance to the cold, so Tim and I erroneously figured that snuggly nestled between fat-arse amps, he might keep his temperature stable. We didn't want him lighting any fires with any of the acoustic instruments.

As far as the loyal entourage went, alongside the band of seven brothers, we knew that en route some of our stalwarts would be joining us. It was almost a given that the president of the Junk Sculpture Fan Club, Mark Dawson, would be there (with a ready collection of spare *Head Injuries* T-shirts for any who needed one) along with partner Jo Galbory, evergreen Sam Tonkin and her buddy Michelle Davison; there was also the entire Browning clan, joining us to bolster the mosh for the Tingha gigs; and Supermum, Kim Stonham, would find the time to put us all into line when she joined us for the final Coonabarabran gig on the return trip.

I did not want our warm-up rehearsals to be overly conventional, and they could not have been less so. We arrived in Coonabarabran with just enough time to get to Whitegum to catch the incredible sunset, and I encouraged the lads to bring what they could for an impromptu concert. (They got used to me wanting to do this, but refused to play 'Khe Sanh' or 'No Second Prize' when we were lunching at Barnsey's Café, Molong. Big bunch of chickens.) Joel had brought with him a portable beat-box called a Cajón, which we decided to use in initial hit-outs such as these, so as to not scare away potential audience with over-amperage. This would include the fearless rock wallaby that lives at the base of Whitegum and who always seems to make an appearance, even if I bring twenty-seven teenagers there with me.

Between trips, it had come to my knowledge that the recently departed David Bowie had filmed portions of his 'Let's Dance' video at Whitegum[2] (as well as inside the iconic Carinda pub, a three-hour drive away). In a 2014 article on BBC's online *News Magazine*, Ed Gibbs details how the video 'made direct references to domestic slavery, the Stolen Generation (the children taken away from Aboriginal families and put into care) and the British nuclear testing of the 1950s'.[3] In a spiritual and political sense we were aligned, and it was good to put on our old red shoes from the eighties and dance the blues, under the serious moonlight, naturally. We had certainly swayed away from crowds into an empty space.

Before we knew it, we were playing out at a spectacular sunset, there at that very spot where I had taken so many students, soccer players and service learners across just short of three decades. Finally, fulfilling a wish to one day sing 'One Country' up there, with the band circled around me, we simply and spontaneously strummed straight into those questions that open the song…

> Who'd like to change the world?
> Who wants to shoot the curl?
> Who gets to work for bread?
> Who wants to get ahead…?[4]

By the second verse, as the surrounds slowly became aglow in lobster-orange, with Joel gently tapping out a rhythmic pulse on the Cajón, under Matt and Rob – who were sitting on boulders gently strumming at their acoustics – we played with a serenity that somehow complemented the silent explosion of gold that was enveloping the valley below. Brownie, baseless (quite literally) and naked (metaphorically), harmonised with me at the refrain – 'So don't call me the tune / I will walk away' – as we were joined by a park ranger at the end of his shift and a curious couple of tourists who saw us lugging in the musical instruments. They didn't walk away and seemed keen for a free concert and spectacular natural light show, in lieu of what I am sure would have otherwise been an early mark from work or sunset smooch, respectively. I felt kingly, standing there on that rock platform from which I had been treated to so many unearthly fireworks, as the horizon's scrim changed from orange to purple to crimson; colour veritably bouncing off, around and between the clouds; and accenting those unpredictable contours of the 'Bungles skyline. I remember singing out from the depths of my soul, as the music echoed out across a regenerating army of eucalypt below: 'Every man must be, what his life can be…'

It was a perfect way to celebrate the beginning of something that we hoped would be similarly transcendent. There certainly existed for me a feeling of redemption after many false starts and transgressions. We followed 'One Country' with 'The Dead Heart' and 'Solid Rock', knowing that we were carrying in our hearts the true country, standing as we were, on sacred ground. Matt Heinrich best captured the moment with an amazing shot on his iPhone, taken in fading light. (The picture was to eventually make *The Coonabarabran Times*.[5] They've evidently not had weird city folk playing at the sunset up there before, so we made the news.)

That night we invited Dick and Sally, along with Sam and Michelle, to our 'family' room, where we played through a selection of Oz rock classics that I had added to the repertoire, just in case playing solely Midnight Oil numbers might be a bit too musically myopic for some audiences. I sprinkled in some of the Angels, Nick Cave, the Church, Cold Chisel, Goanna, Hunters & Collectors and INXS amidst all that good oil. Any fears I had for these less road-tested tunes were immediately abated; the band, champing at the bit, were on song and played these classics like they owned them. I knew Sally would ask for 'Khe Sanh' – as eventually most of northern NSW was to – so we had it ready, despite all my protestations about covering it in the past. It was, this time, not my opinion that mattered. Our poster, after all, had a byline proclaiming that we were 'Drifting north to check things out again'.[6]

Seeing the joy on Sally and Dick's faces, as we left our hearts to the sappers in Khe Sanh, was enough for me. I remember seeing a similar look on both their faces when the Radford boys and I had finished repainting the gates after the fires over a year ago. It was a look that suggested and acknowledged that good people can, do and will come through for each other in the end, in various and unpredictable ways. Even when one is left feeling as if they are going nowhere and they are in a hurry. In the Perrams' eyes, I liked to think that I saw some hope and joy there, two states of being that the band and I wanted to bring to every gig that was to follow.

And I say, see the silence of the ribbons of iron and steel
And I say, hear the punch-drunk huddle as they drive
On a hammer and wheel

The following day saw us trekking north towards Inverell, although the boys knew I would take them on a slight, but significant detour, past the town and further westward to Myall Creek. The group was respectfully silent as I filled them in on the history of Myall and its links to my own story through Midnight Oil and Radford College. It had probably been on G3 when strains of 'The Dead Heart' first entered my head at Myall – 'We will listen, we'll understand…' I read out for the party, once more, those words by Peter Garrett which had become a semi-rationale for the *Blackfella/Whitefella* tour, and which I had wanted to share with all G-trippers:

> To go into the heart of the continent we had to go into our history, because it was so fresh and so recent that the worlds were very real for people, and inhabit that space for a while.[7]

Matt Heinrich, who had been profoundly affected by inhabiting the Myall space, made an immediate connection between it, the Oils, Radford and the band. As he would later share after the tour,

> The words of Peter Garrett quoted earlier about 'going into our history' were reaffirmed in stone at the site's memorial, 'The road to our future travels through the past.' Whilst difficult to describe, this sentiment, and our second day visit to Myall Creek, stimulated my eyes and heart, subsequently heightened and nourished during our tour, particularly whilst playing gigs in Bundarra and Tingha.[8]

I found myself gently whispering the lyrics of 'The Dead Heart' as we wove our way between the information tablets and their terrible story, and completed the song more audibly after we reached the final monument overlooking the plains where 'White man came took everything…' I hoped, as others joined me in singing about walking in the unbroken footsteps of our ancestry, that 40,000 years might make some difference to the state of things; that our collection of songs, set lists and sensibilities might play even a minuscule part in righting the wrongs of places such as Myall. The fact that we were about to play to descendants of the survivors of this place – and others surrounding it – felt like an overwhelming responsibility indeed. I recall looking out at Callum, who was fervently singing along, and thinking that any future responsibility was to inevitably lie with the likes of him and other future Radford visitors. I also hoped that when he played his trumpet on this gig, and at future ones, that it would no longer be as mere flashy embellishment, but a joyous and soulful fanfare for the common man, heralding a more inclusive future prised opened by reconciliation. (A couple of months later, he was to commence his continuing journey to the region by attending G9, and chose to be specifically placed at Tingha Public School where he was about to perform and make connections. After graduating from Radford College at the end of 2015, he immediately returned to TPS to celebrate his finishing with his "buddies" there.)

The Junkies and I had never played a concert through an open window before, but were up for that challenge as we set up in the Out the Back Café in Inverell. Luckily it was a big one. With Matt Pye, the Terrifics and former TPS principal Belinda Eddy[9] in the audience, along with our high-spirited and strictly platonic 'groupies', we set up in a complex configuration to allow us to play to not only the punters outside, but also those enjoying frittatas inside the café. Callum became smitten with a huge art work inside the cafe depicting Louis Armstrong blowing a flock of butterflies out of his trumpet, so I made a mental note to throw some Hunters & Collectors tunes into the set so that he could blow away any lingering butterflies he might have in being the baby on the tour. The fifteen-song gig sizzled alongside owner Abby's cooking and was a chilled affair. The band played reclined in lounge chairs as their lattes provided an effect akin to dry ice in the similarly chilled Inverell early evening air. By the time we got to the final trio of songs – 'Blue Sky Mine', 'Khe Sanh' and 'Read About It' – I was probably the least reclined, bounding onto chairs, swinging around corners and through windows, and unleashing the electric Garrett hand with somewhat reckless abandon, as people looked on delightfully mystified but approvingly over their gourmet tucker.

The previous day, when I inadvertently parked the bus at a Gunnedah servo outside one of those high-flow diesel pumps usually reserved for hugearsed trucks, Rob noticed, snapped and then posted on the band's Facebook site a cheeky picture of the total cost of fuel. It was to leave me feeling extreme pity for the poor and previous truck driver's company – I hoped they had fuel discount vouchers. The final damage was a mere $620.02. I'm not sure if the people at Out the Back Café had read this on Facebook, or had taken to heart the opening lines of our final song ('The rich get richer/ The poor get the picture' from 'Read About It'), but when Julie Terrific took our empty guitar case around to the punters, after I had innocently asked for donations towards petrol costs, the staff and audience were exceptionally generous and well and truly started us on our way.

It hadn't escaped the band's attention that we had not, as yet, pulled out 'Sometimes' to wrap up the evening's entertainment. But I was not ready to unleash it. 'Read About It' was an emphatic storm brewed in a teacup to round off our first gig and I gave it my all – imagine any mix up and the lot would go! I did imagine just that and decided to save my voice and favourite song for the journey ahead.

After all, I needed to leave some fuel in the tank.

> Sometimes you're beaten to the call
> Sometimes you're taken to the wall
> But you don't give in

We didn't have the Warumpi Band around to give us necessary street cred with the locals, but we did have Alex Munro. I still had the Warumpi's lead guitarist, Neil Murray's lyrics ringing in my head and exhorting me to 'Smoke each place for peace', so I was happy when Alex offered, once again, to do just that for the band at the start of the (soulful) business end of the tour. By lunchtime the band, platonic groupies and bubbling Brownings had gathered in front of Tingha Public School – the now traditional greeting spot for Canberrans to be 'welcomed to country' – where we were eventually joined by Alex, his trusty didge and 'smoking' implements. We all walked through the smoke enveloping and protecting us from evil spirits in a symbolically powerful ritual we were fortunate to be part of. There, amidst Alex's own striking artwork which adorns the walkway leading to the school's entrance, a big Yaama sign hangs, similarly welcomingly, near the grey front door. We left TPS all the safer, stronger and spirited for all this warmth.

Alex joined us for the afternoon set-up and sound check at the Tingha Tigers Sport and Rec Club, which president Danny opened for us. I will not quickly forget the moment Alex's didge thunderously droned through Tim's nuclear-powered speakers. The foundations of that modest hall rocked as we played amidst wall-to-wall photographs of generally unsmiling Tingha Tigers of times past, growling at us from benches dating back to the club's inception in 1928. We knew we were onto a great thing. The didge lent itself to tracks like 'The Dead Heart', 'Solid Rock' and even 'Under the Milky Way', to name but a few, but Alex seemed to know when the time was right to fuse it into the mix and envelop the song with that rhythmic, earthy drone that kicks up the dust around your heart and begins to slowly transport you to the Dreamtime.

After the sound check, the band escaped to the Red Rose for pre-gig chicken burgers, but I chose to stay at the club with Rob, who by now had a posse of kids messing with his wah-wah pedal and taking turns to strike power chords on his guitars. Our little mate, Ryan from TPS, who Rob managed to somehow transform from a head-holding-down hobbit to lead-guitar-strutting self-sure superstar, was even promised a solo spot in 'Blue Sky Mine'. In the lead break of that song, he would get his chance to stand totally proud and strong and wah-wah until the cows came home. (As stated, not an uncommon occurrence in Tingha.)

The Minor League Fundraiser was indeed a tiger burning bright. As those larger-than-life personalities from all over the town slowly filtered in, and directly towards the bistro at the far end of the building, I knew that it would not take long for the music to magnetise and draw them closer to the dance floor. We already had a line of TPS kids draped on Tim's foldback wedges, utilising them as nifty black, boxlike, stadium seating. It also helped that in Alex, one of Ruby Street's residents was up there performing with us. Gradually, with much coaxing and taunting from me, I informed those gathered that we had travelled over a thousand clicks to get there, so they could surely work themselves closer to the metaphoric try line (figuring rugby league imagery was the way to go). Indeed, the glory of rock 'n' roll wore away at their defences, possibly heightened to fend off any cuteness that we city folk might be sanctimoniously scattering onto their hallowed home-turf. On top of this, I had deliberately started late, wanting the crowd to build to maximum capacity for what was to be a highly charged first set. Wah-Wah Ryan's grandfather had come over to me, beer in hand, and inquired, 'When yous gonna start? I go to bed at 7.15 but I waited for you lot to get crackin'. I'll buy yous all a beer if yous just start now.' (That was enough to get Brownie, Joel and Matt rushing for their respective instruments.)

We decided to open with 'Solid Rock', and as the band kicked in and Alex's didge took centre stage at the dead heart of the song, we knew we were in for something incredibly special. I threw caution (and myself once more) to the wind and let the music shake every foundation. By the time we got to 'The Dead Heart' and 'King of the Mountain', the place was rocking. My Garrett arms and hands were going berserk, waving frenetically like branches on a withered tree clinging desperately to a hill during a raging thunderstorm. Two-year-old Gavin Little shamed the hesitant dancers when he strutted to the centre of the dance floor and began to mimic my dance moves. (Rob Hirst once memorably said about crowd reactions to the *Blackfella/Whitefella* performances: 'The kids got it first and started dancing like Pete.'[10]) I'm not clucky when confronted by cute, but Garretting-Gavin was pretty damned gorgeous.

And then came 'Blue Sky Mine', with Rob and his ever-expanding fan club ready to exhibit the finer arts of wah-wah pedalling. After the usual and expected hesitation, I slowly taught my own modest posse of backing vocalists the intricacies involved in singing the chorus of either of our 'No'-themed songs: 'No Secrets' and 'No Second Prize'. The band quietened as the kids' confidence grew, and before long the entire club, from grandchildren to grandparents, were (somewhat appropriately) cheering in unison 'OH NO, THERE AIN'T NO SECOND PRIZE!'

as if the Tigers (actually playing away at Goondiwindi) had just won the grand final.

To the left of the stage, there was a lattice upon which a lot of the Indigenous kids were clinging. In the midst of them stood Paulie Munro, arms folded, just taking it all in. He had recently been ill, and may have been making to leave, but the music's pull was strong this evening. I regretted not inviting him to the stage to play with us. So I turned to the crowd and said that forty-five years ago my bass guitarist had been face-planted by a member of the crowd in a game of rugby league on the TPS fields…

> One of those lads, standing near me here on the stage, was the principal's son. Another one of those lads, standing over there near the exit, was the ferocious tackler. Those two little adversaries have not tackled each other in over forty years. But tonight, here at Tingha Tigers Sport and Rec, they're going to have a school reunion of sorts.

Brownie, ever alert to cues, put down his bass, crossed in front of the stage and exacted his revenge on Paul (with a massive bear hug this time). I'm not sure if that symbolic 'tackle' left a dry eye in the house. And I remember feeling so lucky to witness once again, albeit in a different setting, the bringing together of people that distance, time and life have separated. I heard a person in the crowd state, 'What are the odds of that? What a startling coincidence!?' It surely was. How unlikely is it that the guy who has played bass next to me for close to two decades actually went to the very school I visit with Radford's service program? I was reminded of that phrase by DBC Pierre, where he suggested to us that while we may be the author of our own lives, simultaneously these amazing 'accidents write us, linking, honing, dramatising every minute'. The accident of Brownie and Paul's reunion in that rugby club was high drama indeed, and would be considered improbable fiction except that it had occurred, right there in front of many.

By the second half of the fixture, Pat Stewart had slowly migrated closer to the game, with all the stealth of a woolly mammoth, after having spent a lot of the latter set alongside Tim at the sound desk, marvelling at the wonderful atmosphere. He had finally decided to play a part in it all. Tim was filming 'Beds Are Burning' from his iPhone as the crowd were singing along wildly, when I decided I needed to do something special to mark Pat's journey down the Gunbarrel Highway of his heart and out into the front row with all of Rob's wah-wah and my nah-nah kids. No sooner had we blasted the final three emphatic notes of 'Beds are Burning' when I turned to the guitarists and said, 'We're playing Slim Dusty!' (This was probably not as random as some requests that I have made to them in the past, so they did not seem fazed. That, and the fact that they knew they'd only need three chords to get by, probably kept them from getting overly anxious.) To see Pat's face light up when, as an encore, we did an impromptu version of Dusty's iconic 'Duncan', was worth the tour alone. I opened with an improvised lyric about having a beer with 'my mate Pat' (who does not drink alcohol) before dedicating a verse to as many folk in the room I could. All those years making up my own lyrics to existing songs in the bedrooms of childhood had finally paid off.

It was a night of almost too many highlights. Alex's smoking ceremony and playing; Brownie and Paulie's reunion tackle; Pat 'Slow Advance' Stewart's staying on to the end; Wah-Wah Ryan's 'Blue Sky Mine' lead break; his grandpop remaining well and truly past his 7.15 p.m. curfew (I wish I knew his name as he would have copped a verse too); jumping onto the entrance foyer desk, lying down on the bench top and serenading sweetly to Robyn the Receptionist (who should have charged me entry to get back in); being presented with a Tigers plaque by Brad Hickman thanking us for 'playing for the club' – so to speak; or, more poignantly, and as Matt Heinrich was later gently haunted by, seeing those wide-eyed faces of the kids hanging on the lattice near the entrance, observing intently, entering yet not emerging, staying but not playing, mesmerised but distrustful, strangely and safely submerged and distant behind a flimsy barrier, remaining outside of what was occurring, while being paradoxically inside of it. Here was definitely something metaphoric happening, which Matt and the band could sense, because it was so palpable. We quite simply still had work to do here in order to break down the divide. If we had come to bring people together – *all* people together – we had a job to reach out further to draw in those hanging from the metaphoric lattice. It was to come...

And then it was time to unleash 'Sometimes'. I thanked the tiny, tin town for playing such a big part in picking me up when I was down. I hoped that I could do the same for them some time; maybe this song might even be a start tonight... 'So if anyone has had a dog of day, or if the Firsts bottomed out at Goodwindi, let's get past it all with the magic of good ol' redemptive rock 'n' roll.'

You could be certain that nobody behind me on that stage that evening, or hopefully in front of it, felt anything less powerful or poignant than the joy one feels when being reunited with a best mate from childhood.

I know that the cannibals wear smart suits and ties
I know they arm wrestle on the altar

I'm not sure what Slim Dusty would have made of our gig on his custom-built Green Valley stage, especially after our penultimate tip of the Akubra to him at the Sport and Rec (the modern-day 'Town and Country' perhaps?) the previous evening. It was an energetic affair and I had swallowed a jar of Manuka honey to make sure that the voice was as silky and sweet as possible for a string of radio hits and soaring ballads I'd chosen for the sunny afternoon's set on Pat Stewart's splendid wool shed extension.

There was a guy in the modest crowd – which was probably a hundred times smaller than the 3,500 Slim had attracted there on 7 November 1993 – who claimed to have been a roadie for the Oils during their tour to accompany *Place Without a Postcard* and I was a little embarrassed that we didn't have a track to offer from that wonderful album, despite 'I Don't Want To Be the One',[11] 'Basement Flat' and 'If Ned Kelly Were King' coming perilously close. The man was a passionate lover of Oz rock, and was beaming from his deckchair, as we also tipped the Akubra to the recently departed Doc Neeson, and included a couple of Angels' classics (as well as two from the Church to keep it all sanctified.)

But it was the Oils' songs which seemed to radiate and envelop everything from the stage out across all of Green Valley. In honour of the band's surfie culture, I'd often jump from the stage down onto a rickety table – left where a moshpit would have formed if we had had a greater crowd in attendance – and I precariously rocked it back and forth, as if on a forty-footer. Although modest in number, looking out from that lofty height, atop that stage that Slim Dusty once played on, we were certainly among friends: all the Brownings were in full voice and force, Richard behaving with his characteristic lunacy; the wonderful Vickeries, Hickmans, Stewarts, Littles and one Stewart-Little there in droves; Pat, now well and truly near the front, beaming with pride and possibly telling more of his friends that the lead singer of the band was in fact Bing Lee; the Terrific duo, loyal and loud as ever; the entire Pye shop; and of course our adopted fan base family of Mark, Jo, Sam and Michelle. Yes, we were in the right place, at the right time. Those beautiful accidents were once again linking, honing, dramatising. Feeling seriously sentimental, as I recognised so many who had done so much for me over the past year, I reached out once again to this collection of now-familiar and fine families and friends, and said, 'I'd like to dedicate this song to you all – for always making me feel as if I was at home.'

'What? In China?' hollered the politically dubious Pat Stewart, sifting the serious from the sentiment. (No point at all in asserting, once again, my Dutch-Indonesian credentials. For all his cheeky, rapid, potentially risky Chinese chaffing, there is no other person in the district as quick to remind me, particularly when at a low ebb, that I was 'part of the family now'.)

And then we all followed Matt's fingers as they danced across his keyboard playing the stirring introduction to Midnight Oil's 'In the Valley'. When Garrett sings of his mother, I felt it echo in the heartfelt hospitality of so many good people there in front of us:

> She always welcomed the spring
> Always welcomed the stranger
> You don't see too many around like this
> Not many like this…[12]

From there to Alex Munro, reminding us of similarly direct connections to the heart of the country, with his stirring rendition of his original and affecting song, 'Dreamtime'. Its words echoed across Green Valley and out over the mountain and plains beyond it:

> Tribal spirits guiding me
> Over the land so carefully
> Showing me all of the wonders
> And taking me back to the Dreamtime
> Dreamtime stories fill my head
> I remember what they said
> Care for the land your mother
> And don't forget the life that she gives

Listening to Alex sing, it felt as if time had indeed stopped. He really was the Warumpi Band to our Midnight Oil, a man of the local people acting as a conduit to the benign alien visitors who emerged from their silver spaceship. We kept him on stage to sing 'Under the Milky Way' as a duet with me, which we stripped back as we had done recently at the Coonabarabran rehearsal and in Out the Back Café. The bare bones of the song felt raw, honest and exposed as our harmonies lowered the curtains down from Memphis, across the inland seas, to Moree. While the lyrics emphasised a wish to know what exactly it might be that we were looking for, I might have known what we would find. As eight blokes harmoniously played out of a wool shed in the afternoon sun to a motley collection of folk who understood the importance of connections, of family, of working the land, of striving to get beyond the pain of the past, this gig was a mini, but mighty, musical version of reconciliation. I was reminded of a phrase by English psychoanalyst Anthony Storr in which he reflected that music 'is a source of reconciliation, exhilaration, and hope which never fails'.[13] I'm not sure much in this world can have been as sublime as the healing and hope shared at times like these.

I felt like I needed a second jar of Manuka honey after an incendiary 'Beds Are Burning', which we segued into 'Sometimes'. I could not believe that I had almost bypassed the national anthem of my heart, oddly tempted to rip through another Angels number for that Oils roadie in the front row (who had looked like he'd reached a state of nirvana during 'No Secrets'). But Joel, whose skins were still smoking from the previous set, looked me in the eye as I was about to announce 'Am I Ever Gonna See Your Face Again' and said, 'Nah, it's gotta be 'Sometimes', H. You know it.' And it was the correct overrule. I never thanked him for his serendipitous intervention. I turned back to the crowd and dedicated 'Sometimes' to Matt Pye, one man I knew would relate exactly to what I was singing about. Bono once sang about not letting the bastards grind you down,[14] and this song has the same sentiment, different tune. When I got to the bit about (sometimes) being shaken to the core and how (sometimes) your face is going to fall (and not to let it) I looked out at my heroic mate in gratitude and acknowledgement for all those times when both our programs (and rugby league teams: Matt and I both believe supporting the Parramatta Eels and the Canberra Raiders respectively is a massive test of character) felt too heavy for us to carry, yet we persisted and dug deep and hauled each other out of the mud.

I stepped onto Tim's fold-back wedge and passionately spat out the lyrics, as if I was singing at the end of the world. Tim had joined us on the stage and Callum was cajoling him into joining in for the chorus, as Matt strummed the skin off his fingers, Brownie slapped the strings off his bass, and Rob carved the truth out of the notes of his lead riff. Joel, vindicated by his song choice, smashed his kit until it gave off righteous sparks.

For a brief second there, I jumped back onto that rickety table and looked back and up at this glorious band – playing my favourite number from *Diesel and Dust* – and making it their own. I felt an intoxicating, almost sad sense of closure and completeness. From that unusual angle, I also noticed a shape in the outer grounds, near the kiosk. Was that Beryl I saw standing in the shadows of the trees? I hoped so. I hope she experienced some of the joy we all were feeling. (I was told later that she certainly was hoping that the table I was surfing on would hold together for a few more bars.) So I sang from some reawakened compartment of the heart, knowing that going this hard might mean I would regret it in future gigs. But I just had to let go inside a moment so sublime and so perfect.

The table held firm.

Just.

I say don't leave your heart in a hard place.

So there we were in the new Crossing the Divide shed, surrounded by half-built buggies and reconstituted cars, tools hanging from the walls like trophies, and the band firing out a now road-tested set with confidence and guts. Tim had set up a full rig, as I had decided that I didn't want us to scrimp on the amperage, even though the audience would essentially be small: the CTD cohort and some fourth graders from Bundarra Central, who had ventured over with a teacher appreciative of the vintage of the music on offer and who evidently wanted to provide the Hobbits with a musical education.

I warned the band that the CTD boys' reception might be somewhat reserved, as what we were about to do at CTD was far from usual on their timetable or turntable. But I also emphasised that the lads would be onside, despite any outward body language suggesting otherwise. Matt Pye had made sure his staff and students were more than aware of the amount of support and solidarity that Junk Sculpture had given in the past for the program. I was also confident that the CTD participants would get it anyway, as long as we played loud and with 'tude, took no prisoners, and made them understand we felt they were worth coming to play for. As Matt Pye had stated,

> These boys are grounded in a small community which offers very little in the way of recreation and entertainment. The boys are weighed down with fines and for a variety of reasons they don't get their driver's licences at a time when most other youth do. Without public transport, they are stuck, literally.[15]

So, yes, we were quite literally bringing the music and silver spaceship full of gear – to them. And on a school day too.

It was Callum's birthday and what a way to spend it. I often looked at him over to the side of the stage singing/straining – and often found myself crossing over to pat him on the back whenever he raised his trumpet. His solo in 'Holy Grail' was getting better each hit-out, and on his 17th he played it like we were all marching as one on the road to some glittering prize. It had the right effect on the CTD boys too, sitting in the shade of a shed, a few metres away from him, but possibly a thousand miles away in terms of the lives that had brought them to this point of space and time. I recall turning to throw a chorus of 'No Secrets' to Callum and saw the (now) seventeen-year old having the time of his life, no longer living in a tower armed with defences. If anything, happily celebrating his birth with those who could possibly only dream of receiving the presents, attention, care and love that he may well have taken for granted in the past. This would be the best of birthday celebrations any of us blokes could ever muster for him.

Alex arrived at the eleventh hour for the gig, having had to attend to a smoking ceremony at the local TAFE. He was one busy welcomer. As he knew all the boys at CTD, it was wonderful to have him around once more as I handed him the mike to sing 'Dreamtime'. I had tried to get the CTD boys to join us on stage: Neville had his didge with him, Jamahl was never short a stylish dance move, and even Matt Pye had begun refining the art of circular breathing which may have seen him hit the stage for a debut performance. While I felt we had given our all, during the closer, 'Hercules', I skidded across the dirt towards these rough and ragged boys and implored them to sing along with me, 'This is something I will remember.' They didn't. So I stood on a chair and started surfing it (in my now trademark style) and hoped the bravado, the tame/lame anarchy, and my naive enthusiasm for what I was doing, might be enough to break their hardened exteriors. While up there, I thanked them for looking after the Radford kids whenever they visited, and said I would now take a risk and break out into some robot-gone-haywire Garrett moves which I hoped they would like. That certainly did the trick. They had seen nothing quite like it. Sure, they were pissing themselves laughing, but I think it got the job done and those masks starting to drop.

Returning to the shed, I yelled out 'Happy birthday!' to Callum, but he was lost in the moment, with his eyes tightly clenched, passionately hammering out lyrics about the approach of planes and submarines and other massive weapons of destruction, the cost of which would probably keep most of these CTD boys off the streets and out of jails, that is if politicians were brave enough to spend more on the poor, as opposed to armaments. And maybe do something to retrieve sunken South Pacific dreams.

There followed a moment, at the end of the concert, that etched itself as one of my favourite from the tour. The CTD boys, who didn't move an inch during the show, stood up and walked over to the band in single file. Looking each band member in the eye – as explained, something quite rare among young people in this region – the lads filed past and firmly shook the hands of every member of Junk Sculpture and our guests. One of them said to me he didn't realise I could sing. Another told me I couldn't dance. A third said to me he had never heard a live band before and was glad we had been the first. A fourth said to me, 'That was mad.' I heard yet another, as we were bumping out, questioning Matt why the hell would this band be motivated to do something so troublesome just for them? 'Look,' he exclaimed pointing at us loading the silver spaceship, 'it's taking them longer to set up and take down all their stuff than it took them to play!' Heck. I'm not sure we needed any other 'Likes' than these.

Later that night, I remember saying to the JS lads that the CTD boys may not have given away too much, but it was an object lesson in not making assumptions about how an audience is processing a performance. 'It's not often you see them sitting there, without moving and in rapt attention, for as long as they did,' Matt had reassured as we left. 'They were with you for every note. You may not realise just how special that was…'

Maybe not, Matt. But we were certainly starting to.

Sometimes you're beaten to the call sometimes
Sometimes you're taken to the wall

It was Joel's turn to shine and show why he's president of the Kodaly Music Education Institute of Australia. With aplomb, he led a series of music workshops at Tingha Public School, utilising everything from school chairs (in lieu of available percussive instruments) to the human resources of Callum, Matt and me. He emphatically began to instruct TPS on how you could be totally proud and strong through using your own singing voice and/or the sounds that you can bang out on innocent objects. Dividing the school into three groups (easy to do when there's seventy-five kids present) and after some singing and percussive instruction and improvisation, we played 'Beds Are Burning' for each of these three groupings, as a teaser for the evening's concert for the entire school community.

Vice-captain (and high-jumping champ) Kohen came up to me and asked if we were playing it in the evening set. He loved the song and wanted to film every rendition of it that we were to play that Wednesday. I told him tonight would be special, as those TPS kids who were brave enough, would be joining us on percussion (this time with triangles, clapsticks and various jingly items in lieu of plastic chairs). It was also apparent that the more adventurous staff would be fired up by Julie Terrific to relive dance moves from their youth and that maybe this would also be fortuitous to capture on film as well.

While Joel was doing all the work, Brownie, with Rob in tow, wandered through a line of trees in the playground – one of which he planted – reminiscing about past times when cow-like dinosaurs roamed down Ruby Street. He even got to revisit the family house of his youth and possibly reacquaint with neighbours who had not moved on and out.

The walk must have rekindled a nostalgia in Rob as well, who began to open up about his own teenage years in rural Victoria: 'In my first day of school the police came and took away a boy in my class for a violent assault. He never came back. He was Indigenous. The next year I went to a different school and had to travel by train each day to get there. It was a regular occurrence in the evening for the train to have to stop in the middle of nowhere for drunks to be thrown off. More often than not they were Indigenous. I was not sure what to make of the desperation or what it was actually saying to me about this country I had moved to…'

I asked him what he made of it now.

'That desperation and helplessness that I felt from where I grew up… it's not here. Tingha may have its problems, but it has a real community feel which I admit I hadn't expected.'

I told him to expect to see a little of it this evening in a little school hall.

I then moved on to rally the remaining members of the band from the Tingha pub, where Brownie was still reminiscing about prehistoric times, as Callum and Rob went to the playground to relieve some pre-gig excitement with a group of TPS kids. After a quick climb and swing, the group was heading back down Ruby Street for the gig. Walking on the other side of the street, I whipped out my phone and took a shot of them strolling along the path, united and excited, to the impending gig. That is the very moment in time that graces the cover of this book. I remembered thinking, this is our Abbey Road. Albeit a little less leafy.

Entering the school, I was about to show the pic to Rob when he said, 'One little girl asked me to sing her a song. I protested that I was the guitar player, but she insisted and really, who was I to deny her with her wide eyes and huge smile?'

'So, what did you sing her?'

But before he could answer, we were swamped by a wave of Callum's supporters and vice-captain Kohen wanting to make expressly sure that I had included 'Beds Are Burning' on the evening's setlist. I didn't get to hear Rob's answer for a couple of weeks.

Not wishing to be predictable, I had decided to include two new numbers in the setlist, declaring that we'd open with 'Touch' by Noiseworks, the chorus imploring us all to 'Reach out and touch' somebody feeling to me like the best way to open a community gig. Matt Heinrich was on fire with his synth sounds, so I decided to give the Oils time to stew and followed the Noiseworks number with INXS's 'Don't Change' and our tour regular 'Holy Grail' to appease Callum's fan base. (Many Tinghan parents have reprimanded me because their children now want to take up the trumpet. I considered passing on Callum's mobile number.) As always, it was to take a little while into the gig for the audience to come to the party. Playing in the school hall with the back roller-doors opened, I could make out vague figures standing in the shadows – mostly parents – but thankfully their kids and the TPS staff had well and truly joined us by the time we got to Goanna's 'Solid Rock', with Alex didging up a duststorm, followed by his own stirring 'Dreamtime'. And then came the Oils.

Brownie stepped up and the crowd went wild for one of their own TPS alumni. As he blew himself into catatonia during 'Blue Sky Mine', more and more of the community inched forward, in much the same way our relationship with the region had slowly grown. Step by step by little by step. 'Beds Are Burning' did its usual job of calling together the troops for a resounding, anthemic ending – which vice-captain Kohen happily filmed – and this time I knew we couldn't top it. It even put 'Sometimes' on hold.

I wish he had filmed Alex giving Brownie his personally-constructed and painted didge at the end of the gig. Brownie offered to pay for it, but Alex just told him to set it up whenever we played, to remember him and his contribution to the Oil Change tour. It is a wonderful thing, is it not, when you give so much, to every now and again be given something back in return that makes it all seem worthwhile.

> Sometimes you're shaken to the core sometimes
> Sometimes the face is gonna fall
> Don't you let it!

The penultimate gig at the Warrumbungles Mountain Hotel was a corker. I was worried, once again waking without a voice, but the honey and unending support of friends – Sam Tonkin and Kim Stonham were there, having travelled up from Canberra – I knew would be enough to get us all over the line. To this day, I am unbelievably floored by the willingness of our supporters (I hate the word 'fan') to move heaven and earth to be there for us. Tonight had to be a cracker as we finally had a real, live, pre-paying audience – our first on tour. So it was off to the shops for another jar of Manuka.

Around this time, Rob drew my attention to a comment George Harrison had made when writing 'While My Guitar Gently Weeps':

> I was thinking about the Chinese *I Ching, the Book of Changes*. In the West we think of coincidence as being something that just happens... But the Eastern concept is that whatever happens is all meant to be, and that there's no such thing as coincidence – every little item that's going down has a purpose.[16]

So it came that before the gig, I found myself walking along the Castlereagh River, near a spot where an Aboriginal elder had once told me that I was 'one with this country'. He had said that this helped to explain that previously inexplicable pull of mine to return so regularly to walk through these mountains; to periodically bring those of my 'tribe' here; and why, when it became so deeply scorched in early 2013, that I too became a burnt-out, smouldering mess.

'How could you know about my illness? Did someone tell you about it?'

He shook his head.

'You often talk about coincidence, H. No such thing, brother.'

I shook mine.

'You'll be back with more of your tribe soon, H. It's why you've been placed on this earth. You're a conduit. A builder of bridges.'

'A tour guide in a silver spaceship.'

There in the astrological capital of Australia, I suddenly felt like some kind of living, interstellar antenna at this the penultimate gig. Nick Cave was this time crooning in my head:

> Earth and moon and sun and stars
> Planets and comets with tails blazing
> All are there forever falling
> Falling lovely and amazing.[17]

Under Dick and Sally's white marquee, where so many couples have been blissfully married, Junk Sculpture used rock 'n' roll to unite themselves with a congregation of almost total strangers who were going to help us punctuate this mysterious, magical and at times madcap journey of the heart. (Many in attendance were astrologers from Siding Springs Observatory and not all were 'total strangers' either. I had an ex-student in there amongst them. Coincidence again?) Before checking out for the night, after a rousing rendition of 'Beds Are Burning', I thanked the audience for what their town had done for me personally for over a quarter of a century. It went something like this (but wasn't as polished):

> The Warrumbungles and I go back a long way. Some beautiful people have come up and thanked us for what we have done, playing here today and helping with the bushfire remediation earlier in the year. Only a few of you know how deeply I can empathise with your loss, especially as my own heart was scorched when a family member passed away late last year...
>
> This hotel was, in fact, one of the first places where I wanted to be. Here, where I have brought everyone from footy players to service learners to lost souls to immediate family – all to feel the healing power of this incredible spot under the Milky Way. And like the rejuvenation occurring everywhere you look, it's almost as if that regrowth is what is happening inside us all as well.
>
> Inexplicably, when rushing back to my mother's deathbed, it was here of all places, that my car blew a tyre. And it was here – where literally months earlier we had tried to help others pick themselves up from massive adversity – that I was 'picked up' in turn. Rendered inactive with the sinking feeling that I would miss my mother's last moments on the planet, Dick Perram was under my car changing the wheel while Sally made me the best chicken sandwich I've eaten in my life.
>
> It was here, in the Warrumbungle Mountains, that it was confirmed to me that any good you do comes back on you. It can take a lifetime, but it surely does. And that's why we are here. That is why I need to play you this song, to wrap up the evening and an amazing tour that has changed our lives...

Singing 'Sometimes' for the second-last time, images began to flicker through my consciousness: a panoramic view of the Warrumbungles' skyline at sunset; a troupe of boys planting a line of trees out the front of a hotel, removing rocks and repainting a gateway; half of Dick's frame under my car while Sally wandered over with a tray and a cup. And before we knew it, the gig was over and *The Coonabarabran Times* were interviewing us and taking photographs. And some beautiful people who had lost their homes in the bushfires, approached to share their stories with me. I was humbled. I was tearful.

They had listened to us all night. It was time for me to listen to them.

Sometimes you're beaten to the call, sometimes
Sometimes you're taken to the wall
BUT YOU DON'T GIVE IN!

The final gig of the Oil Change tour was to be held at Radford College, at the second Dirrum Dirrum Conference in August 2014, physically but not spiritually distant from the Gamilaraay soil that we had so recently stirred up under the tour bus. Both Matt Pye and Monique Vickery, with Brad Hickman in tow, quite literally followed us back southward to speak, alongside Junk Sculpture and many others, at a conference with the theme 'Be the Change'. They were both to talk passionately and persuasively about Crossing the Divide.

No person or program could have more strikingly embodied the conference's theme than Matt Pye and CTD. His earthy and unromanticised speech, delivered with his characteristic courage, humility and honesty, was for me, and many others, the highlight of the conference. Here was a man who had persisted, against all odds and obstacles, with an unwavering aim to create an alternative educative program that would be the catalyst for positive change needed in the lives of so many lost and desperate young souls around him. That persistence is worthy of knighthood; as Robert Hillman once pointedly stated,

> Working with marginalised kids is going to break your heart after a time, if you have a heart to break. What you want for them and what you can provide – there's a big gulf in between.[18]

That gulf, seemingly gargantuan, was not wide enough to deter Matt Pye. And to have a Bundarra student in Monique Vickery nearby, so deeply supportive and empathetic of the work being done inside her own school and immediate environment, was as inspiring an icing on Matt's cake as could ever be expected.

Junk Sculpture was represented by Matt Heinrich, Rob Marshall and me, and we spoke about the Oil Change tour and how playing music in the Gamilaraay region, with people with whom we had a service relationship, had helped to augment, enrich and celebrate the collaborative work being done there by Radford College. Our hope was that the tour might, like *Blackfella/Whitefella* before it, inspire others to undertake similar ventures and attempt to marry the arts and service in creative and authentic ways. Matt Heinrich reiterated the importance of the band's visit to Myall Creek and how it helped shape our approach for the impending tour, if not beyond it; how it had embedded within us all a deeper understanding of the past and how that past had moulded those to whom we played – across many generations. It was during this talk that I also finally discovered what Rob, somewhat unpredictably, had played that little Tinghan at the playground before the school community gig. In his own words,

> I figured Archie Roach, Midnight Oil, Warumpi Band, Coloured Stone, Kev Carmody or Yothu Yindi? No. I gave her a verse of Joe Cocker's 'Unchain My Heart'. Why? Because the community and kids at Tingha definitely unchained my heart.
>
> You should visit and it might do the same to you.

In many ways, as I wrapped things up on the speech and slide show, I wished Brownie could have been there to share his own moving and unlikely story of homecoming and reunion with the town and people of his early childhood. The knowledge that his youngest son, Pete (less coincidentally named after his TPS-principal grandfather), had signed up for the next G-trip (G9) and was heading to nowhere else but Tingha Public School, must have provided the near-perfect encore to the whole Oil Change experience for my long-standing friend. I also noticed before the gig that he had set Alex Munro's didge in pride of place on a stand next to Joel's formidable drum kit. He reminded us, 'I had promised Alex I'd keep it on stage whenever we played…in his honour.'

The all-Oils set list was a bare, bald, bold, no-holds barred, no-BS, ballistic stand-and-deliver statement of truth. With a brief lull to play (our rockiest rendition yet) of 'In the Valley', made special by Green Valley's own Brad and Monique harmonising in the front row of the mosh, we let fly with a set list consisting of 'The Dead Heart', 'King of the Mountain', 'Best of Both Worlds', 'In the Valley', 'Blue Sky Mine', 'Read About It', 'Beds are Burning' and closing with…well, you know which song.

By the time we got to 'Sometimes', I felt close to collapse. That may sound a tad melodramatic. Perhaps I had overbuilt the significance of this unlikely final rendition of my favourite song of all time, at a gig that was to put paid to just shy of three decades of dreaming. Maybe my body was engaging in a delayed psychosomatic reaction as a result. Or maybe, like a long-distance runner nearing the end of a marathon, I was about to spew up for having pushed myself a little too hard to beat some personal goal, or get within reach of the gazelle-swift Kenyan in front of me. Yet this was such a rare, once-in-a-lifetime opportunity, to be playing in front of so many folk whose songlines irrevocably linked to my own, and were crossing, pulsing and veritably glowing in that hall that evening – brighter with each new song that we started. No. I hadn't come this far to falter before breaking through the ribbon at the finishing line. After all, I had to see out the closing track of a classic album.

Michael Chabon once somewhat scientifically observed when putting music under the microscope that

> more often there is no obvious connection between the song on the radio and the memory that it somehow or other comes to preserve, between the iridescent bubble of the music and the air of the past that it randomly traps.[19]

Here now, as we ripped through our show-stopper, I felt myself wonderfully, magically, deliriously entrapped inside such a bubble, equally nauseated and nurtured, sucking hard at the oxygen of its preserved memory. And as I sang 'Sometimes', there seemed to be a sublime moment of clarity when time was ground to a halt, just before the final cataclysmic chorus, and as I looked out and over the throng. I stepped up on the foldback wedge where I was blinded by beams of coloured light. I swayed, dizzied by the slow-motion surge of the crowd below. Then slipped.

For a moment I could have fallen either way, but like my hero Peter Garrett so many years before, in front of an oil company's high-rise in New York City, I clambered back up again, straightened my back, opened my heart and brought the microphone to my mouth to sing about never giving in, out into that sea of faces, enthusiastic, emblazoned, and one with the energy of those on that stage with me. It was as inspired and as spiritual and as alive and as happening and as aware, and quite possibly as delusional, as I have ever been in this life. It was a moment in time that would never be dampened by any intrusion of scepticism, defeatism, criticism or realism.

Everywhere, songlines were sparking, connecting, plugging in to the real lives of the people sprinkled along this narrative thread. There was Monique Vickery and Brad Hickman, theirs stretching twelve hours north, across the many Green Valley generations, to Irene and Gavin, to Kathy and Adrian, to Beryl and Pat, to Steph. There was Rich Browning, with David Pocock nodding in approval, hurling the idea of Ubuntu into a line-out of his fearless family and all those myriad teams of kids he had challenged to imagine and listen and respect. Out to his Aunt Valerie in the African sands. There was Henry and his team of visitors to Bundarra, shaking their heads as they commenced removal of all the STOP signs, roadblocks and huge, orange witch's hats placed across the middle of pathways that Jamahl, Neville and Lex had hoped to one day travel down. And from Henry out to the Matt Pyes, and so many visionaries like him, who wander and toil in the thankless, dusty corners on the dilapidated back porch of education where nobody seems to desire to take a broom or toolkit. Where the Phillip Heaths and Phillip Toynes, the Frank Fogliatis, Celia Lindsays, Julie Terrifics, Ursula Kims and Jenny Browns dare to dream of quality and equality in education for all.

There, where the Annas and the Ryans have begun to plot, on their own maps and butcher's paper, a way to link their futures with those they wish to serve alongside. There were rows of the many G-kids and teamSUPPORTers, who knew the lyrics of each song carved into the set list from countless reflections and slide shows, mouthing them as if they too had grown-up with them; singing them loudly so that perhaps the words could be heard as far away as the back fences in Armidale, Tingha and Moree, at the Minimbahs and TPSs and Kiahs of this world. Songs dedicated, with humility, to those like Rufus, Kim, Dylan, Motorcycle Mark, Andrew 'Apps' and Kimberley Jane and so many who have recognised and believed in the chord structure of this song, and thought it important enough to be played and paid forward, onward and beyond. There were Declan, Rowan, Meison, Mitchell and Ned and other Ruby Street Rovers, whose bendy songlines traverse beyond teamSUPPORT and G-trips, tracing the bizarre contour of the 'Bungles skyline down into the soil of an old hotel where newly planted and suddenly sprouting trees were beginning to flourish and form, under the wise and watchful eyes of Dick and Sally, and others whose lives had been so suddenly blackened and charred by bushfire.

There were the more ancient lines winding back to my myriad football teams in a journey of jelly snakes and hair gel that lead from Worcester to the Warrumbungles; from the southern to the golden coastlines; and weaving back to the abandoned football fields of Holman Street, Curtin, where my father first sang that sporting song and left it glowing in the gloves of his goalkeeping son. There were those like Vikki, representative of the many – John and Val, Justin, Ryan D, Luisa and Lidia et al. – whose songlines were drawn and intertwined within my mother's quirky orb, fully equipped with Dutch wisdom and a packed-lunch of *speculaas*, *hopjes* and *dropjes*, to be taken along for the joyous ride ahead.

And lastly, there were the sculptors of junk behind me, sporting their 'Still Sorry' shirts, now a little faded and battle-worn, creating raucous music from all that coloured plastic, lacquered wood and shining metal that encircled them; sweating on each and every note, chord, and beat; massaging the song to travel smoothly, like lifeblood, along the arteries of each and every person swaying, shimmering, shining, shouting and singing it sweetly into existence; carrying it like a coloured balloon, out through open doors and into the night sky, disappearing into the gentler dark, somewhere over and beyond the Brindabellas. Callum calling all angels with a shining trumpet; Matt strumming at the strings with his youthful fearlessness, conviction and vitality; Joel beating the skins with a ferocity that could stir even fossilised remains to dance; Rob, his rock acumen on heightened alert, infusing the night with righteous riffs and wah-wah wonder; and my long suffering bass man Brownie, with a grin on his face the length of the Newell, lost in the power of the present as he picked at his fat quartet of strings, always in the knowledge that friendship, like classic rock, must be referred to in terms of decades not days, living rather than talking. There's Tim, collecting it all into his wonderful machines, filtering it like a fine coffee, before plunging it to perfection for the delectation of all. There's Sarah, many miles away in Melbourne, religiously posting the set lists onto a web page weaved from dream for the posterity and the reference of others who, like her, could not but would be there. And last, but never least, there were our loyal Junkettes, Sam and Jo, propping up President Mark in his omni-present *Head Injuries* T-shirt, standing on a chair in the middle of the hall surveying his royal Kingdom of Oil and decreeing that everything's set, everything's fine.

> On behalf of Callum, Brownie, Joel, Matt, Tim, Rob and myself, I would like to thank you for coming to the conference, being here tonight, being the change. Thanks for knowing the words. Thank you for listening and respecting. Now go and imagine. And never, ever, ever, ever leave your heart in a hard place…

And where was mine?

As Rob wrung out the final riff from that stirring song of the soul, it suddenly seemed as if I was being transported back into that CCAE university hall – literally across the road from the school – and back to where the Oils had provided me with a higher education and the promise of an earthier course of study that would transcend anything learnt in those tired tutorial and stifling seminar rooms. Tonight, in a way, was my graduation. Finally. I would have so ideally wished that Dad and Mum (or even savvy and sexy Dorothea Brooke) could have been there in that hall that hot August night as my degree was conferred. Would they have been proud in the knowledge that the potential disaster of a teacher I was so fast becoming, might actually end up being just a little less so? I realised that it can take a lifetime to follow through on your goals and although this drama still had many scenes to be played out, I knew I could now tick (in pencil) the box on a promise I had made in a car park after an Oils concert a lifetime ago. I felt as liberated as those bloody hubcaps.

Michael Chabon also suggested once that

> there was really only one investigation all along. One search, with a sole objective: a home, a world to call my own.[20]

There, amidst that ocean of kids and educators and visionaries and musicians and servers and friends and – dare I say it – family, my search was complete. Jim Moginie's heartfelt and searching lyrics sprang to mind: 'Where is home, where is my home? I'm searching far and wide.'[21] Well, with fingers splayed as if shocked by an electrical charge; with hearts no longer left in a hard, concrete place; tired and out of transmission and commission out on the road; here in fact, for the first time in a long, long, long time, I had tumbled into a place that felt perilously like it. The dusty Gunbarrel Highway of the soul that had led me out and back again, with barely a few cents worth of diesel fumes left from the $620.02 spent, and with just enough juice to get the bus and all its equipment back into the storage shed of existence, had reached the end of a line.

The crowd was cheering. Chanting for more. But I had nothing left to give, except a silent sigh of gratitude to Garrett, Giffo, Hirstie, Jim, Martin and Bones. I remember watching Richard take the cordless microphone from the floor where I had left it and then proceeding to tie a bow on more than just the evening's proceedings. 'They've played until they had nothing left in the tank. LET'S HEAR IT FOR JUNK SCULPTURE…!' There followed more thunderous clapping, some high-pitched whistling, strange hooting sounds. The band and I were incredibly grateful and humbled. We never expect this, or milk it, but by golly, it is nice when it comes.

I found myself joining in the applause. It was an attempt to return it.

To all those who serve others, like these amazing kids. In this happening, haphazardly found community. Our future is secure with them.

To the giant Gamilaraay people and to all who are dispossessed and powerless.

To those who do not flaunt their own good fortune but instead take the hands of those without. And who walk alongside them, with a spring in the step, and perhaps a song. Leaving both totally proud and strong. Each leading the other towards a better place.

Yes, indeed. The time has come.

Now is the time to heal.

Track #9 No Place To Retire

When the dust settled from the Oil Change tour, I found myself lost in the consuming of biographies of seasoned, soulful performers. I came across two quite striking passages. Firstly, Paul Rees quotes from Robert Plant in his biography on the Led Zeppelin banshee:

> You can never have a life plan if you're going to be addicted to music. At this age, when you find you're still getting goosebumps and a lump in the throat when you hear it, how can you tell how it's ever going to go?[1]

Secondly Robert Hillman, reflecting in his biography of Gurrumul, writes that

> In every life there's one legendary journey. It's the journey that makes you feel as if you're heading towards a beacon on a hill; a journey that has a true destination, not just the Point B you've reached after setting out from Point A... Once you set out on this particular road, turning back would be a failure of the imagination.[2]

I knew, on putting these books down, that I would marry the quintessence of both these passages: no longer would I have as structured or unimaginative a roadmap, as I edged towards that shining beacon on the hill of tomorrow. Buoyed, buffeted or gently brought, I would allow that increasingly unplanned itinerary, guided or suggested by the music of songlines – and inspired as much by following coincidence as deliberate design – to be my guide along the next stage of the journey. A sense of scepticism still found me unwilling to label any of this a 'calling', but I would have to admit that the direction suggested from all the sports teams I played in and eventually coached; all the classes taught; all the service ventures explored; all the outdoor activities planned; all the bands joined and gigs played; all the adventures had and people met, outlined from

Not Just Footy through to *Little Life*; all the good stuff stemming from my father and mother's emphatic influences; all seemed, at the end of the inner 'oil change' (and to once more use that phrase of Tutu's) to be *inexorably linked*.

In keeping with my rules of unpacking coincidence, I spent a lot of time after the tour making sure that I did not 'fail the imagination' by not setting off on those roads that were offshoots from goosebumps felt along the 'legendary journey' thus far. While the 2014 Dirrum Dirrum Conference was unravelling, simultaneously opening at the Aboriginal Culture Centre and Keeping Place in Armidale, art works completed by CTD boys, largely concocted from scrap metal, were being exhibited. I visited the exhibition, marvelled at the ingenuity of the work, but could not purchase any of it, as it had all very rapidly sold! Meanwhile, SBS was busy compiling a story on Minimbah's amazing initiative to follow in the steps of their ancestry as they researched, recorded and developed projects based on their students' family trees. I decided, and eventually did, make a trip back to Minimbah later in the year, to speak to Ursula and Jenny, and hopefully to learn more about the project and how it and the Mini-marvels had been progressing. Then in October, I travelled to Sydney Olympic Park, to cheer on TPS's vice-captain Kohen, who had made the state final in his age group for high jump. I suggested he listen to any of his recorded versions of 'Beds Are Burning' to pump himself up pre-jump.

What is telling here, is that all of these successful and inspirational endeavours outlined above have largely evolved free of the expert big-city opinion of reputed tutors, scholars, coaches, educators, specialists, advisors, mentors and philosophers, armchair or otherwise. Larger charitable organisations have had little to do with them. As Kohen lined up amongst some formidable fellow competitors, many with personal trainers who were probably once Olympians, I admired this boy's *natural* athletic talent that had got him and his family to the big smoke in the first place. Without him having to blow any of his own.

This leads one to wonder and question just how many Kohens there are out there in rural Australia, expressing themselves upon the uneven, rocky and dried-up playing fields of the outback; in scarcely resourced weatherboard outback classrooms; and inside messy, under-resourced tin workshops, sweltering in the back of beyond. And how many people actually care enough that these kids get the same chance as someone born thousands of kilometres away and closer to coastlines, skyscrapers and big, impressive, iconic bridges? Surely we all have the responsibility to build a big bridge as well? One that crosses over our own distractedness; occasional apathy; or the delusional belief that our lives are far too busy, thus relegating young leapers like Kohen, the truth-seekers at Minimbah and the arc-welders of CTD, out of mind and out of sight.

As Henry Reynolds reminds us, two different stories need to converge if we are ever to be truly fair dinkum about reconciliation. We may not be able to fix the world, dear reader, but as you've come this far in the book, I implore you to find a story like Crossing the Divide, Minimbah Aboriginal School or Kohen the High-jumping Kid who leaps towards the heavens, and converge it with your own. If you need any inspiration, read some good books, see some inspiring films that are more likely to be screened in independent cinemas, or listen to music that lifts your arse off that seat. Excuse the French.

> It is not sentiment that makes history; it is our actions...

Too right, Kevin. Time to stop clanging gongs. As far as I can see, after forty-seven years on the planet, this is the only way to write a history that all Australian citizens can one day be proud of.

It was while putting the finishing touches to this book that I came across David Pocock's *Openside* at Harbour Town on the Gold Coast. I had been writing and refining at 'Phantom' Oxley's family home in Molendinar, where his immensely tolerant family put up with my seemingly endless stream of hyperbole about the state of education for young Indigenous Australians. (It must have made sense to Pat's son, Ben, who joined me and Declan Pratt for a week at TPS after G10.)

In reading Pocock at the local Zarraffa's, I came across the following passage which put pause to my rants:

> I imagined people trying to avoid me: 'Here comes Dave, wanting to get some money for starving people – here we go again.' I didn't want and still don't want to become that person. I want to be able to invite people into a discussion about how we live, how we think, rather than have everyone write me off as that guy who helps people in Zimbabwe. That's just where I found an opportunity to be useful. I don't want everybody to only support what I've been doing, but rather to get involved with helping others where they feel they can. There are many people in Australia who are doing it very tough and we have many issues to deal with as a nation, so I am not trying to just ask people to help out with our work in Zimbabwe at the expense of people in Australia – I am sure we can do both if we choose to.

Like Pocock, I knew I had to keep my zeal in check and maybe this is a good point in the book to apologise for when I have not. I am often haunted by the Dickens quote that I so often use (to save you going back to chapter 3: 'There were two classes of charitable people: one, the people who did a little and made a great deal of noise; the other, the people who did a great deal and made no noise at all...') as I am aware that in many ways this memoir, like my band, is pretty big on making a ruckus. A justification of one's existence perhaps? I recognised, immediately after reading Pocock's book, a need to now remain still and to stop with all the sound and fury, despite the nagging doubt that any of the noise I have made has been effectively heard by those subjected to it.

Yet the ruckus apparently had not fallen on deaf ears. Two emails arrived at the same time from two men generations apart. One from Phillip Heath, a moving reflection seven years on from Gawura:

> Yet there are also seasons to be still and to listen to the voices of the dispossessed and the disregarded, all the while demonstrating genuine engagement with the depth and legitimacy of the pain of others. There are seasons simply to understand, to respect and to love the lives of others who live in places far removed from our own. There are seasons to stand by the Creek and mourn the heart of darkness that has remained stubbornly hidden to our national consciousness. There are seasons to climb the hills and, together, gaze across

the ancient bushlands and valleys towards the setting sun and, hopefully, experience a moment of cleansing from our shared past. There are seasons to travel into the lives of others, to sit and learn with them, to have them climb on our shoulders and laugh and perhaps for them to say in sentences that need no words, 'It's OK.' Let's be together at last.

I was touched by it and not, if the truth be told, immediately aware that some of the images within were powerful echoes, if not eloquent nods, to the journey we had taken to Myall Creek and Whitegum Lookout, with both the service learners, soccer players and the Junk Sculptors who wanted to walk alongside others. I was touched, a little pathetically, because someone had noticed. Amazingly, before the year was out, Phillip finally found the time and space to meet me on Gamilaraay soil and, after many years, visit the very places and programs his 'green light' had opened to so many others. It must have been the right season.

The second was an emailed link detailing the post-school pursuits of a former student and teamSUPPORTer, Ryan Carters. His songlines have certainly often crossed within the narrative of my previous books. Ryan was in the original teamSUPPORT group playfully described in *Little Life*; has sat at Forster Breakwater, Whitegum Lookout and trekked through the Warrumbungles; and played in many teams I have coached (as outlined in *How to Succeed Without Really Winning*) making me look really good for simply pointing at the field before a game and saying to him, 'Do well.'

Ryan's achievements as a professional sportsman are well documented. In 2013, he opened the batting for the NSW team which went on to win the Sheffield Shield. He hit 861 runs, averaging 53.81, which was described by Andrew Ramsay at Cricket.com.au as 'the best return for a batsman in their first year for NSW since Mark Taylor scored 903 at roughly the same average in 1985–86'.[3] Perhaps less well known is his adventurous, seeker spirit which saw him and two fellow teamSUPPORTers undertake a 1000 kilometre canoe journey, paddling along the Eg and Selenga Rivers from Lake Khovsgol to Russia's Siberian border; and although we keep in irregular touch, I had not been aware of the details of his inspirational work with Batting For Change,[4] which he had recently relaunched. Ryan is immensely modest about the selfless work he does. Enlisting high-profile help from within and outside of the cricketing world, every time a six is hit in the Big Bash, money is raised to improve educational outcomes in impoverished countries:

> People sign up to pledge whatever they can afford – from a dollar or two through to thousands (in the case of philanthropic corporates) – to donate to the initiative's partner organisation the LBW (Learning for a Better World) Trust every time Carters or one of his BBL teammates clears the fence when batting… Carters recalls of the initiative that took shape as he helped pilot the canoe towards Russia's famous Lake Baikal. 'But it's also an opportunity to add another dimension to what hitting a six means.' Last year, opening the batting for the under-achieving Sydney Thunder in the KFC T20 Big Bash League, Carters and his fellow batters landed a tournament total of 23 sixes which enabled them to reach their pre-season target of $30,000.
>
> With this money, the Sydney-based LBW Trust – which delivers educational opportunities for disadvantaged communities throughout the cricket world, and includes among its patrons Greg Chappell, Adam Gilchrist, Rahul Dravid and Kumar Sangakkara as well as ex-Prime Minister Malcolm Fraser and former and current Governors-General Sir William Deane and Sir Peter Cosgrove, was able to build three new classrooms at the Heartland School in Kathmandu, Nepal. This year, having confirmed his signing with the Thunder's cross-town BBL rivals Sydney Sixers, Carters has outlined an even more ambitious (and fitting) target of $66,666 to help support the further education of 500 young women in India… 'Specifically, the women are at the SPRJ Kanyashala Trust which is a women's college in Mumbai, and they'll be attaining degrees in arts, science or commerce at an undergraduate level,' Carters said.

I am very proud of where Ryan has taken his own service journey since leaving Radford College in 2008. I long to sit and have a vegetarian pad thai with him and talk about ways we might also look at somehow improving opportunities inside those classrooms that our Indigenous women attend in our own country, among other things.

In quoting the extract above, I understand I might be accused of self-congratulatory validation, and basking in the stadium-sized light of a former student's glory; yet this is presented as a tonic for all those readers who might work with the young and harbour similar self-doubts and fears that the kids they work with may not, in the present tense, feel or clearly understand the lessons offered, in service amongst other things, with the hope for a better future. As I have outlined more than once, these hopeful seeds, once sown, may take an often excruciatingly long period of time to germinate in the future. If anything, Ryan's finding time amidst an unrelenting schedule of study, sport, travel, friends and family commitments, to look beyond himself into ways of helping others towards feeling empowered, independent and valued, is nothing short of exemplary. It certainly reminds one of the importance of providing ample and sound service learning practice and opportunity squarely at the feet of teenagers in their formative years. Maybe in future times, kids like Kohen, or young adults like Lex, will get others to leap over high bars for similarly sound outcomes. Who knows?

I texted congratulations to Ryan and updated him that my book was in the literary equivalent of the 'nervous nineties', to use a cricket analogy. I told him I felt I was on 94, not out, and considering hitting a six myself. I was just awaiting the right delivery. He replied, 'Good luck in the nineties, H. One ball at a time. Choose wisely.'

After that final gig of the Oil Change tour, I remember sitting with my old mate Brownie and saying, 'I'm not sure it ever can get too much better than that.'

He smiled and had that look on his face that suggested I probably had the next adventure well and truly planned.

'I've written a few songs about up north. Think the time has come to record that album.'

He nodded, seemingly resigned and ready for a new round of H's hair-brained schemes. Ready for a new season to perhaps play the music that is no one else's but my own. Music which arose from out of a slowly healing heart. Music that had been sculpted from junk and shaped by the bumps and dust of miles and miles of dirt road; by landscapes traversed on the whiff of a smelly rag, stained by diesel. Music with earthy melodies and leathery words, telling wondrous stories about serving and learning and acting and sharing, which might – if good enough – somehow heal, in turn, the hearts of the so many wounded that you know only too well, and probably already walk alongside. Or very shortly will.

I could never overstate the effect music has had on my life. While writing the final chapters of this book, I found myself catching up with old friends: those albums outlined in the first chapter I had spent so much of my youth with. I then pored through Mum's dusty photo albums to find pictures revealing either my record collections or those teenage walls overlaid with faces of rock artists I was to eventually cover, in both senses of that word. I began to see with startling clarity where and how their songlines echoed inside and around this narrative, informing it like the anarchic but essentially benevolent mentors they were.

And as I was completing the final edits, I recall coming across a review by Robert Christgau of the much-maligned Bob Dylan album *Self Portrait*, in which Christgau discusses that prolific recording artist's adoption of music he had covered, or in a few cases composed, on it:

> that 'self' is most accurately defined (and depicted) in terms of the artifacts – in this case, pop tunes and folk songs claimed as personal property and semi-spontaneous renderings of past creations frozen for posterity on a piece of tape and (perhaps) even a couple of songs one has written oneself – to which one responds... In other words, you construct your identity through the music you've been exposed to.[5]

I put the book down next to my coffee cup and stood up, visibly shaking with excitement after reading that passage: it could just as easily have been written about me after all. Eureka! I acutely realised how my own 'self' – this fallible and fumbling pseudo maharishi of service – had been constructed: by a somewhat potent collection of musical artefacts. I had to find the original source. For as American author Paul Auster discovered through a quotation he attributed to Proust:[6]

> The past is hidden beyond the reach of intellect, in some material object (in the sensation which that material object will give us) which we do not

suspect. And as for that object, it depends on chance whether we come upon it or not before we ourselves must die.

I knew exactly what that object was. So back under the house I feverishly crawled. After all, I needed to 'come upon' that object before I croaked. (That said, I was momentarily distracted in finding the 'Black Rain Falls' Oils video cassette and wondered if I could make Rob Marshall or Mark Dawson jealous that I owned something so ancient and valuable. I did not realise that it was about to be re-released on DVD to coincide with 'The Making of Midnight Oil' exhibition at Manly Art Gallery and Museum between June and September, 2014.) This time I was absolutely driven. I was dustily directed and deliriously dragged even further back in time. And there, in some old drawer of my teenage years, I finally found a collection of old 45s that Mum had filed for safekeeping, assuming that one day in the future I would be doing exactly what I was doing now. There, inside a plastic wallet designed to preserve and display singles, was a buried treasure – the first record I ever owned: 'A Windmill in Old Amsterdam'. Yes. I was finally to discover, without using Google, the performer of that tune so indelibly caught and preserved in the iridescent bubble of childhood memory.

As I took that prized artefact out into daylight, I thought of that artist, now long dead, who would never know how much he had affected, influenced and brought sunshine to a little life with his music. A relatively unknown singer (outside of the UK) who had left three minutes of gold in this soul with a tune which still, when the moment is right, gives off massive sparks. Unchains a hardened heart. I made a mental note to write some fan-mail to Ronnie Hilton's estate. And then took the little black circle upstairs to spin and to finally complete my research.

Eventually, I will play it for people, perhaps alongside a few tunes of my own, the next time I drift north. And I will talk, more knowingly, about how music can shape you in myriad good ways. The Tingha kids would love it…

The lack of pessimism in the young when approaching those seemingly insurmountable difficulties associated with true reconciliation, real acceptance of the past, and the honest provision of authentic, stimulating and ongoing opportunities for those without, must surely and eventually soften the older, coarser, hardened exteriors of those who might believe otherwise. As that inspirational anthropologist W.E.H. Stanner once proclaimed,

> In the past we were wrong – in some respects grotesquely wrong – about the Aborigines. We thought that they could not possibly survive; that they had no adaptive capacity; that there was nothing in their society of other than antiquarian interest; that there was nothing of aesthetic value in their culture. We could be as wrong about the future.[7]

It is the young, untainted by all that bad history and myopic thinking, whom I encourage older readers to take by the hand and better equip with chisels to attack and hopefully widen the cracks at the base of the apparently insurmountable walls built around Indigenous Australia. Offering them the tools of truth and larger perspective must be the start.

Robert Hillman writes about the beautiful Aboriginal concept of Bapa, an elevated and esteemed love that can place a male

> …amongst those men of his clan who have done the fullest justice to fatherhood in their attention and care. Bapa is the hand that rests on the child's shoulder, the voice that tells the child: 'Like this, do you see?'[8]

What a rich endpoint it must be for any of us older folk to reach, irrespective of gender, when we stand on mountain tops and show our younger generation the better, wiser, wider stuff of existence when it rolls out before us, as the sun sinks gloriously behind other mountains out there on the horizon.

As our finger points and our voice gently sings.

Like this. Do you see?

In the middle of my life... I drew the path of it upon a map and I studied it a long time. I tried to see the pattern that it made upon the earth because I thought that if I could see that pattern and identify the form of it then I would know what my path must be. I would see into the future of my life.

How did it work out.

Different from what I expected.

Cormac McCarthy, *Cities of the Plain*, 1998

Track #10 Court Fines On the Shopfront Walls

Huge portions of this book were written in the following songline hotspots:
Aaronlee Retreat, Mount Tamborine, Queensland.
Clarence Head Caravan Park, Iluka, New South Wales.
Gloucester Caravan Park, Gloucester, New South Wales.
Green Valley Farm, Tingha, New South Wales.
Huitker Studios, Curtin, ACT.
Oxley Residence, Molendinar, Queensland.
Lakeview Cottage, Green Point, New South Wales.
Southport Public Library, Queensland.
Warrumbungle Mountain Hotel, Coonabarabran, New South Wales.

Photographs are by Mel Browning, Mark Dawson, Matt and Mark Heinrich, George Huitker, Andrew Letton, Dylan Mordike, Matt Pye, Steph Stewart-Little and Julie Trevithick. Special thanks to Kate Black, photographer for *Country Living*, for giving permission to use her incredible group photograph of the 2014 Crossing the Divide cohort.

The author would like to thank the following people for their support throughout the writing of the book:
Celia Lindsay for the largely unseen grace, skill, time and care associated with editing
Vikki and Ian Bradfield
Lindy Braithwaite
Chris, Gabrielle, Anthony and Peter Brown
Jenny Brown
Richard, Mel, Sam, Zach and Matt Browning
Ryan Carters

Gayelene Clews
Joel Copeland
Ryan and Kerri Dalrymple
Mark Dawson and Jo Galbory
Justin DeMarco
Richard and Pam Faulks
Frank Fogliati, Sarah Desmond and all the amazing BMS staff
John and Tracy Fraser
Mark Gannon
Chris, Janet, Brock and Jamie Ginman
Fiona Godfrey
Lajos and Susie Hamers
Phillip Heath
Matt Heinrich
Tracey, Russell and Ryan Herbert
Shannon, Jarred, Brad and Irene Hickman
Alison & Danny Jamieson
Ursula Kim
Sarah Kimball
Tim Kuschel
Shauna Lennon
Andrew 'Apps' Letton
John, Val, Josh, Jane and Sam Leyshon
Rob, Alison, Zoe and Angus Marshall
Stephen Matthews
Kate McCallum
Henry Miller
Linda Milligan
Dylan, Sally, Dougal and Jemima Mordike
Alex, Paul and Ella Munro
Ken and Cathy Oldfield
Patrick, Mindy, Ben, Ellie and Nathaniel Oxley
Sally and Dick Perram

Matt, Jen, Jack, Camo, Maddie, Will and Bruiser Pye
Callum Sambridge
Pat and Beryl Stewart
Kim Stonham
Steph, Matt and Gavin Stewart-Little
Sam Tonkin
Staff at all the schools on the G-itinerary
Staff at the Curtin Gourmet Delights, Out-the-Back Café (Inverell) & Red Rose Café (Tingha)
Phillip Toyne
Julie & John Trevithick
Kathy, Adrian, Braydon, Erica, Monique, Breony, Tori, Shanae, Paige and Dakota Vickery, and Jodie
Brad, Claire, Heath and Savannah Walker

Track #11 Build Materials At the Side

Track #1
1. U2, 'God Part II', *Rattle & Hum*, Island Records, 1988.
2. Matthew Sweet, 'Write Your Own Song', *100% Fun*, Zoo Entertainment, 1995.
3. Morrissey, *Autobiography*, Penguin, 2013.
4. T. Creswell, C. Mathieson, J. O'Donnell, *100 Best Australian Albums*, Hardie Grant Books, 2010.
5. Midnight Oil, 'The Dead Heart', *Diesel & Dust*, Sprint/Columbia, 1987.
6. In Australia, it is a little known fact that 'The Dead Heart' (number 4) peaked higher on the charts than 'Beds are Burning' (number 6).
7. The Pintubi Nine, known as the lost tribe, made first contact with relatives near Kiwirrkurra as late as 1984 and are believed to be the last Aborigines to have been living as hunter-gatherers. They were forcibly moved from the Gibson Desert before eventually returning in recent decades to the Kintore Ranges in Northern Territory and Kiwirrkura and Jupiter Well in Western Australia.
8. Midnight Oil, 'Put Down That Weapon', *Diesel & Dust*, Sprint/Columbia, 1987.
9. US pressings closed the album with the additional track 'Gunbarrel Highway' which is now considered the album closer. This was a less than emphatic way to end a classic album in my frequently discredited opinion. The erudite Rob Marshall claims that the live version of 'Sometimes' on *Scream in Blue* (Columbia Records, 1992) is the definitive version.
10. Midnight Oil, 'Sometimes', *Diesel & Dust*, Sprint/Columbia, 1987.

Track #2
1. J. Banville, *Ancient Light*, Penguin Viking, 2012.
2. N. Gaiman, *The Ocean at the End of the Lane*, William Morrow & Company, 2013.
3. DBC Pierre, *Petit Mal*, Faber & Faber, 2013.
4. D. Pearson & C. Webb-Parsons, *Grampians Bouldering: A Guide to Australia's Premier Bouldering Destination*, Sea to Summit, 2010.
5. D. Tartt, *The Goldfinch*. Little Brown & Company, 2013.
6. G. Huitker, *Little Life*, Ginninderra Press, 2010.
7. The previous PM, John Howard (1996–2007) did not wish to reside at the Lodge. He also

did not wish to apologise to those who had camped on its grounds many centuries earlier.
8. Department of Foreign Affairs and Trade 2008, speech by Prime Minister Kevin Rudd to the Parliament 13 February 2008, Australian Government, accessed July 2015, <http://dfat.gov.au/people-to-people/public-diplomacy/programs-activities/Pages/speech-by-prime-minister-kevin-rudd-to-the-parliament.aspx.>
9. D. Cooke 2008, "Sorry' statement should acknowledge cultural loss, says state leader', *The Age*, 1 February.
10. Gurrumul's musical collaborator and soulmate.
11. R. Hillman, *Gurrumul, His Life and His Music*, ABC Books, 2013.
12. DFAT, op. cit.
13. Midnight Oil, 'Put Down That Weapon', *Diesel & Dust*, Sprint/Columbia, 1987.
14. Elvis Costello & the Attractions, 'Lip Service', *This Year's Model*, Radar, 1977.
15. A. McMillan, *Strict Rules*, Hodder & Stoughton, 1988.
16. M. Okie 2008, 'Oz Captain! My Captain!: An "Ode" to Midnight Oil & An Interview with Midnight Oil's Jim Moginie', *Identity Theory*, 19 September, accessed July 2015, <http://www.identitytheory.com/oz-captain-captain-ode-midnight-oil-interview-midnight-oils-jim-moginie/>.
17. On whose escape from the Moore Creek Settlement *Rabbit Proof Fence*, Mirimax, 2002 is based.
18. Director of *Bran Nue Dae*, Roadshow, 2009.
19. I'd better footnote here that Peter Garrett taking coffee at the Curtin shops is apocryphal.
20. G. Huitker, *Little Life*, Ginninderra Press, 2010.
21. G. Huitker, *How to Succeed Without Really Winning*, Ginninderra Press, 2005.
22. Patrick, who flew in from the Gold Coast, was to play the man behind the mask in a Savoyards production in Brisbane in 2013.
23. The Beatles, 'Dear Prudence', *The Beatles*, Apple, 1968.
24. In many ways, it was impossible to express in words. I came across a photograph in Robert Hillman's book, op. cit., capturing Soft Sands Band member Keith Garadhawal Garrawurra teaching a young boy how to play the drums. It comes close to mirroring Connor's joy. It's on page 69.
25. L. Andrews, 'Fab Concert Swings In to Help Children', *The Canberra Times*, 22 November 2009, p. 5.
26. Principal of Black Mountain School Canberra from 2007 to the present day.
27. B. Obama, *The Audacity of Hope*, Crown/Three River Press, 2006.
28. *Utopia*, Dartmouth Films, 2013.
29. DFAT, op. cit.

Track #3

1. Richard encourages readers to check out Sam's bestseller, *Head Over Heels*, ABC Books, 2006, or visit his website at http://www.sambailey.com.au/head-over-heels-a-best-

seller. As he recounts, 'There is some stuff in Sam's book about the days of our visits. Lots came from visiting Sam. In our wedding video, Sam Bailey crows about being the reason Mel and I got together. I reckon he is probably right. I also reckon it is one significant reason behind the name of our first son.'
2. Richard was assistant curate, Christchurch Anglican Church, St Lucia, Brisbane, 1997–8, followed by five years as associate priest of Gold Coast North Anglican Church and as Director of Spirituality, Coomera Anglican College, 1999–2003.
3. Robert Hillman, op. cit.
4. Founded amidst some controversy, pickets and protest. See Jenny Murphy's Radford history, *A Matter of Choice*, Goanna Print, 2004.
5. In 2013, Richard received recognition for his work in Timor Leste and service learning in the Educational Leadership Excellence Awards from the ACT Branch of the Australian Council for Educational Leaders (ACEL).
6. http://www.eightytwentyvision.org
7. D. Pocock, *Openside*, New Holland, 2011.
8. B. Franklin, 'On the Price of Corn and Management of the Poor', *The London Chronicle*, 29 September 1776.
9. C.R. Hyde, *Pay It Forward*, Simon & Shuster, 1999; Warner Brothers, 2000.
10. V. Browning, *Maalika: My Life Among the Afar Nomads in Africa*, Macmillan, 2008.
11. Ibid.
12. Ibid.
13. Ibid.
14. P. White, *Flaws in the Glass*, Jonathan Cape, 1981.
15. My Everyman Library edition published in 1992, translated from the Russian by Richard Pevear and Larissa Volokhonsky.
16. Directed by Steven Spielberg for Dreamworks Pictures, 1997.
17. Current Director of Leadership Development at the Australian New Zealand School of Governance.
18. V. Browning, op. cit.
19. G. Huitker 2014, 'Radford's G-Trips', *Anglican Schools Australia News*, June.
20. Matt Pye, the founder of Crossing the Divide initiative (discussed later in the book), recently endorsed this approach to service when he explained about his own programs, 'We didn't choose Crossing the Divide. It chose us. So I guess in terms of effecting change, sometimes it is thrust upon you and you simply choose to run with it.'
21. Watson may be uncomfortable with being credited with this quotation. See 'Attributing Words': <http://unnecessaryevils.blogspot.com.au/2008/11/attributing-words.html>.
22. Nick Cave & the Bad Seeds, 'Sweetheart Come', *No More Shall We Part*, Mute Records, 2001.
23. National Archives of Australia, Opportunity and care, dignity and hope: Prime Minister Paul Keating at the launch of Australia's celebration of the 1993

International Year of the World's Indigenous Peoples, Redfern Park, 10 December 1992, Australian Government, accessed July 2015, < http://primeministers.naa.gov.au/galleries/audio/transcript-m3983-749.aspx>.
24. National Archives of Australia, op. cit.
25. R. Hillman, op. cit.
26. R. Hillman, op. cit.
27. D. Pocock, op. cit.
28. National Archives of Australia, op. cit.
29. V. Browning, op. cit.
30. *The Silence of the Lambs*, Orion Pictures, 1991.
31. H. Kureishi, *Intimacy*, Faber & Faber, 1998.
32. V. Browning, op. cit.

Track #4

1. http://www.sbs.com.au/programs/first-contact/article/2014/10/30/ray-martin-great-divide
2. T. Keneally, *Woman of the Inner Sea*, Hodder & Stoughton, 1992.
3. http://gunawirra.org.au
4. F.W. Putnam 2006, 'The Impact of Trauma on Child Development', *Juvenile and Family Court Journal*, 57.
5. C.Y. Johnson, 'Lasting Impact of Early Stress', *The Canberra Times*, 25 September 2012
6. M. Chabon, *Maps and Legends*, McSweeney's Books, 2008.
7. A village of around 400 goodly folk, found between Guyra and Armidale.
8. Except for 'Bakerman' (from *Red Sails in the Sunset*, Sprint/Columbia, 1984), you can rarely pull off a tap dance to Midnight Oil songs.
9. C.Y. Johnson, op. cit.
10. At the time of printing, we are up to G14. The reduction of the number of days Tingha Preschool was to be open in 2014 made it logistically impossible for us to continue with volunteers there.
11. The ultimate go-to man during early trips, Andrew would have a phone app to answer all of our questions. He always new the best apps to determine the exact distance to places, where the nearest petrol stations were, if cows were blocking or raging torrents were gushing over the roads, which astrological constellation we were under or how to best doctor a photo to make it look like it was taken in the wild west or as if it was framed by a florist of the 70s. Since graduating, Andrew's continued support of the development of the program with the Collegians has been considerably helpful.
12. National Archives of Australia, op. cit.
13. Safia actually consists of a trio of gifted Radford lads: www.facebook.com/safiamusic. Like them now!
14. www.animalsonbikes.com.au
15. G. Brooks, *March*, Viking, 2005.
16. National Archives of Australia, op. cit.
17. The Treaty Republic website (http://treatyrepublic.net) provides the following information about Slaughterhouse Creek, which is also known as Waterloo Creek or as the Australia Day Massacre:

The official reports spoke of between 12 and 80 killed but the missionary Lancelot Threkeld set the number at 120. Major James Nunn later boasted they had killed from two to three hundred natives, a figure endorsed by historian Roger Milliss. Whatever the numbers, most of the Kamilaroi/Gamilaraay were wiped out.
18. M. Da Silva, 'Aboriginal Massacre Site Commemorated', *Australian Geographic*, 15 November 2010.
19. DFTA, op. cit.
20. H. Reynolds, *Forgotten War*, New South, 2013.
21. D. Pocock, op.cit
22. P. Stewart. *Demons at Dusk*, Sid Harta, 2007
23. Neil Murray, 'Myall Creek', *Going the Distance*, ABC Music, 2003.
24. P. Stewart, op. cit.
25. H. Reynolds, *Why Weren't We Told*, Penguin, 1999.
26. D. Pocock, op. cit.
27. DBC Pierre. op. cit.
28. Robert Hillman, op. cit.
29. National Archives of Australia, op. cit.
30. H. Reynolds, *Forgotten War*, op. cit.
31. N. Murray, op. cit.
32 P. Smith, *Woolgathering*. Bloomsbury, 1992.
33. M. Pye, 'But for the grace of God...go I and go you'. Presented at the 2014 Dirrum Dirrum Conference and available for viewing at: www.dirrumdirrum.org.au
34. Tingha Public School's indomitable Front Office Lifeforce,

Julie Trevithick, made it all as clear as mud for me in a recent email: 'I've been pondering on how to write the pronunciation of Tingha! I've been walking around saying it (I know – sounds slightly weird!) Now I hope you don't think me presumptuous, but I think you should write it as "Ting-gha" for the correct pronunciation, and the way you say it as "Ting-ah". Try it – sit there and say it a few times!'
35. Evonne Goolagong, a member of the Wiradjuri, was the only mum to have won Wimbledon since before World War I. Career highlights include winning 7 Grand Slam titles and appearing in 18 Grand Slam finals.

Track #5
1. Midnight Oil, 'Time to Heal', *Breathe*, Sprint/Columbia, 1996.
2. It was in fact a VH-PGA Italian Piaggio. It was apparently a TAA passenger plane. Pat Stewart, whom you are about to meet, bought its exoskeleton back from Port Macquarie.
3. Around the time of the wedding, the Fab Four were apparently sampling Tasmanian apples at Australian House with Australian High Commissioner Sir Eric Harrison. What a great, possibly fruitful, image for a record label.
4. Also see http://www.australia.gov.au/about-australia/australian-story/chinatowns-across-australia
5. My favourite parts of the museum are the many slightly eerie examples of taxidermy, such as the two-

headed calf, or perhaps the bottled specimens, such as an eight-legged kitten. And a glistening collection of minerals of all the colours of the rainbow, including the world famous Star of Bethlehem quartz exhibit. In November 2014, a savage storm removed the room from the museum causing considerable damage to it.

6. Richard Browning once 'controlled' the giraffe for me so that I could experience it at full, fast and maximum stretch. I subsequently produced, in my undies, some fertiliser for the gardens.
7. After a bit of googling, I discovered the band, formed in 1995, were Golden Guitar winners from 1996 to 1998.
8. http://www.daretolead.edu.au/ Minimbah_Aboriginal_School
9. http://www.abc.net.au/local/ stories/2014/07/03/4038728. htm and http://www.abc.net.au/ local/audio/2014/06/26/4033952. htm?site=newengland
10. D. Tartt, op. cit.
11. Adapted from a text of his speech he submitted to the 2013 Radfordian.
12. D. Purvis-Smith 2014, 'Crossing the Divide', *New England Country Living Magazine*, July.
13. M. Pye, op. cit.
14. V. Browning, op. cit.
15. A. Cox, *On Purpose Before Twenty*, Four Corners Press, 2012.
16. P. McLaren, *Sweet Water… Stolen Land*, Queensland University Press, 1993. Rob Marshall spotted this book in a second-hand bookshop and knew it would interest me when he saw a picture of the Breadknife on the cover and when he read the blurb on the back: 'Racial brutality and the tragic account of the Myall Creek massacre underscore the story of Ginny and Wollumbuy, Kamilaroi people of the Warrumbungle range.'
17. D. Purvis-Smith, op. cit.
18. M. Pye, op. cit.
19. National Archives of Australia, op. cit.
20. Ron Sexsmith, 'For the Driver', *Retriever*, Nettwerk, 2004.
21. M. Pye, op. cit.
22. D. Purvis-Smith, op. cit.
23. Ibid.
24. Ibid.
25. M. Pye, op. cit.
26. Bruce Springsteen, 'Reason to Believe', *Nebraska*, Columbia Records, 1982. It became a regular, particularly at the close of a lot of UTE gigs in 2013.
27. D. Purvis-Smith, op. cit.
28. M. Pye, op. cit.
29. http://www.beyondq.com.au
30. Words: David Purvis-Smith, Images: Kate Black.
31. Like Ryan's passionate reflection about his experience at Minimbah, this all occurred at Richard's student reflection space within the Foundation Day service, exactly one year later. This opportunity always seems to allow for quite profound reflection to be loosened up, opened and released.
32. A more benign one than the one spat out by Nick Cave on the 1992 album/song of that same name.

33. Midnight Oil, 'Star of Hope', on the vastly underrated *Breathe* album, Sprint/Columbia, 1996.
34. D. Purvis-Smith, op. cit.

Track #6
1. J. Atkinson, *Trauma Trails: Recreating Song Lines*, Spinifex Press, 2002.
2. Ibid.
3. J. Atkinson, op. cit..
4. Please don't judge me. See the latter stages of *Little Life*, once more, for how travelling with a Time Lord can have its poignancy and be deeply affecting.
5. H. Als, 'The Art of Theatre No. 17', *The Paris Review*, No 201, Summer 2012.
6. B. Bruford, *The Autobiography*, Jawbone, 2009.
7. I had met lead singer Shane Howard after his own 'lounge room' gig at Manning Clark House in August 2010. I had been playing an intensely personal song he wrote called 'Here and Now', from his 1990 solo album *River*, at my own home gigs as a tribute to my parents – and simply wanted to thank him for its creation and for what the tune and its words stirred in me. Howard was polite and grateful that I had discovered it, but shared with me that he rarely played it himself due to its deeply personal associations. This song and album are very hard to find these days.
8. Karla Grant/SBS Productions, *Living Black Conversations*, Ep. 1 – Peter Garrett, 9 October 2013, SBS One.
9. Tim's business, Guz Box Design and Audio, can be explored at http://www.guzbox.com.au
10. In 2012 it was a Restaurant & Catering National Award Winner in the Best Entertainment Restaurant category.
11. M. Okie, op. cit.
12. Midnight Oil, 'Read About It', *10 9 8 7 6 5 4 1*, Columbia Records, 1982.
13. B. Zuel, 'Midnight Memories', *Sydney Morning Herald*, 1 November 2012, accessed July 2015, <http://media.smh.com.au/entertainment/music/blackfellawhitefella-3761832.html>.
14. M. Dodshon, *Beds are Burning: Midnight Oil, The Journey*, Penguin Viking, 2004.
15. U2, 'One Tree Hill', *The Joshua Tree*, Island Records, 1987.
16. Thanks to Sam Tonkin for sending me this quotation.
17. See G. Huitker, *Not Just Footy*, Ginninderra Press, 2005.
18. Glen Campbell, 'A Better Place', *Ghost on the Canvas*, Surfdog, 2011.
19. U2, 'Red Hill Mining Town', *The Joshua Tree*, Island Records, 1987.

Track #7
1. J. Barnes, *Levels of Life*, Jonathan Cape, 2013.
2. L. Murray, *Killing the Black Dog*, 2nd edition, Farrar, Straus and Giroux, 2011.
3. F. Dostoevsky, *The Brothers Karamazov*, 1880.
4. C. McCarthy, *Cities of the Plain*, Picador, 1998.
5. I really am not kidding. It's by Barry Stone, Pier 9, 2010.

6. C. McCarthy, op. cit.
7. F. Dostoevsky, op. cit.
8. Johnny Marr, 'New Town Velocity', *The Messenger*, Warner Bros, 2012.
9. It featured in that *Anglican Schools Australia News* article previously referenced, June 2014.
10. Rugby league legends. Blacklock scored many many tries for the St George Illawarra Dragons and represented Australia in 2001; Campbell played for Cronulla Sharks, Penrith Panthers and finally the Gold Coast Titans, and was a New South Wales Country and Indigenous Dreamtime representative. In 2008, Preston was awarded the Ken Stephens Medal for his commendable work amongst Indigenous communities, which continues to this day.
11. Absolutely no factual truth in this.
12. B. Mould with M. Azerrad, *See a Little Light: The Trail of Rage and Melody*, Little Brown, 2011.
13. G. Ritchie (with E. Sherrill), *Return From Tomorrow*, Spire, 1978.
14. D. Tutu, *No Future Without Forgiveness*, Rider & Co., 1999.
15. L. Shriver, *We Need To Talk About Kevin*, Text Publishing, 2003.
16. F. Dostoevsky, op. cit.
17. Jon & Vangelis, 'I'll Find My Way Home', *The Friends of Mr Cairo*, Polydor, 1981.
18. A third of the way through his set on 7 April 2013 at the Factory, Sydney.
19. Mike Nesmith, 'Rio', From *A Radio Engine to the Photon Wing*, Pacific Arts, 1977.
20. Ibid.
21. M. Dodshon, op. cit.
22. N. Gaiman, *Anansi Boys*, Headline, 2005.
23. G. Dayal, *33 1/3: Brian Eno's Another Green World*, Bloomsbury, 2009.
24. J. Pallington West, *What Would Keith Richards Do?: Daily Affirmations from a Rock 'n' Roll Survivor*, Bloomsbury, 2009.
25. Midnight Oil, 'Warakurna', *Diesel & Dust*, Sprint/Columbia, 1987.
26. F. Dostoevsky, op cit.

Track #8

1. Section starters in this chapter are the lyrics of Midnight Oil's 'Sometimes' from *Diesel & Dust*, Sprint/Columbia, 1987.
2. http://cosmic-horizons.blogspot.com.au/2012/01/anglo-australian-bowie.html
3. http://www.bbc.com/news/magazine-26577308
4. Midnight Oil, 'One Country', *Blue Sky Mining*, Columbia, 1990.
5. *The Coonabarabran Times*, Thursday 24 July 2014, p. 8.
6. A lyric from the sixth verse of 'Khe Sanh'.
7. M. Dodson, op. cit.
8. M. Heinrich, G. Huitker & R. Marshall, 'Say fair's fair, pay the rent, pay our share', presented at the 2014 Dirrum Dirrum Conference: www.dirrumdirrum.org.au
9. As Brownie points out, 'Belinda's mum, Doreen Dean, taught me in 4th class, in the room Joel was to run his music lessons. She was the school piano player. She used

to work in the classroom after school and I pestered her to teach me to play the recorder and to read music. I remember a couple of times walking home with her, which was across the road from where the hospital was. She is also the author of the classic *Well Well! Goanna Oil and Other Tingha Tales.*

10. K. Grant, op. cit.
11. I did include this song as a cameo during 'King of the Mountain' at some Vivaldi's gigs.
12. Midnight Oil, 'In the Valley', *Earth and Sun and Moon*, Sprint/Columbia, 1993.
13. A. Storr, *Music and the Mind*, Ballantine, 1992.
14. U2, 'Acrobat', *Achtung Baby*, Island Records, 1991.
15. M. Pye, op. cit.
16. J. Guesdon & P. Margotin, *All the Songs, The Story Behind Every Beatles Release*, Black Dog & Leventhal, 2013.
17. Nick Cave & the Bad Seeds, 'As I Sat Sadly By Her Side', *No More Shall We Part*, Mute Records, 2001.
18. R. Hillman, op. cit.
19. M. Chabon, *Manhood for Amateurs*, Harper Collins, 2009.
20. M. Chabon, *Maps and Legends*, op. cit.
21. Midnight Oil, 'Home', *Breathe*, Sprint/Columbia, 1996. As previously mentioned, vastly underrated.

Track #9

1. P. Rees, *Robert Plant: A Life*, Dey Street Books, 2014.
2. R. Hillman. op. cit.
3. http://www.cricket.com.au/news/feature/ryan-carters-batting-for-change-sydney-sixers/2014-11-06
4. http://www.battingforchange.com.au
5. D. Dalton, *Who is that Man? In Search of the Real Bob Dylan*, Omnibus Press, 2012.
6. P. Auster, *The Invention of Solitude*, Faber & Faber, 1982.
7. W.E.H. Stanner, *The Dreaming & Other Essays*, Black Inc, 2010.
8. R. Hillman, op. cit.

Postscript

In November 2015, the Gamilaraay Trips received an Order of Australia Group Award for their 'outreach and development of relationships with schools and communities in northern New South Wales'.

In March 2016, the author finally got to meet members of Midnight Oil and have a chat about music and other matters over pretzels. That is a story for another day.

About the Author

George Huitker is a writer, musician coach and teacher closing in on completing his third decade at Radford College, Canberra. He has published three collections of poetry and two sporting memoirs, *Not Just Footy* (adapted for the stage in 2004 by Canadian director Walter Learning) and *How to Succeed Without Really Winning*, winner of an ACT Writing and Publishing Award in 2006.

He has formed various theatre companies and bands over the years, finally settling with his own independent theatre company, Huitker Movement Theatre (HMT) and his rock group, Junk Sculpture. In 2007, with Rachael Bishop, he founded teamSUPPORT, a project designed to encourage young people, particularly boys, to participate in charitable work.

George's website is at www.georgehuitker.com.au

Junk Sculpture's Facebook page is at https://www.facebook.com/junksculpture

It is refreshing to be reminded just what sport is all about. In the relaxed, insightful and entertaining style made famous by Bill Bryson, George Huitker recounts a lifetime of sporting experiences and anecdotes – delivering messages so often forgotten in these days of decreasing sports participation and increasing sports contracts.

Robert de Castella

Football is life and, as George Huitker says, not just footy. Huitker as a fan, a son of a fan, a player and a coach, narrates a classic every-man football story. The highs, the lows, the joys, the frustrations, the rewards and the ingratitude are all there in ways and doses we can recognise all too well. We have all played this game.

Les Murray

For George Huitker, footy is certainly not just footy. Coaching his kids allows George to express himself as a writer, and a teacher… George displays the kind of Australian passion and intensity for sport that must go a long way in explaining the incredible success this nation has enjoyed for many decades. His prose and poetry are sensitive, humorous and informative.

Dick Telford

I opened this book with trepidation… But by the end of the introduction I was excited. Here was passionate writing about sport as romance and fairy tale, that decried those who seek success at any cost and the commercialism of the game… Here is a writer who can unlock for me the mystery of why anyone has the slightest interest in sport… The book is a lovingly rendered meditation on a son's relationship with his father, as mediated by the game of soccer. It is a window into the strange world of school sporting competition. It edges towards being *Zen and the Art of Coaching a School's Sports Team*...

Not Just Footy is well worth a read, especially for a sports coach or a young player. Or a sports cynic.

Robin Davidson, *Muse*

George Huitker's book *Not Just Footy* allows our soccer community to celebrate its commitment and vitality. Outsiders can get some inkling of the human galaxies which revolve around that bouncing narcotic called, simply, 'ball'. The spirit of community, the conflict between success and ethics, the complacency of the winner, the desire of the loser. All of these emotions tumble out of Huitker's simple and special retelling of his experiences... In these days of inflated soccer industry egos and unimagined salaries, the people who matter are left behind. Huitker reminds us, sometimes hilariously, sometimes humiliatingly, but always with humility, of what it's really all about. His writing is part of the social cement which keeps us together. It puts things in context. It made me feel better. Buy it, read it, and you'll feel better too.

Danny Moulis

In the world of sport, published memoirs abound. Yet they are rarely worth reading. Such trips down memory lane usually deserve a flick through, but not close scrutiny... George Huitker's *Not Just Footy* is a shining exception to this trend. It is replete with questions about the socio-cultural significance of sport, reflections on the appropriate role of the coach, and criticisms against the idea that sporting acumen compensates for poor educational and social skills. His sense of what is possible moves from pessimism, to fatalism, and eventually to realism; that is, the players more so than the coach are responsible for their destiny. The coach, nonetheless, has a vital leadership role – not just by helping to develop sporting attributes, but also by promoting to young people valuable skills-for-life.

Dr Daryl Adair, *Sports Coach*

First-rate, original, distinguished by a congenial tone throughout. Includes an outstanding bibliography. If only we could all be so lucky as to have had George Huitker for a coach.

2006 ACT Writing & Publishing Awards Citation

If Bill Shankly's famous 'life and death' credo was about the destination, then Huitker's yarn is about the journey. The sequel to *Not Just Footy* continues the Canberra teacher, writer and football buff's coaching odyssey through the wild landscape of junior sport. It is one of the infinite intersections where stakeholders have the choice of embracing the inherent beauty and life-enforcing ways of the contest, or heading down the path to boorish beahviour and madness – a narrow tract between balance and obsession. Funny, tragic and richly sourced, it is not just a must-read for anyone like Uday Hussein, but all of us who've been temporarily unhinged by our sporting passions.

Neil Jameson, *Inside Sport*

The author's *leitmotiv* is that a win-at-all-costs attitude is positively harmful. As Huitker puts it, 'You can genuinely grow, develop and succeed through loss.' It seems to me that there is so much practical wisdom in this book that it should be required reading for all those involved in the vital task of coaching and supervising children's sport.

J. Neville Turner, *Sporting Traditions*

In *How To Succeed Without Really Winning* George Huitker has truly given us a gift. He has taken the time to reflect on our tendency to invest so much in the outcome of a 'measly game' of junior sport that the behaviour of adults – coaches, managers, parents and supporters – leaves much to be desired. This book should be required reading for everyone involved in junior sport, much the way that coaches are required to sign a Code of Ethics. A copy should be shared among the associates of every team! If the book is used as a guide, even once, it will have saved some juniors from the horrors most of us remember only too well.

Rae Wells, *Sports Coach*

Many sports, such as cricket, have – until recently, anyway – stressed that 'the game's the thing', and that the result should be secondary. But what's different about Huitker's book is its presentation, drawing on a frame of reference from Shakespeare to the Dalai Lama to lyrics from the pop group Kiss. In fact, in its gently didactic style, the book is reminiscent of Alain de Botton's *The Consolations of Philosophy* set in a sporting context.

Philip O'Brien, *The Canberra Times*

Turning 40, Huitker had the minor crisis that men are supposed to have at that age. He wondered whether teaching classes or directing actors around a stage or players around a football pitch was all he would do with his life. He describes the route that led him to set up teamSUPPORT, an outreach group among Year 10 boys at his school. Inspired by the book and film *Pay It Forward*, the boys – and now also the girls – organise and run activities with Black Mountain School and other organisations working with people with disabilities… I loved *Little Life*. The writing is fresh, the story uplifting… No doubt our city has many stories of quiet service like this one. It is our loss that we do not hear more of them.

Frank O'Shea, The Canberra Times

I read it within hours… *Little Life* showed me with clear-eyed objective attention to detail the terrible cost of dementia not only on George himself, but on all his relationships… In the face of suffering that marks human existence, we can take one of two paths: we can give in and give up, or we can take the experience and use it to transform the mess of our lives into something that lights the darkness. This is what *Little Life* does. It shows us vividly that all experience, no matter how harrowing and terrible, can be transfigured.

John Foulcher

www.ingramcontent.com/pod-product-compliance
Lightning Source LLC
Chambersburg PA
CBHW071813080526
44589CB00012B/775